346. (K)

MODERN LEGAL

The Law Book Company

Ottawa • Toronto • Calgary • Montreal • Vancouver

NEGOTIATING TRAGEDY:
LAW AND DISASTERS

MODERN LEGAL STUDIES

NEGOTIATING TRAGEDY: LAW AND DISASTERS

by

CELIA WELLS

LONDON
SWEET AND MAXWELL
1995

Published in 1995 by
Sweet & Maxwell Limited of
South Quay Plaza
183 Marsh Wall London E14 9FT
Typeset by Selwood Systems,
Midsomer Norton
Printed and bound in Great Britain
by Butler & Tanner Ltd, Frome and London.

No natural forests were destroyed to make this product;
only farmed timber was used and replanted

A CIP catalogue record
for this book is available
from the British Library

ISBN 0 421 47380 0

Preface

Like most of us, I travel by road, rail, car-ferry and aeroplane. I had just moved to Wales when the Chernobyl nuclear reactor discharged its waste over Europe, affecting the western parts of the UK more than the east. None of this explains my interest in law and disasters but it ensures a constant engagement with the issues dealt with here. Doubtless, a complex mixture of personal history, intellectual curiosity (not, I hope, prurience) and a coincidence of events has led to my thinking about the subject of disasters.

Without the focus of the Economic and Social Research Council seminar programme on risk and hazard held at the London School of Economics in 1991–2, it is unlikely that I would have pursued this project. I was tremendously grateful to Barry Turner for involving me in the series and it was with great sadness that I learned of his premature death on 24 February 1995. Tom Horlick-Jones has ensured a continuing exchange about the cultural interface between risk, disasters and law and encouraged me to pursue this research. Many others, including Hazel Genn, Diana Leat, Bob Lee, Hector McQueen and Keith Stanton, have supplied useful references, suggested avenues of thought or given support in other ways.

In keeping with the spirit of the Modern Legal Studies series, this book traverses traditional legal boundaries and suggests different ways of looking at topics familiar either to lawyers or to other disciplines. It has the modest aim of providing the framework for further debates and of displacing some common misconceptions about the ways in which law does and does not work. The Modern Legal Studies Board has given me much encouragement in writing this, a relationship handled with great discretion by its Chair, Hugh Beale, given that I am also a Board member. Hugh additionally contributed with his astute editorial comments.

Cardiff Law School has funded research assistance and I thank Phil Smith, Mike Edwards, Tess Newton and Wayne Dellimore for the work they have done and Dawn Morgan for her secretarial support. At home, Derek Morgan has asked his usual challenging questions, and our children, Alice and Lydia, have taken up his mantle to varying degrees – thanks! Joe Wells has been a brilliant chauffeur and soothing influence. All the mistakes are mine.

Celia Wells
6 March 1995

Contents

Table of Cases

Table of Statutes

Table of Statutory Instruments

Rules of the Supreme Court

1. Disasters: Types, Causes and Effects

Most of us can recognise a disaster when we see one. People have written books on disasters without feeling the need to define what is meant by the word or to explore the variety of meanings it has acquired. We might apply the description to a temporary inconvenience such as dropping a full milk bottle on the doorstep or to the personal catastrophe of losing a day's work on the word processor. But there is clearly a scale against which misfortune can be measured and the milk bottle episode would easily be trumped by a house fire, or a traffic accident. There is a category beyond personal disasters which includes events which are recognised both as personal disasters for those involved and as occurrences which lead to shared responses, which are publicly acknowledged. One reason why it is impossible to draw a precise line is that disasters by their nature are relative, contingent and often indeterminate. For example, the London Ambulance service introduced a new computerised dispatch system in 1992. It was a spectacular failure and had to be abandoned after 36 hours. This was a disaster of a kind, with a public and a private face.[1]

While a dictionary might define a disaster as "anything ruinous or distressing that befalls; a sudden or great misfortune, or mishap; a calamity,"[2] to speak of "disasters", as opposed to describing a single personal mishap as a disaster, is to speak of cataclysm, catastrophe, tragedy or devastation.[3] Many different factors contribute to the construction of an untoward event as a disaster, but here I take the following as necessary ingredients: multiple deaths or serious injuries occurring more or less simultaneously for which there is no one obvious human agent. Although disasters do not

---

[1] *London Ambulance Service Inquiry,* (1994); see Flowers, "One Huge Crash" *The Guardian,* 28 April 1994, p. 21.

[2] *Shorter Oxford English Dictionary* (1971).

[3] See Horlick-Jones, T., *Acts of God? An Investigation into Disasters* (1990).

necessarily involve loss of human life, most of the examples I use and most of the analysis does presume either death or serious physical injury.[4] I have excluded events where there is an obvious human agent, for example in random killings, because many of their legal sequelae are familiar. Not all disasters fit neatly into these definitional boundaries. There was sufficient doubt about the individual causation of the bomb which led to the Pan Am air crash at Lockerbie to regard it as a disaster.

One of the themes which will emerge in this book is that the clarity of the distinction between individual and collective responsibility and accountability is becoming increasingly clouded.[5] Another is the cultural relativity of attitudes to risk and therefore to reactions to events. Disasters are perceived as such because previously adequate precautions are no longer seen to be effective; they represent forms of "cultural collapse" which take place because of inaccuracy or inadequacy in the accepted norms and beliefs.[6] Although both these themes inform the book as a whole, they are drawn together in the last chapter. In this introduction I aim to establish some of the ideas and concepts which inform those themes. Writing about how law deals with disaster involves an enterprise which combines two fields of study which rarely meet. Disaster studies traverse a number of disciplines, ranging from the scientific and technological to the sociological and psychological. The interface between these fields and law is inevitably complex, especially as law itself is not a discipline of determinate boundaries. The attraction of a contextual and interdisciplinary work of this kind is that it demonstrates how legal study can be viewed through the prisms of different types of analysis surrounding a particular type of event.

Using the risk analysis distinction between levels of scale and levels of frequency, it can be seen that disasters usually involve high magnitude, low-probability events. In other words, where large numbers of deaths, or extensive damage or destruction occur infrequently, a disaster is made. Lower magnitude and higher probability incidents, for example, domestic and road accidents,

---

[4] And sometimes the epithet "disaster" can itself exacerbate problems; the Braer tanker which ran aground off Shetland Islands in 1991 was widely reported as a disaster. Before the anticipated damage to fisheries, a hurricane dispersed the oil. The economy was devastated more by the myths than the reality of the damage.

[5] See especially Chap. 7.

[6] Turner, "The Organisational and Interorganizational Development of Disasters" (1976) *Administrative Science Quarterly* 378 at 381.

do not usually attract the epithet.[7] When 10 children were killed in a minibus accident, however, the magnitude was far enough outside the normal expectation for road crashes that it attracted the attention accorded to a disaster.[8] This demonstrates the linkage between two important attributes of disasters, in the sense I have laid out, that they cause unpredicted and unexpected harm and are worthy of public attention. Although most of the examples used here are rapid in onset, slow-onset disasters such as famine or disease are also recognised in the extensive literature on disaster.

The most comprehensive bodies of disaster literature have been developed in the United States, Italy and Japan. These are all highly industrialised countries covering large land masses and are subject to a wide range of disaster agents.[9] Their disaster responses are civilian and somewhat decentralised. They all have a social science community with pragmatic attitudes to research and strong international connections. Other European countries have a narrower range of natural disaster concerns. According to Dynes, the first empirical study of disaster was published in 1920 and took as its subject an explosion in Halifax,[10] while the first theoretical work appeared in 1942.[11] This marked the beginning of a period in which significant attention was paid to such phenomena in the disciplines of human and behavioural sciences. In his poetic account of the Buffalo Creek dam break, an ethnography of a community following a disaster, Erikson wrote that "the term refers to a sharp and furious eruption of some kind that splinters the silence for one terrible moment, and then goes away". He continued that disasters have a distinct beginning and a distinct end, and that by definition they are extraordinary.[12]

However, the nuclear reactor radiation escapes at Chernobyl and Three Mile Island have disturbed the certainty of that particular image of disaster. While they had a beginning, their end was less easy to identify.[13] Other features of those "technological" catastrophes were their invisibility and their lack of geographical containment. No environmental disaster, such as earthquake or

---

[7] Royal Society, *Risk: Analysis, Perception and Management* (1992), p. 135.

[8] The Hagley school tragedy, November 1993; see Appendix for details of disasters referred to in this book.

[9] Dynes, "Cross Cultural International Research: Sociology and Disaster" (1988) *International Journal of Mass Emergency and Disaster* 101 at 118.

[10] Dynes, *ibid.*

[11] Sorokin, P., *Man, Society and Calamity.*

[12] Erikson, K., *In the Wake of the Flood* (1979), p. 200.

[13] In 1994, world leaders debated how to assist Russia in dismantling Chernobyl; and a quarter of a million Welsh sheep were still confined to their holdings in January 1994.

flood, respects political boundaries, but chemical or radiation damage can present a different scale of challenge.

In referring to disasters as out of the ordinary, Erikson used the phrases "freak of nature" and "perversion of the natural processes of life". By this he did not mean that they were necessarily natural in origin, for that was clearly not the case with Buffalo Creek, but that what gave them the characteristic of disaster was the effect on people's lives, that the two major properties of disasters are that they do a good deal of harm and they are sudden, unexpected, acute. A more detailed account is found in the following comprehensive definition offered by Kreps, an elaboration of an earlier attempt by Fritz:

> "Disasters are events, observable in time and space, in which societies or their larger sub-units (*e.g.* communities, regions) incur physical damages and losses and or disruption of their routine functioning. Both the causes and consequences of these events are related to the social structures and processes of societies or their sub-units."[14]

1. Classifying Disasters

This discussion of the definition of disaster has already touched on the sensitive issue of how to classify disasters into types. A simple division is often made between man-made and natural disaster. In making historical sense of attitudes to death and destruction, it can be helpful to recall that attributing misfortune to human causes is relatively recent. Human agency has always been capable of sparking large-scale destruction, as the Fire of London bears witness, but there was then a much stronger tendency to invoke religious or spiritual meaning to explain events which would now be seen as man-made. Paradoxically, however, death is now more problematic with people displaying a reluctance to accept its inevitability or at least its unpredictability. It has been brought under the control of medicine with a much larger percentage of deaths now taking place in hospital.[15] This has clear implications for bereavement reaction following deaths in disasters. That which was seen as uncontrollable now demands expla-

---

[14] Kreps, "Sociological Inquiry and Disaster Research" (1984) 10 *Annual Review of Sociology* 309 at 312.

[15] In 1992, 54 per cent of deaths in the UK took place in hospital or other institutions (*Mortality Statistics* Series DHI no. 27, Table 7).

nation and account. There are really two separate points hiding behind the apparent simplicity of this historical account of the emerging notion of man-made disaster and of secular accounts of death. The first is that the causes and consequences of death were more firmly grounded in magical and religious belief, with less sense (or illusion) of control than now. The other is that industrial, followed by technological, advance has unleashed much greater mobility, and thus a greater potential for large scale transport accidents, as well as introducing the possibility of collisions, explosions and so on which are of near universal threat.

Those same developments have also altered the perception and reality of "natural" hazard. The interaction of technology and environment leads to and exacerbates the detrimental impact of natural phenomena such as floods. Thus, more help is gained from a typology which goes beyond the two categories of natural and man-made. A tripartite version replaces them with environmental, technological and social hazard.[16] "Natural" here is supplanted by "environmental" in recognition of the role of human activity in distorting the effects. "Technological" comprises those disasters emanating from human designed technological systems, and "social" those arising from human behaviour such as terrorism, arson or crowd violence.

Dividing disasters into categories allows for more sophisticated analysis in terms of understanding risk perception, risk management, disaster prevention, civil protection, and other related issues. A legal review has to take account also of questions such as employment status (as between the driver of a train and its passengers, for example), relational matters (as between parent, child, or spouse following accidental death, for example) and jurisdictional divisions (as between Scotland and England and Wales, for example). For these reasons, a further refinement suggested by Cohen of the three-part framework already outlined, is useful:

1. Environmental—including hurricanes, earthquakes, floods;[17]
2. Ordinary—including rail accidents, where there is low risk perception by passengers;
3. Technological—including radiation escapes such as Three

---

[16] Royal Society, *op. cit.*, p. 135.
[17] Cohen, D., *Aftershock: The Psychological and Political Consequences of Disaster* (1991). Cohen actually calls this category "natural" but for the reasons given earlier, environmental is preferable.

Mile Island and Chernobyl, where high technology institutions place ordinary citizens at risk;
4. Industrial—for example, oil installations and mining where workers know their job is hazardous;
5. Crowd violence—such as that at Hillsborough and Heysel.[18]

Although these typologies indicate variations in causal factors, it is possible nonetheless to point to some common features of the build-up to disasters. In a useful analysis of the Aberfan, Hixon Level Crossing and Summerland disasters Turner notes the following pattern. First, there were what he calls rigidities in belief in organisational settings so that the accurate perception of disaster was inhibited by cultural and institutional factors. He cites Aberfan as "a powerful and tragic instance of the manner in which a failure of perception may be created, structured, and reinforced by a set of institutional, cultural, or subcultural beliefs and their associated practices."[19] Secondly, he describes the phenomenon of the decoy: because of pre-occupation with an altogether different problem often no action was taken to deal with a perceived hazard. At Aberfan a slip was anticipated but deposits of "scalings" were thought to be the relevant antecedent. Once these deposits ceased, the slip hazard was thought also to cease. Another example comes from the perceived shipping hazards in the English Channel. Shipping experts anticipated a major shipping incident, but they expected a mid-Channel collision, not a near harbour capsize as occurred with the *Herald of Free Enterprise*.[20] Thirdly, organisational exclusivity tended to lead to disregard of outside advice. Again, later disasters back this up, with Bradford City football club ignoring the fire safety advice of the local council. Fourthly, information difficulties lead to management adopting an idealistic and unrealistic view of problem areas which can be compounded by interpersonal difficulties blocking effective dissemination of information. Other common features identified include failing to comply with existing regulations and, a factor which is presumably partly connected, minimising or under-estimating emergent danger.[21] Based on this pattern, Turner also develops a

---

[18] *Ibid.* p. 18.
[19] Turner, *op. cit.*, p. 388.
[20] Hamer reported that Lloyds, post-*Herald*, assessed the risk to the 75 ferry fleet as one collision per year with every fifth year a collision with the appropriate ingredients for a major loss of stability ("The Risks of Ferry Travel" *New Scientist* 18 August 1990).
[21] Turner, *op cit.*, p. 378.

chronology of disaster, beginning with initial beliefs and norms reflected in a failure to comply with regulations or violation of existing precautions, followed by an incubation period, leading to a precipitating event, then onset, and next rescue and salvage, and lastly, full cultural re-adjustment.

This analysis gives a helpful framework in which to consider the legal implications of disasters and reminds us that while the consequences are tragic and many features are unique, the causal antecedents are often ordinary and mundane.[22] High technology compounds the effects but does not explain the incidence. The causes and the consequences are located in a process, a response *continuum*, beginning with preparedness, mitigation efforts, emergency response and finally recovery and reconstruction. However, questions of causation are not easy; they are deeply embedded in cultural attitudes to risk and danger and that is the next layer of analysis to consider.

2. Attitudes to Disaster

A number of disasters occurring in or affecting the UK in the last 25 years provide the background for this account of the legal responses to such events. That period has seen significant changes in social and legal perceptions of disasters. A number of writers assert that we are witnessing an increased tendency towards blaming collective institutions for the misfortunes which befall us.[23] In particular, the argument that there has been a cultural shift towards blaming corporations has been eloquently made by Mary Douglas.[24] Perceptions of corporate organisations and their responsibilities for mass death have, it is argued, undergone a change. It is clear that corporate negligence is more likely to be translated into calls for manslaughter prosecutions. There appears to be less blind faith in the ability or willingness of corporate organisations to take safety seriously.[25] Business corporations are

---

[22] See Pearce and Tombs, "Bhopal: Union Carbide and the Hubris of the Capitalist Technocracy" (1989) 16 *Social Justice* 116.

[23] A process anticipated in the debates about tortious principles of causation: see Bush, "Between Two Worlds: the Shift from Individual to Group Responsibility in the Law of Causation of Injury", (1986) 33 *University of Cal L.R.* 1473 1986 and Rabin, R., "A Socio-legal History of the Tobacco Tort Litigation" (1992) 44 Stan. L.R. 853; see also Chap. 7.2.

[24] Douglas, *Risk and Blame* (1992).

[25] *Ibid*. Douglas has argued that all cultures share the same basic repertoire of explanations for explaining misfortunes (blaming the victim in a "moralistic" style, blaming unpopular groups or forces in an "adversarial" style or deflecting blame in a "no fault" style).

increasingly expected to provide compensation for injuries that in earlier times would have been attributed to individual fault or fate.[26] This itself is possibly part of a move towards greater legalisation resulting from a decline in confidence in major institutions, business and government.[27]

Speculation about contemporary sources of strain has led to a range of suggestions: that this is an age of moral relativism; that it is an age of impotence in which fewer people can derive meaningful satisfaction from the act of producing something needed by the rest of the community; and that it is an age of sensory overload, leading to "a flattening of affect, a sheer anaesthetisation of the moral and cognitive senses, as if one were suffering from a kind of psychological concussion."[28] How we relate to disasters is part of a series of much wider questions concerning the social construction of risk, and the emergence of a "risk society" as Beck puts it.[29] Disasters symbolise outrage and betrayal in the struggles people make to cope with their vulnerability in the modern world.[30]

These may or may not command support as explanations of changes in a disaster perception. What is less in doubt is that as a result of those changes a new vocabulary has developed which encompasses terms such as "disaster litigation", "corporate manslaughter" and also "post-traumatic stress disorder". The phenomena which these phrases describe are not necessarily new, of course, but they both reflect and affect the way we think about them. The apparently seamless web of legal response to death and injury belies important changes in the roles played by the different components. This can be seen in a number of different legal arena, including regulatory schemes which seek to ensure higher safety standards in industry and in public transportation; institutional arrangements such as inquests and inquiries which accompany some deaths; compensation provisions, the establishment of charitable or other funds to assist those affected, social security provision, criminal injury compensation; tortious actions, fatal accidents payments and attempts to pursue criminal charges for those seen to be at fault.

---

[26] Bush, *op. cit.*

[27] Galanter, "Law Abounding: Legalisation around the North Atlantic" (1992) 55 *Mod. L.R.* 1.; Lipset and Schneider, *The Confidence Gap: Business, Labour and the Government in the Public Mind* (1987) and Giddens, *The Consequences of Modernity* (1990). See also Horlick-Jones, "Modern Disasters as Outrage and Betrayal", paper at *International Institute of Sociology Congress*, Paris, June 1993.

[28] Erikson, *op. cit.*, pp. 204 *et seq.*

[29] Beck, *Risk Society* (1992).

[30] Horlick-Jones, *op. cit.*

Cause is a persistent issue for legal analysis: who or what caused the accident from which legal liability might flow. However, it is important to underline the point that attributing cause is as much a psychological and cultural matter as it is a legal or scientific question. Research tends to show that attributions of fault often follow the decision to seek legal redress rather then the other way round.[31] Knowing that there is an insured potential defendant tortfeasor may lead to a different attribution than knowing that an accident was caused by one's best friend. Explaining an event, seeking a cause for it, is a way of giving it meaning.[32] Assigning it to a benign or non-human cause disposes of it; self-blame or seeking to blame it on others are other avenues. Cultural selection determines which dangers are recognised, and the institutions of public inquiry and legal avenues of blame (including tortious and criminal proceedings) are ways in which this selection is activated.[33] Whether victims are blamed, whether misfortunes are regarded as "natural" rather than "man-made" and the types of official institutional response to them are, it is suggested, functions of the type of social system in which they arise.[34] Blame is only invoked where an event is perceived as unnatural: "If a death is held to be normal, no one is blamed."[35] Yet the perception as natural or unnatural is culturally produced; attitudes to disaster are both the result and the cause of acceptable ideas about risk in everyday activities.

There is a complex relationship between public reaction, media responses, risk perception and causal attribution. It comes as no surprise that there is empirical evidence that newspapers report violent and homicidal events disproportionately resulting in bias in public perceptions of their frequency.[36] Lee suggests that, in addition,

> "[T]he criteria used by the public in assessing the seriousness of an event often include not merely biological states but ethical and moral convictions. The awfulness of a catastrophe may lie not merely in the loss of life and suffering involved, but in the violation of people's sense of justice or moral right-

[31] Lloyd-Bostock, "Fault and Liability for Accidents: the Accident Victim's Perspective" in Harris *et al*, eds, *Compensation and Support for Illness and Injury* (1984).
[32] Taylor, *Disasters and Disaster Stress* (1989), p. 148.
[33] Douglas, *How Institutions Think* (1985), p. 54.
[34] *Ibid.*, p. 64.
[35] Douglas and Wildavsky, *Risk and Culture* (1983), p. 35.
[36] Combs and Slovic "Newspaper Coverage of Death", (1979) 56 *Journalism Q*. 837.

ness. They are indeed intangible matters and they change with time."[37]

Thus, attitudes to safety and risk affect both the propensity to blame and the target of it. The importance both of risk perception and of the part played by perception in what have hitherto been accepted as objective risk assessments is being increasingly recognised.[38] In their account of media reaction to the nuclear reactor failure at Three Mile Island, Baum, Fleming and Davidson suggest that technological disasters are particularly newsworthy.[39] Three Mile Island, along with Hiroshima, Seveso, Bhopal and Chernobyl, are names which reflect "the uniquely twentieth century phenomenon of man's capacity to catastrophically poison himself and his natural environment."[40]

Compared with so-called natural disasters which, though powerful and sudden are familiar and inflict damage which is visible, technological disaster can be invisible, and universally threatening.[41] In terms of control, technological catastrophes arise when systems which were thought to be under control fail.[42] "Not having control when one expects to have it appears to have different psycho-physiological consequences than does not having control when one had no expectations for it."[43] Connected to this is the finding that the risks which people are prepared to take vary in relation to their voluntariness; there is far greater tolerance of chemicals when consumed voluntarily in food than of lower risk environmental chemicals.[44] Familiarity also alters our perception of risk which perhaps explains how we ever manage to bring ourselves to make a journey by car and why people are resistant to move from earthquake prone areas. High personal cost is traded off (although not in algebraic terms) against benefits such as maintaining a lucrative lifestyle and not having to move. People select and distort what they attend to, in order to reduce conflict so that they may completely suppress any thoughts about the undesirable aspects of a hazard.[45]

[37] Lee, "The Public's Perception of Risk and the Question of Irrationality" in Warner, ed., The Assessment and Perception of Risk (1981), p. 7.

[38] Royal Society, op cit.

[39] Baum, Davidson and Fleming, "Natural Disaster and Technological Catastrophe" (1983) 3 Environment and Behaviour 333.

[40] Hodgkinson P. and Stewart M., Coping with Catastrophe (1991), p. 55.

[41] Baum et al, op. cit., p. 334.

[42] Ibid., p. 346.

[43] Ibid., p. 348.

[44] Katzman, "Chemical Catastrophes and the Courts" (1986) The Public Interest 91.

[45] Lee, op. cit., p. 12.

In the attribution of responsibility, the identification of a human cause is significant. Pre-existing hostility also leads to a stronger inclination towards blame.[46] Hostility can arise from a sense of having authority imposed unilaterally, a perception which many people share in relation to governments, scientists and industrialists.[47] With more sophisticated forecasting techniques, even meteorological disasters can lead to allegations of blame if there has been a perceived failure to warn or prepare.[48] The more we come to rely on experts, the more sense of control we feel, and therefore the greater sense of loss when the apparently controllable breaks down.

Attribution, blame and consequent behaviour are not therefore easy matters and it is important to emphasise that legal explanations of events are products of a complex process which has a variety of perceptual, psychological and other ingredients. In noting the role of public sentiment in shaping legal responses, sight must not be lost of power discrepancies between the competing forces at each stage of the legal process.[49] It is easier to blame an individual employee than the system which has left a person overworked and affected by stress, or the systems defects resulting from poor design, or from inadequate maintenance or other management led cost-saving decisions.[50]

3. Consequences of Disaster

It seems clear from what has already been said that a disaster represents more than the sum of a number of individual or personal tragedies. It is the simultaneous (or near) loss of life or profound physical devastation which signifies the event and provides it with its powerful imagery. But of course, disasters do affect individuals and they affect them in different ways.[51] A graphic demonstration of the ripple effect has been supplied by the repercussions on the insurance market of disasters such as Piper Alpha, the 1987 storms in south-east England, the Exxon Valdez oil spill, and Hurricane Hugo in North America. Until then catastrophe

---

[46] *Ibid.*, p. 13.

[47] *Ibid.*, p. 13.

[48] These issues will be discussed further in Chap. 3.

[49] Calavita, *et al*, "Dam Disasters and Durkheim: An Analysis of the Theme of Repressive and Restitutive Law" (1991) 19 *Int. Jnl. of Sociology of Law* 407.

[50] Horlick-Jones (1993), *op. cit.*, p. 21.

[51] Littlewood, *Aspects of Grief: Bereavement in Adulthood* (1992), p. 147.

insurance had been spectacularly remunerative for investors.[52] It is thought that the insurance costs of the *Estonia* ferry disaster in 1994 will dwarf the £45 million bill following the *Herald* sinking. Catastrophes in the developed world cost more to the insurance industry because more victims have life insurance cover.[53]

Although severe property damage caused by flood or storm can be traumatic even where there is no loss of life, most of the discussion in this book assumes that there has been loss of life or at least the very real threat of it (as of course is nearly always the case where property is severely damaged). Broadly speaking, in most disasters there are three groups of people who are immediately and directly affected:

1. The immediate victims, the dead and injured,
2. their relatives and friends, and
3. any rescuers, including those involved in disaster planning, those employed in rescue services as well as passersby.

The types of damage which any of these might experience will range from death and physical injury to recognised stress disorders. In order to understand social and legal reactions to disasters we have to know something about the emotional significance of death. However, again, the cultural contingency of these reactions has to be underlined. Emotions used to be conceived as instinctual and therefore unchanging and uncontrollable.[54] They were primitive and common to both animals and humans.[55] Recent writing asserts their cultural relativity and locates the social construction of emotions into more general theories of socio-cultural constitution of individual experience.[56] Death raises profound social and cultural issues. Modern reactions to death suggest underlying beliefs in death's avoidability providing one meets certain behavioural standards.[57] As Illich explains, rather than seeing death as natural and inevitable we seek to attach blame to someone or something because we hold the irrational belief that death, particularly premature death, should

---

[52] One group of Lloyds Names successfully sued the Gooda Walker agency for negligent underwriting, *Deeny & Others v. Gooda Walker Ltd & Others, The Independent*, 5 October, 1994.

[53] *The Independent* 29 September, 1994.

[54] Harre, *The Social Construction of Emotions* (1986).

[55] Based on Darwin's theories, see Harre, *op. cit.*

[56] Armon-Jones, in Harre, *op. cit.*, p. 32.

[57] Gorer, *Death, Grief and Mourning in Contemporary Society* (1965).

ultimately be avoidable.[58] The experience of loss is not peculiar to disasters, but in disasters what people lose additionally is faith, "faith in the fact that A and C follow B—that life has a certain consistency or probability."[59]

Wittgenstein gave us a profound and troubling thought when he observed that we do not live to experience death: "Death is not an event in life itself. Death is not lived through."[60] Leaving aside accounts of near-death experiences, there is something appealingly apt about this. For, of course, death is not a state which we can directly *know* for ourselves. What Wittgenstein failed to capture, however, is the intense emotional impact that the death of others can have upon us.

The death of a close relative can induce emotions of shock and denial, distress, helplessness, and images of death and destruction. These are intense emotional experiences including fear, anxiety and anger.[61] In addition to the denial, distress, and helplessness which characterise the psychological reactions to trauma and shock, profound images of death and destruction emerge. This, argues Illich, is attributable to the coming to the fore of all the fears and anxieties, the destruction and mutilation, associated with death. Death "with its inevitability and power, death that cannot be controlled, evokes primitive fears and magical thinking, dreads of contagion and the search for protective omens."[62]

Death by disaster compounds these reactions. Unexpected death, death outside the natural order (child before parent, for example) is associated with complications in the bereavement process.[63] It seems that all deaths of children are regarded as outside the "natural" order and that death of adult children often provokes a response of anger in the bereaved parents.[64] The grief associated with all violent deaths is intensified in deaths by disaster.[65]

The commonest causes of death of an adult child are accidents and cancer. A study of parents whose children had died in accidents found that they felt more depressed and guilty and found the loss more painful than those where the death was caused by cancer.[66] Even between parents, death had differential impact with

---

[58] Illich, *Limits to Medicine: Medical Nemesis and the Expropriation of Health* (1977).
[59] Hodgkinson and Stewart, *op. cit.*, p. 2.
[60] Wittgenstein, *Tractatus Logico-Philosophicus*, trans C.K. Ogden (1922) 6.4311; echoed in the title to Lifton's account of Hiroshima, *Death in Life*, (1967).
[61] Raphael, "Personal Disaster" (1984) 5 *Austr. and NZ Jnl. of Psychiatry* 183.
[62] Illich, *op. cit.*, p. 189.
[63] Littlewood, *op. cit.*, p. 27.
[64] *Ibid.*, p. 143.
[65] *Ibid.*
[66] *Ibid.*, p. 140.

mothers more often than fathers reporting that the death of an adult child was the most painful experience of their lives. Mothers who lost a daughter also reported relatively more anger and guilt following the death.[67]

Relational, circumstantial, historical, personality, and social factors contribute to potential grief problems, many of which are present in disasters. Disasters are events outside everyday expectations. Particularly relevant factors, some of which have been touched upon already, are these: deaths outside the natural order; unanticipated deaths; uncertainty whether the loved one is dead or alive; and multiple deaths.[68] Since viewing the body is associated with better recovery outcome, failure to recover the body also exacerbates grief recovery.[69]

Grief is seen as complicated when it is delayed, chronic, absent or distorted. In complicated grief, "Anger is frequently directed against the self, the dead person, the environment in general or specific other people who are believed, usually erroneously, to have been the instrumental in either causing the death or failing to prevent it."[70] If the disaster can be regarded as man-made this provides a target to focus anger upon.

Aside from bereavement, other effects from disaster arise from those who are involved as survivors, rescuers or witnesses. They share five central experiences, first described by Lifton, a psychiatrist who studied Hiroshima survivors.[71] The "death imprint" is an intrusive image of the disaster which may intercept a survivor's waking or sleeping moments with startling and distressing intensity. Survivor guilt is common. This can take the form of "why me?", of the kind which partly accounts for difficulties which parents have when their children pre-decease them. It also takes the form of responsibility: was it the survivor's fault, should they have done more to help and so on. This can lead to further tragedy as in the case of a lorry driver who survived Zeebrugge; although he spent seven hours in the water assisting with the rescue of others, he could not forget the screams of his fellow drivers whom he was unable to reach. He committed suicide three years later.[72] "Psychic numbing" is a common reaction at the time

---

[67] *Ibid.*, p. 141.
[68] Hodgkinson reported that some bodies were never recovered after Zeebrugge, and some took five weeks or more; "Technological Disaster-Survival and Bereavement" (1989) 29 *Social Science and Medicine* 351.
[69] Littlewood, *op. cit.*, pp. 54–55.
[70] *Ibid.*, p. 54.
[71] Lifton, *op. cit.*
[72] Hodgkinson and Stewart, *op. cit.*, p. 4.

of traumatic events and is the term used to describe the often observed phenomenon of calm, controlled, disconnected behaviour. If this persists, it can leave survivors emotionally disabled from participating in life.

A fourth effect is that of distrust of those outside the experience; resistance to the help of others and paranoia may develop, leaving victims isolated in their own trauma. Lastly, there is a response which resonates with much of what has already been said about attitudes to disaster and that is the "quest for meaning". Questions of how and why compete as survivors seek to make sense of what happened. "The true meaning of survival involves finding a place for the experience in a new view of the world, and its institutions and authorities, the value of life and family relationships, and risk and hazard".[73]

4. Differential Effects

Just as any one disaster will affect people in different ways, so also disasters vary in terms of the stress they are likely to engender. Predictability and controllability are key features in affecting people's ability to cope with the effects of a disaster, or indeed other catastrophic events.[74] Determining the range of potential damage of any future disaster is also of course of prime concern to those engaged in emergency planning. For both the purposes of effective response and in order to make useful comparisons once the damage has occurred, it is useful to consider the key variables. Berren *et al* identified five, some of which were adapted to take account of the invisible and unknown impact of the Chernobyl nuclear accident: (1) the type of disaster (natural versus human induced), (2) the degree of personal impact, (3) the scope (temporal and geographical dimensions), (4) whether there is an identifiable low-point and (5) disaster size.[75]

The idea that natural disasters are "Acts of God" and therefore predictable in the sense of expected to occur, compared with man-made which are unexpected and "not supposed to happen" has already been mentioned.[76] The differential effects of each is supported by the observation that while any loss is associated with

---

[73] *Ibid.*, p. 9.
[74] Raphael, *op. cit.*
[75] Berren *et al*, "A Classification Scheme for Disasters" in Gist and Lubin, eds, *Psychological Aspects of Disaster* (1989).
[76] Hodgkinson and Stewart, *op. cit.*, Chap. 2.

some anger "it is likely that technological mishaps may engender more focused anger than will natural disasters."[77]

However, it is not just attributed cause which determines the response. Some types of accident produce particular difficulties either for the survivors, or for the rescuers or for those bereaved by them. In an examination of mass transport accidents Hodgkinson and Stewart pointed to the paradox that travel by road, rail, air and sea is now accepted as a key feature of the modern world despite the perception of boats, one of the oldest forms of transport, as engaged in never-ending battle against the mighty powers of the sea. Pointing to particular characteristics of mass transport disasters they note a number of aggravating features.[78] Lack of warning increases the sense of shock; the disasters often occur in locations inaccessible to rescuers; the environment is often unfamiliar to survivors; some are totally catastrophic, air crashes for example; they may involve impact at speed which severely damages bodies making identification difficult and with a consequent increase in stress on rescuers. Unidentified or unrecovered bodies are known grief complicating factors; re-entering the situation (e.g. travelling by train again) has a re-sensitizing effect yet cannot easily be avoided. A particular feature of post traumatic stress disorder is phobic avoidance of the situation in which stress occurred; the sense of loss of control and helplessness is high; anger, often directed at the operator, is prominent; guilt is common for survivors and may be particularly strong for crew; importance of post disaster cohesion amongst survivors is often frustrated by dispersal over a wide geographical area, with little community focus, leading to an intense sense of isolation compounded by difficulties in organising psychological support.

Disasters vary in the extent and type of damage, with some resulting not only in death and injury but also damage to victims' property or devastation to their immediate environment. While physical damage is relatively easy to quantify, it is only comparatively recently that the psycho-social detriment has been recognised and subjected to analysis. One of the most comprehensive studies of the psychological reaction to disasters was made following the Buffalo Creek dam break in 1972. 132 million gallons of black slag, debris-filled mud and water cascaded down the valley when the dam gave way. People scrambled up the hillside and watched helplessly as relatives, friends and neigh-

---

[77] Baum et al, op. cit., p. 351, discussing natural and technological disasters.
[78] Hodgkinson and Stewart, op. cit., p. 38. They also examine fire, pp. 50–54, and environmental poisoning, pp. 55–58.

bours were propelled past them. 125 were killed and many thousands were made homeless; the valley was re-contoured in the space of hours. Two years later the degree of psychological impairment was severe to the extent of interfering with effective daily functioning. Only one in six was asymptomatic and 35 per cent were moderately to severely disturbed.[79] Buffalo Creek brought together a horrific combination of amplifying effects. Not only had the presence of the dam implanted a fear of its collapse such that when it did occur it was a nightmare come true but also, in losing their homes and their valley, people were denied the therapeutic benefit of returning to their own homes.[80] As Rangell comments, "ground" is profoundly important to a person's well-being, it is "the background into which self can merge, [which] is the base for his security."[81]

Gleser *et al* suggest six factors which influence the degree of psychological effect:

1. The extent to which the event poses a serious and unexpected life threat to individuals, family and friends, leading to existential fears, feelings of powerlessness and vulnerability, and threat of sudden loss;
2. the degree of bereavement suffered by victims;
3. prolongation of physical suffering, life threat and the lack of normal necessities over an extended period, coupled with the impossibility of changing or ameliorating situation;
4. the extent to which disaster victims must face displacement or changes in the former environment and new modes of living;
5. the proportion of community or group affected by the disaster. Victims who are part of the community relatively unaffected by disaster will recover better;
6. cause—whether it was perceived as natural or man-made. The latter is likely to result in a widespread feeling of having been betrayed by those who were trusted. Loss of trust can lead to conflicts, recriminations and alienation that lessen the sense of community.[82]

---

[79] Gleser, Green and Winget, *Prolonged Psychosocial Effects of Disaster: A Study of Buffalo Creek* (1981).

[80] Rangell, L., "Discussion of the Buffalo Creek Disaster: The Course of Psychic Trauma" (1976) 133 *Am. J. Psychiatry* 313, 314.

[81] *Ibid*.

[82] *Ibid*., p. 148.

Thus, in addition to the causal factors already mentioned, the particular damage which results is a variable affecting responses to disasters. Many of these examples also demonstrate the interactive nature of these different factors. The community loss in Buffalo Creek may have assisted in preventing the sense of isolation felt by transport accident victims and facilitated the aftercare support services. However, the daily exposure to the scene of the disaster aggravated the effect, as did the dislocation and powerlessness caused by the loss of the victims' homes. A distinctive characteristic of disasters is that they are often multi-factorial in terms of both cause and consequence. They are not simple events.

Support groups may be a particularly useful focus where disasters take place outside established communities.[83] And in this sense, those individuals bereaved in non-disaster accidents may be worse off, given the evidence that increasing secularisation of western societies is an important factor which contributes to difficulties associated with coping with dying.[84]

Of course, not all the outcomes of disasters are negative. As well as sometimes providing useful data paving the way for better prediction, prevention, or mitigation in the future, disasters, economists suggest, produce winners and losers. "Some persons, families, organisations, and communities get specific economic benefits as a result of disaster."[85] Similarly, the development of community groups, self-help and support groups and individual gains in terms of understanding can themselves be seen as positive outcomes, without in any way suggesting that those benefits outweigh the costs through which they were achieved. Survivors commonly report an enhanced perception of the value of life and of friends and family as a result of their experience.

5. Conclusion

This chapter has presented some of the background features which have a particular relevance to any consideration of the ways in which law responds to or otherwise affects aspects of disasters. Mention has already been made of different stages at which the law may play a role. It is not only the settling of claims or the demand for criminal prosecution which have to be considered. An

---

[83] Littlewood, *op. cit.*, p. 27.
[84] Turner, *op. cit.*
[85] Scanlon, "Winners and Losers: Some Thoughts about the Political Economy of Disaster" (1988) *Int. J. Mass Emergencies and Disasters* 47 at 50.

elaborate framework of public law captures disaster in various ways, through safety regulation, emergency planning, inquiries into the aftermath and so on. In the next chapter, five disaster case studies are outlined, which give an idea of some of the different legal consequences arising from recent disasters in the United Kingdom and set the arena for the subsequent analysis. Chapter Three outlines the public law dimension, while Chapter Four introduces the question of compensation from charitable funds, from social security and national insurance schemes. The role of the media and of support groups is also considered there. Compensation as a result of legal actions for death and injury, including post traumatic stress and exemplary damages are discussed in the following two chapters. And lastly, Chapter Seven considers moves towards blaming collective institutions and compares the aims of criminal responses to disasters and those of compensatory systems.[86]

The cultural and historical contingency of the legal aftermath of disasters has been emphasised in this introduction. Legal responses are both reactive and procreative, both dependent on as well as influencing cultural understandings. Calls to blame individuals and collective institutions, demands for "justice", claims for compensation and pressure for increased safety: all these reverberate in and bear witness to the echo-chambers of the cultural process. As well as addressing a readership drawn from different disciplines and sub-disciplines, this book has to overcome the challenge of all contextual studies. While law is heavily categorised in abstract ways, procedural versus substantive law, public versus private, civil versus criminal and so on, individuals are confronted with only their own experiences, histories and stories. Because there is a dearth of legal writing about disasters from this contextual angle, I have included the case studies in the next chapter to provide a resource against which the subsequent categories of legal response can be measured. The material, presented in this somewhat unusual format, can be approached either as a precursor or a point of reference to the remaining chapters. Because the legal responses are multi-layered they are inevitably complex and often span several years. Through a combination of the case-studies and the categorised explanation which follows, it is hoped that the fascinating intricacies are exposed and clarified and that a basis is laid for continuing discussion of the cultural significance of disasters.

---

[86] The Appendix gives brief details of the disasters mentioned in the book.

2.   Disaster Case Studies

Five recent British disasters have been selected as the basis for case studies which illustrate the interaction between legal responses and the particular circumstances in which disasters arise. Although they span 25 years, most of the disasters have occurred in the last decade. Between them, the legal history of each disaster is valuable in a number of ways. First, they show the types of legal consequences which can arise, ranging from those over which the victims' relatives have no control, such as the inquiry and inquest, to those where they are active litigants. Secondly, they demonstrate the complexity and interplay between these legal responses. Finally, they provide a descriptive context in which to place the rest of the book. Each case study analyses a disaster under the following headings: Inquiry, Safety Changes, Inquest, Legal Actions (civil, criminal, other), Support group and Disaster fund. Below is a summary of the characteristics of the five case study disasters, including location, victim type, and perceived risk:

Aberfan (1966)—mining village, public victims, mainly children, perceived high-risk.

Herald of Free Enterprise (1987)—vehicle ferry, public and employee victims, perceived low-risk.

Piper Alpha (1988)—off-shore rig, male employee victims with dependents, perceived high-risk, Scottish procedural focus.

Hillsborough (1989)—leisure, public victims, mainly young adult males, perceived low-risk.

Marchioness (1989)—leisure, public victims, mainly young adults, perceived low-risk.

1. Aberfan

116 children and 28 adults died when a waterlogged coal tip slid down and engulfed a village school in South Wales, in October 1966. The tip was owned and run by the National Coal Board. 20 years on, a local person commented that the victims died "through the negligence and stubbornness of man."[1]

INQUIRY

A Tribunal of Inquiry, chaired by Lord Justice Edmund-Davies, was appointed, under the Tribunals of Inquiry (Evidence) Act 1921 which bestows High Court powers to summon witnesses and send for documents. The Tribunal's Report was published in July 1967.[2]

The following are extracts from the Report (numbers in brackets refer to paragraphs in the Report):

(17) We found that many witnesses ... had been oblivious of what lay before their eyes. It did not enter their consciousness. They were like moles being asked about the habits of birds.

(18) ... our strong and unanimous view is that the Aberfan disaster could and should have been prevented.

(34) [T]here was no lack of water in the tipping area ... It was this water that counsel for the Tribunal, summarising the experts' opinions, rightly characterised as "for long recognised as the destroyer of the stability of refuse tips." [F]ailure to prevent [water at the base of the tip] was the real explanation of the disaster. Lest it should be thought that there is any hindsight about any of this, it is worthy quoting the ... questions to and answers given by [a soil mechanics expert called on behalf of the NCB]:

Q. [Was the means of knowledge of the water on the mountain available] to the NCB in 1957 when they were considering a tip site?
A. This information would have been available at that time.

Q. The information as to the taking of proper drainage measures which would have obviated this disaster was available to them?
A. Yes.

(47) The Aberfan disaster is a terrifying tale of bungling ineptitude by many men charged with tasks for which they were totally unfitted,

---

[1] *The Times*, 20 October 1986.
[2] Report of the tribunal appointed to inquire into the Disaster at Aberfan on 21 October 1966 (1967 H.C. 553).

of failure to heed clear warnings, and of total lack of direction from above.

(64) There was no regular inspection of the tips; their inspection (such as it was) was wholly haphazard ... and had no reference to their stability at all, but simply related to such matters as the condition of the mechanical equipment for tipping.

(135) [It had become clear that the tip had moved in 1963 although the NCB denied this for much of the hearing] The *insouciance* of the NCB regarding this substantial slide, late in 1963 is remarkable. After the 1944 slide, tipping on Tip 4 was stopped. Yet, as we have already remarked, after the 1963 slide there was no cessation of tipping; material continued to be tipped in the same way ... there were no tipping instructions, and there was no inspection for stability.

(161) One of the most striking discoveries emerging from our investigations has been the degree of extent to which the views expressed by the experts in relation to the causes of the Aberfan disaster were anticipated 27 years earlier by the Powell Duffryn memorandum of 1939. [following a slip at Abercynon, the company prepared an illustrated memorandum "The Sliding of Colliery Rubbish Tips."]

(81) Had its points and warnings been observed, the probability is that there would have been no disaster in 1966.

(82) On the issue of blameworthiness, the 1939 slide "... is of vital importance, both in relation to organisations and to individuals ... It caused damage in the region of £10,000 ... It could not fail to have alerted the minds of all reasonable prudent personnel employed in the industry of the danger lurking in all coal-tips unless they were so remote as to be incapable of causing harm ... Even had they no knowledge of the existing literature regarding the precautions called for when tipping on mountain slopes, all those connected with the Powell Duffryn Co, in particular, should have learnt therefrom an unforgettable lesson. On the contrary, the lesson if ever learnt, was soon forgotten."

[A slide in 1965 at Tymawr led to an amended form of the memo going to Area Chief Engineers. But the Tribunal found no proper communication between civil engineers and mechanical engineers.]

Conclusion

(178) However belatedly, it was conceded by the NCB that the Aberfan disaster stemmed from their failure to initiate any policy in relation to the siting, control, inspection and management of tips.

(188) ... we cannot escape the conclusion that the Board must at national

level also be blamed for its neglect of the stability of tips ... Theirs was the overall responsibility for the initiation of policy, which involved that at national level there should have been due consideration of the proper methods to dispose of the waste of the coal-mining industry.

(190) [The NCB in its opening statement had stated that the disaster was due to a coincidence of a set of geological factors] The Tribunal is in no doubt that this was the starting-point of an attempt, persisted in for many weeks by the NCB, to persuade acceptance of the view that the concatenation of geological features on Merthyr Mountain was such as could not reasonably have been expected to exist ... It might conceivably have had some bearing on our task had there ever been an attempt to ascertain what the geological features were; but, since there was no investigation and no thought devoted to the subject, the claim carried one nowhere.

Summary

The Report was persuasive and unequivocal in its condemnation not only of the National Coal Board not only for failures which led to the disaster, but also for the attitude it displayed to the Inquiry.

SAFETY CHANGES

A National Tip Safety Committee was set up to advise the Minister of Power.

The Mines and Quarries Act 1954 was amended to give to the Minister and Mines Inspectorate additional powers and duties recommended by the Tribunal. Tips forming part of active mines and quarries were to be regularly inspected by persons competent to judge their stability: Mines and Quarries (Tips) Act 1969.[3]

INQUEST

Adjourned until October 1967, the inquest then lasted four minutes. The coroner stated that "the tribunal assessment is tantamount to a finding of accidental death in each case." Verdicts of accidental death were returned.

---

[3] ss. 3–6.

LEGAL ACTIONS

Civil

The Board's liability was not contested, but with few of the victims having dependents, the compensation payable was limited (see Chapter 5.4.1).

The NCB were said to be liable for the damage caused under the principle in *Rylands v. Fletcher*.[4] This had been applied to coal tips by the House of Lords in *Att.-Gen. v. Cory Bros and Co. Ltd*.[5] Claims in negligence would also have been sustainable.

Post Traumatic Stress Disorder: Aberfan predated general recognition of PTSD.[6] However, a woman who witnessed the disaster as a child of 11 has sued British Coal (legal successors to the NCB) for damages, claiming that the horrific scenes caused her to suffer a nervous breakdown 12 years later. She said that she blanked out the memory of the day, until she read newspaper reports about a man and his children who died in a fire.[7]

Incidental actions

Use of the phrase "Aberfan-type disaster" led to a libel case in 1984.[8] A local newspaper reported, under the head-line "Landslip feared as ash-hill moves when it rains" that new home-owners feared an "Aberfan" type disaster. The court, awarding damages to the builders, said that the word "Aberfan" has passed into "the currency of ordinary language" and required no explanation and that to say of a local builder that he develops sites in such a way as to create the risk of an "Aberfan type disaster" is about as serious a libel as could be published.

Criminal

There were no criminal proceedings.

After Aberfan while it was accepted that there might be the basis for prosecution, to institute proceedings was not thought to be appropriate. The Attorney-General explained to the Commons that those implicated "have suffered enough by their own neglect". Neither criminal proceedings nor the Chairman's resignation would be desirable. He quoted from the Report:

---

[4] (1868) L.R. 3 H.L. 330; see Chap. 5.
[5] (1921) 1A.C. 521.
[6] See Chap. 6.2.
[7] *Crocker v British Coal Corpn*, Cardiff High Court, QBD, 20–22 Feb 1995, judgment reserved.
[8] *Kerria Developments Ltd and another v. The Reporter Ltd*, 31 July 1984, H.C.

Whether or not named or adversely referred to in this report, there must be many today with hearts made heavy and haunted by the thought that if only they had done this, that or the other the disaster might have been averted. Of these, some will blame themselves needlessly; others, while blameworthy in some degree, will condemn themselves with excessive harshness; yet others must carry the heavy burden of knowing that their neglect played an unmistakable part in bringing about the tragedy.[9]

The Aberfan Parents and Relatives Association decided that they did not want to pursue prosecutions because that would be "to bow to vengeance". They appeared to be thinking in terms of prosecutions of individuals.

It can be noted, however, that the first known prosecution for corporate manslaughter in England and Wales was brought against Cory Bros, a South-Wales colliery company in respect of an overground accident at a private mine not far from Aberfan.[10] This is discussed further in Chapter 7.1.2.

SUPPORT GROUP

The Aberfan Parents and Relatives Association was formed. See Chapter 4.2 for discussion of such groups.

DISASTER FUND

£1.75 million was donated. Bitterness persisted in the village that £150,000 of it was taken back by the Government to pay towards the cost of clearing the remaining tips. The fund is discussed in Chapter 4.3

2. Herald of Free Enterprise

154 passengers and 38 crew members died when the *Herald of Free Enterprise* capsized just outside the harbour at Zeebrugge in March 1987. The *Herald* was a Roll on/Roll off passenger and freight ferry, owned by Townsend Car ferries, a subsidiary of P&O.

---

[9] *Op. cit.*, para. 207.
[10] *R. v. Cory Bros* [1927] 1 K.B. 810. This same company was involved in the civil case mentioned above.

INQUIRY

A Formal Investigation, under section 55 of the Merchant Shipping Act 1970, was set up with Mr Justice Sheen as Wreck Commissioner. Its report was published in July 1987.[11]
The following are extracts from the report:

(7.3) [The *Herald* was designed to operate between Dover and Calais.] The ramp at Zeebrugge was designed for loading on to the bulkhead deck of single deck ferries. In order to load the upper deck of the *Herald* it was necessary to raise the ramp so that it led upwards to E deck. When loading or unloading at high water spring tides the ramp could not be elevated sufficiently to reach E deck. As the ships berthed bows to this berth it was necessary to trim the ship by the head to allow the raised ramp to reach E deck ...

(7.4) ... At Zeebrugge only two deck officers were available, only one deck could be loaded at a time, it was frequently necessary to trim the ship by the head and the bow doors could be closed at the berth. Because of these differences, with proper thought the duties of the deck officers at Zeebrugge would have been organised differently from their duties at Calais. No such thought was given to the matter, with the result that immediately loading was complete the Chief Officer felt under pressure to leave G deck to go to his harbour station on the bridge.

(8.1) On the night of the casualty the *Herald* was trimmed by the head in order to load E deck ...

(10.1) The *Herald* capsized because she went to sea with her inner and outer bow doors open. From the outset ... the assistant bosun ... has accepted that it was his duty to close the bow doors at the time of departure from Zeebrugge and that he failed to carry out his duty ...

(10.3) The questions which arise are: why was the absence of [the assistant bosun] from his harbour station not noticed? and why was there not a foolproof system which would ensure that the vital task of closing the bow doors was performed irrespective of the potential failure of any one individual? This was not the first occasion on which such a failure had occurred ...

(10.4) A general instruction issued in July 1984 prescribed that it was the duty of the officer loading the main vehicle deck (G deck) to ensure that the bow doors were "secure when leaving port". That instruction

[11] *M.V. Herald of Free Enterprise, Report of the Court*, No. 8074 Dept. of Transport 1987.

had been regularly flouted. It was interpreted as meaning that it was the duty of the loading officer merely to see that someone was at the controls and ready to close the doors. That is not the meaning of the instruction ... If it had been enforced this disaster would not have occurred ...

(10.9) [There was some confusion about the precise facts surrounding the Chief Officer's departure from the loading deck to harbour station on the bridge.] The precise facts are of no consequence because, on either version, [the CO] failed to carry out his duty to ensure that the bow doors were closed. He was seriously negligent by reason of that failure. Of all the many faults which combined to lead directly or indirectly to this tragic disaster that of [the Chief Officer] was the most immediate. This Court cannot condone such irresponsible conduct. For this reason his certificate of competency must be suspended.

(11.1) The Court found some difficulty in finding a clear answer to the question: Why could not the loading officer remain on G deck until the doors were closed before going to his harbour station on the bridge?

(11.3) ... The Court was left in no doubt that deck officers felt that there was no time to be wasted. The Company sought to say that this disaster could have been avoided if the Chief Officer had waited on G deck another three minutes. That is true. But the Company took no proper steps to ensure that the CO remained on G deck until the bow doors were closed. On 6 March they were running late. The *Herald* sailed 5 minutes late. This may have contributed to the COs decision to leave G deck before the arrival of the AB, which he anticipated.

(12.1) [The] Master of the *Herald* on 6 March 1987 ... was responsible for the safety of his ship and every person on board. [The Master] took the *Herald* to sea with the bow doors fully open, with the consequences which have been related. It follows that [the Master] must accept personal responsibility for the loss of his ship.

(12.5) ... before this disaster there had been no less than five occasions when one of the Company's ships had proceeded to sea with bow or stern doors open.

(12.6) The system which was in operation in all the Spirit class ships was defective. The fact that other Masters operated the same defective system does not relieve [t]he Captain] of his personal responsibility for taking his ship to sea in an unsafe condition. In so doing he was seriously negligent in the discharge of his duties. That negligence was one of the causes contributing to the casualty ... the Court would be failing in its duty if it did not suspend his Certificate of Competency.

(14.1) At first sight the faults which led to this disaster were the aforesaid errors of omission on the part of the Master, the Chief Officer and the assistant bosun ... But a full investigation into the circumstances of the disaster leads inexorably to the conclusion that the underlying or cardinal faults lay higher up in the Company ... All concerned in management ... were guilty of fault in that all must be regarded as sharing responsibility for the failure of management. From top to bottom the body corporate was infected with the disease of sloppiness.

(16.2) ... But as this Investigation progressed, it became clear that the shore management took very little notice of what they were told by their Masters ... the Court heard of four areas in which the voices of the Masters fell on deaf ears ashore. Those areas [included]:—

... b. The wish to have lights fitted on the bridge to indicate whether the bow and stern doors were open or closed.

(18.5) [One Captain wrote a memorandum to shore management suggesting that indicator lights be fitted, which was distributed amongst managers.] It was a serious memorandum which merited serious thought and attention, and called for a considered reply. The answers ... received will be sent out verbatim. ... "Do they need an indicator to tell them whether the deck storekeeper is awake and sober!" "My goodness!" ... "Nice but don't we already pay someone!" ... "Assume the guy who shuts the doors tells the bridge if there is a problem." ... "Nice!" It is hardly necessary for the Court to comment that these replies display an absence of any proper sense of responsibility ...

(18.8) Enough has been said to make it clear that by the autumn of 1986 the shore staff of the Company were well aware of the possibility that one of their ships would sail with her stern or bow doors open. They were also aware of a very sensible and simple device in the form of indicator lights which had been suggested by responsible Masters. [Such lights were fitted within days of the tragedy].

Summary
The immediate cause was failure by crew. The vessel was short-manned and the loading officer was also officer for the watch, who not only had to be responsible for seeing that the bow doors were closed, but also had to be on bridge 15 minutes before sailing.

Penalties

The Captain's and Chief Officer's certificates were suspended.

The company was ordered to pay £400,000 towards costs of the Inquiry (£350,000 to Secretary of State for Transport and £50,000 to the seamen's union).

SAFETY CHANGES

Counsel argued at the inquiry that no offences were committed under the Merchant Shipping Act 1979, s. 44 or under the Merchant Shipping (Load Lines) Act 1967. No reference was made to the Merchant Shipping Act 1970, s. 27 which covers masters and crew. The Inquiry recommended an offence of leaving the berth with either bow or stern doors open (see Merchant Shipping (Closing of Openings in Hulls and Watertight Bulkheads) Regulations 1987).[12]

The Merchant Shipping Act 1988 sharpens up existing as well as introducing new offences (sections 30–33).

Section 30 (superseding Merchant Shipping Act 1979, s. 44) renders owners and masters liable in respect of dangerously unsafe ships.

Section 31 creates a new offence: "It shall be the duty of the owner of a ship ... to take all reasonable steps to secure that the ship is operated in a safe manner. See *Seaboard Offshore Ltd v. Secretary of State for Transport, The Safe Carrier*,[13] where the House of Lords held that shipowners were not vicariously liable for the actions of all their employees. The House of Lords said, *obiter*, that a charge could be based on allegation of failure to lay down a system for securing that what happened did not happen (see further chapter 7.1.1.)

Section 32, refers to conduct endangering ships, structures and individuals (replacing the Merchant Shipping Act 1970, s. 27). See the *Marchioness* case study below.

Section 33 establishes the Marine Accident Investigation Branch headed by a Chief Inspector of Marine Accidents, thus giving a formal structure to the system of inspection which previously operated.

New international standards on ship stability are being phased in by 2007.[14] These standards do not make transverse bulkheads

---

[12] S.I. 1987 No. 1298.
[13] [1994] 2 All E.R. 99.
[14] Safety of Lives at Sea 90 (SOLAS 90).

compulsory, an omission which was further criticised in the wake of the sinking of the *Estonia* in the Baltic Sea in 1994.[15]

INQUEST

The inquests were held in October 1987. A challenge was brought by way of judicial review of the coroner's initial ruling that there was no such offence as corporate manslaughter or, that if there were, there was no evidence of gross negligence necessary for such a finding. On the second point the Divisional Court agreed but was prepared to assume for the purposes of the appeal that a corporation was capable of committing manslaughter.[16]

The inquest jury returned unlawful killing verdicts on 188 of the victims. Because of the coroner's ruling, these have to be assumed to be based on individual rather than corporate culpability.

NUS (the seamen's union) reacted by seeking to bring a private prosecution against the company, while NUMAST (the officers' union) instructed solicitors to investigate the possibility of having the inquest verdicts overturned. The NUS said "If there is to be any prosecution it should be against the company itself for allowing a system of work which cost the lives of 188 people when an individual overslept."[17]

LEGAL ACTIONS

Admiralty

Following the Sheen Report, the Master's certificate was suspended. He appealed to the Admiralty Division. Suspension is authorised under the Merchant Shipping Act 1970, ss. 52 and 56, where the investigation is satisfied that an officer "has been seriously negligent in the discharge of his duties" and that that caused or contributed to the casualty. Even though he followed the normal practice of masters of ferries of this class, the court held that "that standard fell below the standard of the reasonably prudent cross-Channel ferry master" and his appeal was dismissed.[18]

---

[15] *The Independent*, 30 Sept 1994.
[16] *R. v. HM Coroner for East Kent, ex p. Spooner* (1989) 88 Cr. App. Rep. 10.
[17] *The Times*, 10 October 1987.
[18] *Herald of Free Enterprise Appeal*, *The Independent*, 18 December 1987, Q.B.D.C.

Civil

The main compensation agreement agreed by the steering group of solicitors included a payment of £5,000 to everybody whether injured or not.[19] 10 survivors were reported to have been awarded sums of between £9,100 and £150,000. This last sum was paid to a 54 year-old man whose mother, wife, daughter and grandchild died and included a sum for the psychological effects. 116 of 299 surviving passengers accepted settlements. Of 154 deaths, 86 cases settled. The settlements also went over the Fatal Accidents limits and allowed £10,000 to be paid in all cases. A compensation settlement of £165,000 was approved by the High Court in January 1988; it was paid for the death of a breadwinner who left a wife and dependant children. By May 1994, there were still 20 outstanding claims. Crew claims come under ordinary negligence and it was reported that the insurers were seeking to reduce the claims from a global £2.4 million proposed by the crew's lawyers to £1.4 million. See Chapters 5 and 6 for an account of the legal principles and processes leading to these settlements.

Post Traumatic Stress Disorder: Survivors were reported to have been awarded between £1,750 and £30,000 for psychological injuries. Relatives sought to claim for PTSD caused by TV transmission of the rescue attempts. These failed in light of the House of Lords' ruling in relation to the similar Hillsborough claims.[20] PTSD claims are also discussed in Chapter 6.

A claim for psychiatric damage arising from the rescue was dismissed by the Court of Appeal in 1991.[21] The appellant, who had succeeded in the High Court, was a member of one of the crews which worked on the *Herald* but was not on the ship on that sailing. Within three days he went as a volunteer to Zeebrugge where he was required to identify the bodies of two colleagues. The claim had proceeded without showing the causal or temporal relationship of the psychiatric damage with the activities he undertook when he volunteered to go to Zeebrugge. Without an examination of those facts, the case could not be decided.

Family

The question arose whether it was contempt of court for a newspaper to identify a child, orphaned in the disaster, as a ward

---

[19] *The Times*, 29 April 1989.
[20] *Alcock v. Chief Constable of South Yorkshire Police* [1991] 4 All E.R. 907; see Chap. 6.2.2.
[21] *Rapley v. P&O Ferries*, 21 February 1991, Lexis.

of court, in the absence of a specific order restricting publication of any information. It was held that neither common law nor section 12 (1) of the Administration Act 1960 in themselves made contemptuous publication of the fact that a child was a ward of court.[22]

Criminal

Unusually, the decision to prosecute was taken after both the inquiry and the inquest findings. Seven P&O employees and the company itself were indicted for manslaughter in 1989 and tried in 1990. The judge directed acquittal of the company and the directors on the ground that the prosecution were unable to show that they had ignored an obvious and serious risk of the ferry sailing with its doors open. The charges against the Chief Officer and the assistant bosun were then withdrawn by the Crown. There is no direct provision for appeal against acquittal, but under the Criminal Justice Act 1972 the Attorney-General may refer a point of law to the Court of Appeal. Despite pressure from some quarters, the Attorney declined to do so.[23]

There were also criminal investigations in Belgium arising from the *Herald* disaster.

Tax

P&O, who had agreed to pay all the legal costs of the defendants in the corporate manslaughter trial, attempted unsuccessfully to claim input tax on the fees paid to the firms of solicitors representing the individual defendants. These fees amounted to £3.5 million. The company argued that the services were not supplied to the company, but to the individual employees and thus were not used for the purposes of the company's business. The VAT Tribunal disagreed, holding that although the individual employee was client of the particular solicitor, the company was a client as principal in relation to each solicitor. This was because the company not only approved the choice of solicitor, it also instructed and agreed to pay him, and the solicitors' rights to recover costs would be from the company. The Tribunal agreed that the legal representation conferred substantial benefits on the individual employees, the expenditure also benefited the company, whose Board had taken the view that in order to mitigate the real risk of being driven out of business, it had to guard against the conviction of any of the employees. Therefore, the legal

---

[22] *Re L (a minor)* [1988] 1 All E.R. 418, Fam.D.
[23] Criminal Justice Act 1972, s. 36.

services were used for the purpose of the company's business within section 14(3) of the Value Added Tax Act 1985.[24]

SUPPORT GROUP

The Herald Families Association was founded in August 1987 with the objectives of helping members come to terms with the effects of the tragedy, improving the safety of ro-ro ferries and to "seek justice" by making the company legally accountable. A charitable off-shoot, the Herald Charitable Trust, has been instrumental in the establishment of Disaster Action, an umbrella group committed to safety causes. The Trust has commissioned three published works, including one on the *Herald* disaster.[25]

3. Piper Alpha

Piper Alpha, an off shore oil rig, exploded in July 1988, killing 167 men. Of those who died, two were on the support vessel *Sandhaven*. There were 81 survivors. It was the world's worst off-shore disaster and insurance claims ran to between $1 billion and $1.5 billion. Combined with heavy claims for storm damage in 1987, this undoubtedly contributed to the Lloyds insurance collapse in the early 1990s. Off-shore oil is a high-risk industry, with an estimated 500 deaths in the 25 years since North Sea oil and gas exploration began.[26] The operator of the platform was Occidental Petroleum (Caledonia) Ltd. Occidental pulled out of the North Sea in January 1991, selling their interests to Gulf Aquitaine.

INQUIRY

Lord Cullen was appointed by the Secretary of State for Energy to conduct a public inquiry.[27] With three assessors, Lord Cullen's task was to report on the circumstances of the accident and its cause and to make any observations and recommendations with a view to future preservation of life and prevention of further

---

[24] *P&O Ferries (Dover) Ltd v. The Commissioners of Customs and Excise* [1992] VATTR 221.

[25] Crainer, S., *Zeebrugge: Learning from Disaster* (1993); Bergman, D., *Disasters: Where the Law Fails*, (1993) and Young, P., *Focusing on Management Responsibility* (1993).

[26] Miller, K., "Piper Alpha and the Cullen Report (1991) 20 *Industrial Law J.* 176–187.

[27] Under the Offshore Installations (Public Inquiries) Regulations 1974 (S.I. 1974 No. 338).

33

accidents. The report of nearly 500 pages was published in November 1990.[28]

The following was taken from the "Executive Summary":[29]

(1.5) [The explosion resulted when condensate leaked following a pump being restarted by night-shift workers before replacement of a pressure safety valve taken off during maintenance.] The lack of awareness of the removal of the valve resulted from failures in communication of information at shift handover earlier in the evening and failure in the operation of the permit system in connection with the work which had entailed its removal.

(1.7) The initial explosion put the main power supplies and the Control Room at Piper out of action. It appears that the emergency shutdown system was activated and the emergency shutdown valves on the gas pipeline risers probably closed ... The other emergency systems of the platform failed immediately or within a short period of the initial explosion. In particular the fire-water system was rendered inoperative either due to physical damage or loss of power. However, even at the time of the initial explosion the diesel fire pumps were on manual mode so that, even if they had not been disabled, they would have required manual intervention in order to start them.

(1.8) ... Of the 226 men on the platform, 62 were on night-shift duty; the great majority of the remainder were in the accommodation. The system for control in the event of a major emergency was rendered almost entirely inoperative. Smoke and flames outside the accommodation made evacuation by helicopter or lifeboat impossible ... At no stage was there a systematic attempt to lead men to escape from the accommodation. To remain in the accommodation meant certain death.

(1.10) [From the 135 bodies recovered, the main cause of death was smoke inhalation. 14 died during an attempt to escape from the platform.]

(1.11) [T]he failure in the operation of the permit to work system was not an isolated mistake [and] there were a number of respects in which the laid down procedure was not adhered to and unsafe practices were followed. ... The evidence ... indicated dissatisfaction with the standard of information which was communicated at shift handover. This had been the subject of criticism in the light of a fatality in September 1987. [Occidental were prosecuted for breach of the Health and Safety at Work Act 1974 .]

---

[28] *Public Inquiry into the Piper Alpha Disaster* Cm. 1310 (1990). See McEldowney, J., "Public Inquiry into the Piper Alpha Disaster" (1991) 2 *Utilities Law Review* 2.
[29] Chap. 1.

(1.13) [Emergency training was criticised as cursory and inconsistent]. The OIMs and platform management did not show the necessary determination to ensure that regularity was achieved.

(1.14) ... Occidental management should have been more aware of the need for a high standard of incident provision and fire-fighting. They were all too easily satisfied that the permit to work system was being operated correctly, relying on the absence of any feedback of problems as indicating that all was well. They failed to provide the training to ensure that an effective permit to work system was operated in practice ... They adopted a superficial attitude to the assessment of the risk of major hazard. They failed to ensure that emergency training was being provided as they intended ... The safety policies and procedures were in place: the practice was deficient.

(1.15) Installations such as Piper Alpha were subject to regular inspections [by the Department of Energy], the purpose of which was, by means of a sampling technique, to assess the adequacy of the safety of the installation as a whole. [A visit in 1988] was also used to follow-up what Occidental had done in the light of the fatality, which was in part due to failures in the operation of the permit to work system and the communication of information at shift handover ... Even after making allowance for the fact the inspections were based on sampling it was clear to me that they were superficial to the point of being of little use as a test of safety on the platform ... [T]he evidence led me to question, in a fundamental sense, whether the type of inspection practised by the DEn could be an effective means of assessing or monitoring the management of safety by operators.

(1.17) The disaster involved the realisation of a potential major hazard ... Although such remote but potentially hazardous events had been envisaged Occidental did not require them to be assessed systematically; nor did the offshore safety regime require this.

(1.19) The safety of personnel on an installation in regard to hazards at large is ... critically dependent on the systematic management of safety by operators. The present off-shore safety regime does not address this in any direct sense, and current measures are, in my view, ineffective for the purpose of ensuring that the management of safety by all operators is adequate.

Summary
The Report contains 106 recommendations covering many technical areas, the availability of emergency control facilities, means of escape, standard of standby vessels and the provision of personal survival suits.

It also makes recommendations about the management of off-shore facilities by the operators themselves and by the UK regulatory authorities.

Cullen recommended that operators should be required to carry out formal assessments of major hazards, the formal safety assessment to be in the form of a *Safety Case*. A temporary safe refuge for personnel should be a central feature. Regular auditing of compliance with safety management should be for the operator to carry out rather than the regulatory body. This is new for the offshore industry, but is consistent with the Robens philosophy on which the 1974 Act was based, *i.e.* that the inspectorates responsible for health and safety should be replaced by a single body.[30] There should be a single regulatory body and existing restrictive safety regulations should be replaced by the type which set objectives rather than solutions.

SAFETY CHANGES

At the time of the disaster, safety was the responsibility of the Department of Energy, which administered the Mineral Workings (Offshore Installations) Act 1971 and the Health and Safety at Work Act 1974. This was contrary to the general approach of the latter which emphasises unitary regulatory responsibility. A plethora of different regulatory schemes covered exploration,[31] off-shore installations,[32] off-shore pipelines,[33] and vessels.[34] Health and Safety at Work Regulations only applied outside Great Britain if expressly provided and, at the time, only one set applied.[35] In respect of these, the Health and Safety Commission had an agency agreement with the Department of Energy to enforce them.[36]

The Secretary of State for Energy announced in 1990 that all Cullen's conclusions and recommendations were accepted by the Government. Formal responsibility for off-shore safety was transferred to the Department of Employment and administered by

---

[30] *Report of the Committee on Safety and Health at Work* Cmnd. 5034 (1972).

[31] Petroleum Production Act 1934.

[32] Mineral Workings (Offshore Installations) Act 1971.

[33] Petroleum and Submarine Pipelines Act 1975.

[34] Under the Merchant Shipping Acts this responsibility falls on the Department of Transport.

[35] Offshore Installations and Pipeline Works (First Aid) Regulations 1989 (S.I. 1989 No. 1671).

[36] For a detailed account of the off-shore safety regime, see Barrett, B. and Howells, R., "Legal Responsibilities for Industrial Emergency Planning in the UK" in Parker, D. and Handmer, J., eds, *Hazard Management and Emergency Planning: Perspectives on Britain* (1992).

the Health and Safety Commission (HSC) and Executive (HSE). Cullen recommended that more resources be devoted to safety and the increase in the HSC's budget from £12 million in 1990–91 to £20 million in 1991–92 has allowed a fourfold increase in the HSE personnel working on offshore safety. Evidence to the Select Committee on Energy was that new safety expenditure since the Cullen Report was in the region of £850 million.[37] Up to 80 per cent of that expenditure is expected to come from petroleum revenue tax receipts. Numerous regulations have been passed to implement detailed recommendations on matters such as standby vessels, and emergency pipeline valves as well as other HSE Codes of Practice.[38] For example, the Offshore Installations (Prevention of Fire and Explosion, and Emergency Response) Regulations require operators and owners to take action to prevent fires and explosions, to think through the consequences of all major accidents, and to structure their emergency response arrangements to deal effectively with the reality of those consequences.[39]

The Offshore Safety Act 1992 represents the main response to the Cullen Report and gives legislative backing to the transfer of safety responsibility to the HSE. However, there are still areas of potential uncertainty, particularly with respect to vessels working near installations.[40]

A recommendation to deal with concerns about victimisation if workers raise safety issues was not included in the 1992 Act on the ground that it was an employment and not a safety issue. This was rather pedantic. However, the Government did support a private member's Bill which was enacted in 1992.[41]

FATAL ACCIDENT INQUIRY

The Scottish equivalent of an inquest is a Fatal Accident Inquiry (FAI). Under the Fatal Accidents and Sudden Deaths Inquiry (Scotland) Act 1976 the hitherto unresolved issue of jurisdiction over deaths on North Sea oil and gas installations was clarified. Section 9 extends the application of the Act to deaths in connection with exploration of the seabed for natural resources occurring on

---

[37] Seventh Report of the Energy Committee on Offshore Safety Management, 17 July 1991 (1990–1991, H.C. 343, para. 13).

[38] See Gaskell, N., Annotations to Offshore Safety Act 1992, *Current Law Statutes Annotated* (1992) Vol. 2, Chap. 15–7.

[39] Draft regulations were issued in September 1993.

[40] Gaskell, *op. cit.*, 15–13.

[41] Offshore Safety (Protection against Victimization) Act 1992.

that part of the Continental Shelf to which Scots law applies.[42] The potential overlap with the provision for enquiries under the Mineral Workings (Offshore Installations) Act 1971, first invoked in relation to Piper Alpha, was anticipated. The 1976 Act amended the 1971 Act to the effect that unless the Lord Advocate so directs, no fatal Accident Inquiry shall be held where there has been a 1971 Act inquiry.

LEGAL ACTIONS

Civil

The Chair of the Aberdeen Bar called a group meeting, attended by 90 solicitors, nine of whom formed a steering committee.[43]

Lawyers representing 135 families and 50 survivors formed the Occidental and Piper Disaster Group, which consisted of 142 solicitors' firms. Full details of the settlement have not been disclosed, but it was estimated to be worth nearly £100 million based on a "mid-Atlantic" settlement. Dependants of workers received £600,000, although for families of those on higher than average earnings, the sum reached £1 million.[44] Although an action in the US might have yielded higher awards, the obstacles and cost would have been stiff, possibly prohibitive.[45] Nonetheless, the compensation levels were much higher than those following many disasters, partly because the victims were more likely to have left dependants but also because of the pull which the possibility of litigation in the States gave to the negotiations.

Criminal

The Secretary of State for Energy referred the question of a manslaughter prosecution to the Lord Advocate who has the prerogative over such matters. The failure of the P&O case militated against the likelihood of prosecution and in July 1991, it was announced that the evidence which Cullen had mounted would not pass the test of a criminal burden of proof.[46] Although the relatives' association considered mounting a private prosecution,

---

[42] This extends the effect of the Continental Shelf (Jurisdiction) (Amendment) Order 1975 which was restricted to deaths caused by some other person.

[43] McBryde and Barker, "Solicitors' Groups in Mass Disaster Claims" (1991) 141 New Law Journal 484.

[44] "Piper Alpha Settlement" (1989) Law Soc Gazette No. 27, p. 3.

[45] Kolman, "The Piper Alpha Oil Rig Disaster" (1989) Scots L.T. 293, and see Chap. 6.5.

[46] See above under Herald of Free Enterprise and also Chap. 7.1.3 for further details of the P&O case.

they abandoned the quest in 1992. It was reported that lawyers advised that difficulties with the evidence and the sale of the company made a prosecution unlikely to succeed.[47]

SUPPORT GROUPS

The Piper Alpha Families and Survivors Association met regularly.[48] A new union, the Offshore Industry Liaison Committee was set up in 1991.

DISASTER FUND

A discretionary trust set up by Aberdeen's Lord Provost received an immediate gift of £1 million from the Chairman of Occidental and eventually received £4.59 million. Each of the bereaved and the survivors received an early payment of £3,500. The decision was then taken to distribute the remainder to the bereaved, excluding the survivors. Sums awarded were confidential but distribution was in proportions of three units to a widow, two to a child and one to a surviving parent.[49]

4. Hillsborough

95 people were crushed to death at Sheffield's Hillsborough football ground when too many were allowed into one part of the terraces. The ground was host to the FA Cup semi-final between Liverpool and Nottingham Forest in April 1989. Those who died were mainly Liverpool supporters. The match, which was being televised, was abandoned five and a half minutes after the 3 p.m. kick-off.

INQUIRY

An inquiry, chaired by Lord Justice Taylor, was set up by the Home Secretary. As a departmental inquiry, evidence was not given on oath (see further Chapter 3). It was the ninth official

---

[47] (1992) 142 New Law Journal p. 115.
[48] See Sheridan, G. and Kenning, T., Survivors (1993), Chap. 4.
[49] (1988) 138 New Law Journal p. 716.

report covering crowd safety and control at football grounds.[50] Three years earlier, the Popplewell Report into the Bradford Fire had been published, which also looked at the Heysel stadium riots which had occurred shortly after. Between them, Bradford and Heysel left 91 dead.

Both the Bradford and Hillsborough grounds were subject to the safety provisions introduced by the Safety at Sports Grounds Act 1975. The Act provides for local authority certification of designated stadia.[51] At the time of the Bradford fire, the only stadia designated were those in Divisions One and Two of the Football League with over 10,000 capacity.

The following is taken from the Interim report[52]:

(58) At about 12 noon Chief Inspector Creaser asked Superintendent Murray whether the pens on the west terrace were to be filled one by one successively but was told that they should all be available from the start and the fans should find their own level.

(63) In the 20 minutes from 2.30 p.m. to 2.50 p.m. there were crucial developments both inside and outside the ground. In pens 3 and 4 there was a steady increase in pressure as more fans came through the tunnel to the favoured area behind the goal. By 2.50 p.m. these pens were already full to a degree which caused serious discomfort to many well used to enduring pressure on terraces. The numbers at the time were clearly in excess of the maximum density stated by the Home Office Guide to Safety at Sports Grounds [1986 edn, the Green Guide], i.e. 54 persons per 10 square metres. (Although the Green Guide has no statutory or legal force, it is the only official advice available about safety at sports grounds.) In the wing pens of 1, 2, 6 and 7, there was still ample room and bare patches of concrete were visible.

(67) [The police control room was requested to allow the gates to be open because the pressure at the turnstiles was creating a potentially dangerous situation outside the ground.] Mr Duckenfield gave the order [to open the gates]. Neither the Club control room nor any police officers inside the turnstiles were told of this order before or after it was given or of any action it would require.

---

[50] Shortt Report, Cmd. 2088 (1924); Moelwyn Hughes Report, Cmd. 6846 (1946) (set up following the disaster at Bolton Wanderers, where 33 died); Chester Report (1966); Harrington Report (1968); the Lang Report (1969); Wheatley Report, Cmnd. 4952 (1972) (following the Ibrox disaster where 66 died); McElhone Report (1977) Scottish Education Department, HMSO; Department of Environment Official Working Group on Football Spectator Violence (1984); Popplewell, Cmnd. 9710 (1986) (following the Bradford fire, where 53 died).

[51] The Fire Safety and Safety of Places of Sport Act 1987 extends this system.

[52] *The Hillsborough Stadium Disaster*, Interim Report, Cm. 765 (1989).

(70) In the five minutes it was open about 2,000 fans passed through [gate C] steadily at a fast walk ... [A] large proportion headed straight for the tunnel in front of them.

(144) [The Club's safety certificate contained no maximum figures for the pens. Section 2(1) of the Safety of Sports Grounds Act 1975 provides ...: "A Safety Certificate shall contain such terms and conditions as the local authority consider necessary or expedient to secure reasonable safety at the stadium when it is in use ..." [Section 2(2) required a maximum for the stadium but left discretionary the fixing of maxima for different parts] ... Section 2(2) was repealed by the Fire Safety and Safety at Places of Sports Act 1987, section 19, which gave power to the Secretary of State to lay down, by order, terms and conditions. No order has yet been made and guidance from the Home Office has recommended local authorities to approach their function under section 2(1) in accordance with the criteria in the repealed section 2(2).

(146) [In accordance with its obligations under the 1975 Act, the Club had notified the local authority of its plans to alter the pens and barriers] ... Having received notice of the alterations to the pens and the barriers, the local authority ought, in my view, to have amended the Safety certificate accordingly. They did not do so.

(149) ... If proper maximum figures had been inserted in the certificate for each of the pens, the Club and the police might well have been prompted to find some means of limiting the numbers entering those pens other than by visual monitoring:

(161) [Who should monitor the terraces] Should it be the host club via its stewards? Should it be the police? Should it be both? Or should it be by arrangement, depending upon the ground or section of the ground in question?

(162) In principle, a football club which invites the public to a match on its premises for reward is responsible for securing safety at that event...

(164) [Quoting from the Popplewell Report, para 4.13] ... Those responsible for organising a private function, however, have the primary and continuing obligation and responsibility to ensure reasonable safety for those who are invited on to their premises ... It cannot be too strongly emphasised that it is upon the club or the occupier of the ground who is putting on the function, that the primary and continuing obligation rests."

(165) There remains, however, the question whether there are some grounds or parts of grounds where the club may need to rely upon

the police (whom they pay to attend) to control filling of pens and monitoring ... [W]hilst the duty in law to ensure safety rests upon the club, they may need, ... to employ the police to act as their agents in certain circumstances.

(169) [In *Harris v Sheffield United Football Club Ltd*] the South Yorkshire Police Authority obtained a judgement against the [club] for money due for police services provided at Sheffield United's matches.

(285) [Having concluded that neither the choice of venue nor the allocation of sections of the ground were causative of the disaster, the report continued] It is a matter of regret that at the hearing, and in their submissions, the South Yorkshire Police were not prepared to concede that they were in any respect at fault in what occurred. Mr Duckenfield [the Chief Superintendent in control of policing at the match], under pressure of cross-examination, apologised for blaming the Liverpool fans for causing the deaths. But that apart, the police case was to blame the fans for being late and drunk, and to blame the Club for failing to monitor the pens ...

(286) The performance by the City Council of its duties in regard to the Safety Certificate was inefficient and dilatory. The failure to revise or amend the certificate over the period of three years preceding this disaster, despite important changes in the layout of the ground, was a serious breach of duty.

(290) [Although the Club had a responsible and conscientious approach to its duties] ... there are a number of respects in which failure by the Club contributed to this disaster. They were responsible as occupiers and invitors for the layout and structure of the ground ... The Club knew best what rate of admission the turnstiles could manage and ought to have alerted the police to the risks of the turnstiles being swamped.

(292) Although the police had assumed responsibility for monitoring the pens, the Club had a duty to its visitors and the Club's officials ought to have alerted the police to the grossly uneven distribution of the fans on the terraces.

Summary

The disaster occurred because gate C was opened without cutting access to the central pens which were already overfull. That was because there was no safe maximum capacity specified in the safety certificate. The operational order and police tactics on the day failed to provide for controlling the foreseeable arrival of a concentrated number of spectators in a short period before the match.

The final report added other contributory factors. The lessons of previous disasters were unheeded because of insufficient concern for safety of spectators, and because of complacency that disasters could not strike twice.[53]

The interim report made 43 separate recommendations (brought up to 76 in the Final Report), 28 of which were to be implemented before the start of the football season.

Disciplinary measures

These were not within Taylor's remit. Chief Superintendent Duckenfield was transferred from his post as divisional commander to head of community liaison and later suspended on full pay. He was retired early two years later because of persistent depression and mental stress.[54] The Superintendent in charge of the police control box has moved to a different division. Disciplinary action, taken against him and against Duckenfield, was dropped in 1992 following the latter's retirement. The Police Complaints Authority was reported to have said "It would be an injustice to the superintendent, who conducted himself with dignity at the inquest and throughout the investigations, for him to stand alone ... and thus appear to be a 'scapegoat' for faults which may well be attributed to others."[55]

The Chief Constable's offer to resign after publication of the interim report was not accepted, but he took early retirement two years later.[56]

SAFETY CHANGES

The recommendation was that stadia designated under the Safety of Sports Grounds Act 1975 should work towards converting to all-seat accommodation. For first and second division clubs, Scottish premier league and national grounds, that goal was to be achieved by the 1994/95 season.

While local authorities remain responsible for safety, certification of grounds is overseen by the Football Licensing Authority (FLA).[57] Six clubs have been granted an extension on the 1994 season deadline for all-seat accommodation by the FLA. In addition, a Trust distributes the £23 million raised annually from

---

[53] *The Hillsborough Stadium Disaster*, Report Cm. 962 (1990).
[54] *The Guardian*, 30 October 1991.
[55] *The Guardian*, 14 January 1992.
[56] *The Times*, 5 August 1989.
[57] Described in more detail in Chap. 3.1.1.

the Pools levy and from "Spot-the-Ball" competitions, currently at the rate of £1 for every £3 spent by the Clubs on ground improvements.

A private individual has made a number of applications for judicial review to compel the Home Secretary to implement the Safety at Sports Grounds Act 1975: one action was an attempt to get him to make regulations under section 6; another to invoke the powers of inspection of sports grounds under section 11(d) which states that "A person authorised by ... the secretary of state may ... enter a sports ground at any reasonable time, and make such inspection of it ... as he considers necessary for the purposes of this Act ..." These were unsuccessful.[58]

INQUEST

The inquest was opened formally on 18 April 1989. Rather than prolong the adjournments until after the D.P.P. had completed investigations into the possibility of a criminal prosecution, the coroner proceeded with the inquests on a limited basis. "Mini-inquests" dealing with issues such as "who" the victims were and "where" they had died, but not "how", were held in April and May 1990. The South Yorkshire police insurers agreed to fund the cost of "block" representation of the bereaved. Described as solely an "information dissemination exercise", with no cross-examination allowed, eight mini-inquests were held each day on a set pattern; the pathologist gave a brief account of findings and an opinion on the cause of death, police evidence was then given of movements of the deceased prior to death and of witness statements.[59]

By September the D.P.P. had ruled out prosecutions and the main inquests resumed in November. The coroner decided to limit evidence to events which occurred before 3.15 p.m. on the day of the disaster, although not all the victims were dead by then. This meant also that the emergency response was not considered. The families had to fund their representation, estimated to cost £100,000, at this full inquest. Police counsel were paid from public funds.

Before the inquest jury retired, the Coroner told them only to consider unlawful killing verdicts if they found that the management of the match involved a degree of recklessness. After two

---

[58] See *R. v. Lord Chancellor ex p. Edey* C.A. 2 July 1993, Lexis.
[59] Coleman and Scraton, "Unanswered Questions" (1990) November *Legal Action*, p. 8.

days of deliberation, verdicts of accidental death were returned.[60]

After an unsuccessful request to the Attorney-General to use his powers under the Coroners Act 1988 to apply to the High Court for the verdicts to be quashed and a fresh series of inquests held,[61] relatives sought an application for judicial review in the High Court.[62] McCowan L.J. refused to strike down the coroner's decision to impose the 3.15 p.m. cut-off time (see the discussion in Chapter 3.5.2).

LEGAL ACTIONS

Civil

The Hillsborough steering committee was formed in Liverpool with 50 law practices representing 92 families. A writ alleging negligence was served on the South Yorkshire Chief Constable in June 1989. The police sought a contribution from Sheffield Wednesday FC and Eastwood and Partners (the civil engineers employed by the club) in respect of the compensation they voluntarily agreed to pay the bereaved. They alleged negligence and breach of common duty against the club and negligence against Eastwood.

The apportioning was settled out of court in October 1990.

Post Traumatic Stress Disorder: Hillsborough gave rise to three important decisions, two of which concerned claims for post traumatic stress disorder. The other arose in respect of the duty to keep alive a person in a persistent vegetative state.

It was held by the House of Lords in *Alcock v. Chief Constable of S. Yorks. Police*[63] that damages for psychiatric illness brought about by witnessing or apprehending physical injury or risk to another person could be claimed from the person whose negligent act caused the injury or risk if:

(i) their relationship to the primary victim was close enough for it to be reasonably foreseeable that they might sustain nervous shock;

(ii) their proximity to the accident was sufficiently close in time and space;

---

[60] 28 March, 1991.
[61] s. 13(1)(b).
[62] *R. v. HM Coroner for South Yorkshire ex p. Stringer and others* Q.B.D. [1994] 17 BMLR 92.
[63] [1992] 1 A.C. 310.

> (iii) they suffered nervous shock through seeing or hearing the accident or its immediate aftermath.

Watching TV or listening to the radio was not sufficiently proximate. Of those claimants at the match, there was not a sufficiently close relationship: one lost two brothers, and another his brother-in-law. There was no evidence that there were particularly close ties of love or affection: see Chapter 6.2.2 for a full discussion.

Hicks v. Chief Constable of S. Yorks. Police[64] was a claim by a father present at the ground when two teenage daughters died. It was made on behalf of the deceaseds' estate, under the Law Reform (Miscellaneous Provisions) Act 1934, for pre-death injury, including suffering from awareness of impending death.[65] Whether they suffered injuries before death was purely one of fact, the House of Lords held, and both the High Court and the Court of Appeal found that no physical injury had been caused before the fatal crushing, and that unconsciousness and death occurred in a very short space of time after onset of asphyxia. Fear itself cannot give rise to damages, only pain and suffering. This case is discussed in more detail in Chapter 5.4.1.

Withdrawing treatment to patients in a persistent vegetative state Tony Bland, one of Hillborough's victims, died in 1993 following a landmark case in which the House of Lords authorised the hospital where he had lain in a persistent vegetative state since the disaster to withdraw life-sustaining treatment.[66]

Criminal

The D.P.P. announced in August 1989 that there would be no prosecutions. He said that after an investigation by West Midlands Police, he found that there was insufficient evidence to bring a prosecution against any of the following: South Yorkshire police, Sheffield Wednesday Football Club, Eastwood and Partners (the club's civil engineer advisors) or Sheffield City Council.

Lawyers representing relatives had said that they expected unlawful killing verdicts at the inquest and that the C.P.S. would then decide on manslaughter charges against the police and the club. However, neither of those predictions proved to be accurate.

---

[64] [1992] 2 All E.R. 65.

[65] This head of claim replaced damages for loss of expectation of life: Administration of Justice Act 1982, s. 1(1)(b). See also Chap. 5.4.2.

[66] *Airedale N.H.S. Trust v. Bland* [1993] 2 WLR 316. See Alldridge, "Who Wants to Live Forever?" in Lee, R. and Morgan, D., eds, *Death Rites* (1993) p. 11.

A Police Complaints Authority investigation found that the Chief Constable had no criminal offences to answer, nor had he committed a breach of discipline.[67]

Support Group

The Hillsborough Family Support Group was active in providing advice, social and other support and in campaigning for changes in the inquest proceedings and the level of bereavement payments.

Disaster Fund

An appeal raised more than £10 million.[68]

5. Marchioness

51 people died when a Thames dredger, the *Bowbelle*, collided with a pleasure cruiser, the *Marchioness*, in August 1989. The *Bowbelle* had a gross tonnage of 1494.94 and a length of 79.91 m; the *Marchioness* was 46.19 gross tonnage and 26.06 m in length.

Inquiry

An inquiry was conducted by Captain Peter Marriott, chief inspector of the newly established Marine Accident Investigation Branch.[69] The investigation was conducted in private and completed in February 1990 but was not published until August 1991.[70] The explanation given for the delay was that it was necessary to prevent any prejudice to the trial of the *Bowbelle*'s captain on charges under the Merchant Shipping Act (see below).

The report found that the accident occurred on a fine moonlit night, that both vessels were bound down river, in both the wheel-houses were properly manned, but neither was aware until too late of the presence of the other to take avoiding action.

In each vessel the maintenance of a good look-out was seriously hampered as a result of the design (in the case of *Bowbelle* alarm-

---

[67] 28 April 1990.
[68] *The Times*, 29 March 1991.
[69] Merchant Shipping Act 1988, s. 33.
[70] *Report of the Chief Inspector of Marine Accidents into the Collision between The Passenger Launch Marchioness and MV Bowbelle with the loss of life on the River Thames on 20 August 1989*, Dept. of Transport (1991).

ingly so)[71], so that visibility from the wheelhouse was seriously restricted, and in neither vessel were sufficient steps taken to overcome this. This was the main cause of the collision.[72]

A further major contributory factor was the failure of the *Marchioness* to keep to the starboard side of the channel.

Poor lighting was a further contributory factor and the Report noted that "no particular attention" has been paid by the Department of Transport to consideration of "any steps to improve the conspicuity of passenger launches".[73] The failure in the look-out, especially in the *Bowbelle*, which as the overtaking vessel had the overriding duty to keep clear, the design faults and failure of the *Marchioness* to keep starboard all stemmed from bad practices which had grown up over many years.

The investigation disclosed earlier collisions between similar vessels in 1981 (involving the *Hurlingham*, a sister cruiser of the *Marchioness*) and two in 1983, (one of which involved the *Bowbelle*). In addition, the *Bowbelle* had been involved in three incidents serious enough to be reported to the Port of London Authority. The Report concluded that it would have been unrealistic for the Department to respond to potential risks from poor visibility.[74] However, the accident occurred partly through the failure of the Department and the shipping industry to look at design and operation as integrated matters.

The decision to licence the two vessels was questioned. Boats with such design faults "ought not to have been allowed by the department in the first place. But to attach responsibility to any individual ... would be impossible, for the fault was simply part of a malaise which for many years affected not just the department but the entire maritime community."[75]

SAFETY CHANGES

27 recommendations for safety improvement were made in the Marine Accidents Investigation Branch's interim report, 20 of these were implemented within five weeks of the accident. The Port of London Authority introduced new navigational regulations requiring:

vessels to be equipped with VHF radio telephones,

---

[71] Paras. 7.4, 7.5 and Annex 5, photograph B.
[72] Para. 18.4.
[73] Para. 17.11.
[74] Para. 17.11.
[75] Paras. 58–9.

vessels such as the *Bowbelle* to have forward lookout at all
times,
vessels to have white identification lights on the bow.

The remaining recommendations came into force in January 1992.

INQUEST

The inquest began with a preliminary review hearing in February 1990 at which the coroner indicated that he would take the
inquest in two parts: the forensic and personal details of each
victim in the first, followed by an inquiry into all the deaths
including eye witness and technical evidence. The first stage was
completed for 44 of the 51 victims. However, in April 1990, the
D.P.P. intervened because the *Bowbelle* captain had been charged
(see below). In June 1992, when all criminal proceedings had been
abandoned, the coroner had to consider whether to reopen the
inquest. His decision not to do so was set aside by the Court of
Appeal in 1994, on the grounds of potential bias.[76] A new coroner
re-opened the inquests in March 1995 and adopted an unrestricted
policy on the evidence admitted from relatives and survivors.
Much of the evidence contradicted the M.A.I.B.'s findings on the
precise location of the accident, casting doubts on the alleged
failure of the *Marchioness* to keep starboard. On 7 April 1995 the
jury returned verdicts of unlawful killing with 12 safety recommendations appended.

LEGAL ACTIONS

Civil
    A group of solicitors formed the Marchioness Disaster Solicitors'
Steering Group. Owners of the *Marchioness* agreed to pay up to £6
million without waiting to establish blame, in October 1989. Both
shipowners admitted liability in May 1990 and interim damages
of £3,000 per claimant were paid. This followed the claimants'
decision to arrest two sister ships in an effort to force the negotiations.[77] East Coast Aggregates responded with a writ against
the survivors to set the limit of compensation from the *Bowbelle*
to £852,000. This is the maximum payable under the Merchant
Shipping Act 1979 unless reckless conduct is proved. Tidal Cruises,

---

[76] *R. v. Inner West London Coroner, ex p. Dallaglio and others The Times* 16 June 1994,
discussed further in Chap. 3.5.2.
[77] An appropriate procedure to avoid such an arrest was laid down by Sheen J. in
The Bowbelle (Q.B.D.) 9 March 1990, *The Times*, 21 March, 1990.

who owned the *Marchioness* waived their limit of £5 million (larger because they were carrying passengers).[78]

To speed up the process, claims not settled out of court were put through an informal assessment, undertaken by the Admiralty registrar. The first claim resulted in a payment of £9,500, twice that originally offered by the insurers. The High Court set up an informal procedure to assess compensation in August 1990.

Criminal

The captain of the dredger, *Bowbelle*, was prosecuted under the Merchant Shipping Act 1970.[79] At two successive trials juries could not agree on the charge that he had failed to ensure a proper lookout.

The D.P.P. in September 1990 ruled out the possibility of charges against the *Bowbelle*'s owners, South Coast Shipping.[80] A private prosecution for corporate manslaughter was launched by the widower of one of the victims, once the case against the captain was dropped. He estimated that it would cost up to £70,000.[81] This prompted the D.P.P. to ask for papers from the private prosecutor's solicitor with a view to taking over and dropping the prosecution.[82] After receiving protest at this unprecedented move, the D.P.P. decided not to intervene. It was at this point that publication of the MAIB Report took place.

The defendants attempted to stop the proceedings before committal with an application for judicial review on the grounds of abuse of process and lack of locus standi on the part of the prosecutor. Neither went in favour of the applicants.[83] Committal proceedings finally began in June 1992, but the case was dismissed by the Chief Metropolitan Stipendiary and came to an end there.

---

[78] The Convention on Limitation of Liability for Maritime Claims 1976 came into force in 1986: Merchant Shipping Act 1979, Sched 4.

[79] s. 27(4)(b), as substituted by the Merchant Shipping Act 1988, s. 32. No use was made against the *Bowbelle*'s owners of the offence under s. 31 of failing to ensure the safe operation of their ship, a new provision introduced following recommendations of the Sheen inquiry into the *Herald* disaster.

[80] An application for judicial review of this was rejected: *R. v. D.P.P., ex p. Langlands-Pearse* (Q.B.D.) 30 October 1990, Lexis.

[81] *The Times*, 3 August 1991.

[82] *Ibid.*

[83] *R. v. Bow Street Magistrate, ex p. South Coast Shipping Co. Ltd* [1993] Q.B. 645.

SUPPORT GROUP

The Marchioness Action Group was set up shortly after the disaster. As with the Hillsborough Group, much of their energy has been devoted to attempts to procedural and other reform campaigns. Unlike the other disasters chronicled here, no public inquiry has been held and it was five and a half years before the full inquests were eventually held. The group's persistence illustrates the complexities and multi-layering of the legal avenues open to disaster survivors in their efforts to achieve what they regard as a "just" response to the tragedy.

DISASTER FUND

The appeal raised £86,000. The relative lack of success was attributed to the media reports of the victims as young "yuppies". The mother of one of the victims claimed that this was a misrepresentation as they were mostly in low paid work.[84]

---

[84] *The Times*, 1 August 1991.

3. Disasters: Prevention, Preparation and Post-Mortem

In this chapter I discuss the various strategies states employ to reduce the incidence of disasters, to lessen the impact of them when they occur and to investigate and learn from them afterwards. All the issues discussed here fall broadly into the sphere of public law; they are not activated by particular individual litigants but are powers exercised by regulatory agencies, local authorities or central government. Safety and emergency policies are becoming increasingly trans-national in focus. 1990 marked the beginning of the United Nations International Decade for Natural Disaster Reduction, leading to a number of initiatives and international co-operation. Disaster prevention can be seen at different levels: global, continental, national, regional and local. Inevitably, the concentration here is national and local, but since the United Kingdom has been somewhat slow to develop an overall strategy, with respect to planning at least, reference will be made to other jurisdictions where helpful.

The prevention, preparedness, and inquiry phases form a rolling process. Prevention or mitigation is reflected in safety laws which themselves often follow the recommendations of inquiries set up in the aftermath of a particular disaster. So in a sense, it does not matter where I begin, but the safety framework seems to be as appropriate as any.

A word or two first about the use of the term "mitigation". I have separated the safety framework from that of emergency planning, but of course they are both concerned partly with mitigation. The disaster literature tends to use mitigation in the sense of policies designed to reduce the effect of a potential disaster (land-use schemes, for example). However, it is also used in the emergency response literature to refer to efforts to ensure that once a disastrous event has occurred, the results are not exacerbated by, for example, poor rescue responses. These two meanings can be distinguished by use of the terms prevention-mitigation and response-mitigation. Both safety regulation and emergency planning are inevitably based on forms of risk assessment, itself a rapidly evolving science. Whereas it was once the province of traditional pure and applied sciences, the psychology of human behaviour and socio-cultural theories are now impressing themselves on and influencing ideas and practical applications of risk management.[1]

Human factors such as land use, the density and location of population and of building structures all affect the impact of environmental disasters and, as we have seen, many disasters are themselves the outcome of technological development. Scientific understanding about meteorological and other natural phenomena is constantly unfolding, so that even if the precise moment an earthquake will occur may still defy prediction, knowledge of its likely effect and of the areas in which it might strike has greatly improved. Weather-based phenomena such as hurricanes, floods and fire are capable of greater predictability, although the warning signs may only be counted in hours. High risk technology-based industries are also continually advancing in analysis and comprehension of the elements in their processes which might lead to breakdown. Unusual weather patterns and technological failures do not always spell disaster, but they are generally significant, necessary precursors to it.

1. Prevention

(1) The Safety Law Framework

Studies of disasters reveal a consistent mixture of bad design, poor safety procedures and human error.[2] Human error arises from factors such as fatigue, boredom, lapses of attention and occasionally inexplicable inaccuracy in reading instruments.[3] An analysis of 251 accidents in the chemical industry by a Lloyds surveyor showed that although human failure accounted for about a third, poor design and inadequate basic maintenance played a significant role. Operational, as opposed to operator, failure accounted for nearly half.[4] It is useful to bear these findings in mind in considering safety policies.

---

[1] See Royal Society Study Group, *Risk: Analysis, Perception and Management* (1992).
[2] Singleton, W., *The Mind at Work* (1990).
[3] *Ibid.*
[4] Pearce and Tombs, "Bhopal: Union Carbide and the Hubris of the Capitalist Technocracy" (1989) 16 *Social Justice* 116, 132.

Numerous statutes have as their central aim the promotion of greater safety. One of the most significant in terms of the numbers potentially affected is the Health and Safety at Work Act 1974, but many others deal with areas of wide concern, including the Environmental Protection Act 1990, the Civil Aviation Act 1982, the Merchant Shipping Act 1988 and the Offshore Safety Act 1992. Road traffic legislation is largely motivated by safety worries; building regulations also have a safety angle, as does the Consumer Protection Act 1987. The Food Safety Act 1990 reflects growing anxieties about hazards in the food chain.

Many recent disaster inquiry reports have revealed weaknesses in management strategies in relation to health and safety at work.[5] In their study of the work of the health and safety inspectorate, Hutter and Lloyd-Bostock refer to the "power of accidents" both to assist in the effective enforcement of safety laws and sometimes to interfere with it.[6] Disasters are accidents writ large (although it has to be noted that many disaster survivors are profoundly irritated when their tragedy is referred to as an accident, with the implications that the difference is one only of quantity and, perhaps more importantly, that it was unavoidable). The contrast between the dramatic and the routine is reflected in media attention which directly affects the responses of the Health and Safety Executive (HSE). Where members of the public as well as employees are affected in a workplace incident, the media interest will be increased.

In terms of safety prevention, more may be gained from patient observation of data about minor incidents than from a particular major accident. Inspectors gain their information from extensive accident reporting which is required under the legislation. Any accident occurring at or in connection with work and resulting in three or more days' incapacity and any injury requiring 24 hours in hospital are reportable to the HSE.[7] Hutter and Lloyd-Bostock found that inspectors tended to investigate accidents on the grounds of seriousness of injury and whether it occurred as a result of a breach of specific regulations. The 1974 Act provides both a general offence of failing to ensure health, safety and

---

[5] The EC Framework Directive is implemented in the Management of Health and Safety at Work Regulations 1992 (S.I. 1992 No. 2051).

[6] Hutter and Lloyd-Bostock, "The Power of Accidents: The Social and Psychological Impact of Accidents and the Enforcement of Safety Regulations" (1990) 30 *Br J. of Criminology* 409.

[7] (RIDDOR) Reporting of Injuries, Diseases, and Dangerous Occurrences Regulations 1985 (S.I. 1985 No. 2023).

welfare as well as specific regulations, breach of which will be an offence.[8]

Some of the different inspectorates managed by the HSE operate additionally under specific legislative frames; for example, parts of the Railways Act 1871 are still in force.[9] As part of a tendency (often seen, it has to be said, in the aftermath of disaster) to transfer previously discrete inspectorates to the HSE, railways moved from the Department of Transport in 1990. Some of the legislation applying to off-shore installations and the Nuclear Installations Inspectorate has also been brought within the HSE framework.[10]

An important aspect of safety work is the communication of risk and hazard findings. In the professional and expert sphere, communication of the wider implications of accident investigations is done through National Industry Groups (NIGS) which are part of the Factory Inspectorate. Each NIG has a specific industry to watch, for example, chemicals, or steel. Investigation of accidents can draw attention to areas of risk and therefore may lead to prevention, but investigation is time-consuming and may distract inspectors from preventive visits.[11] The resources available for either of these types of preventive work are limited, with 638 Factory Inspectors for 400,000 workplaces, 171 Agricultural Inspectors for 300,000 workplaces, and 52 Railway Inspectors for the entire railway network.

The work of the HSE has attracted far more attention as an area of in-depth regulatory behaviour than that of other agencies which also engage in preventive work, such as the fire service.[12] Somewhat surprisingly, it is only in the last twenty years that fire prevention has been placed on a statutory footing.[13] The Fire Precautions Act 1971 was a direct result of concern generated by a series of fires in places of entertainment in the previous decade.[14] It has been supplemented by the Fire Safety and Safety of Places

---

[8] s. 33. Regulations are increasingly European in origin, see Goddard, "European Law: New Origins for Health and Safety Regulation" [1994] *Jnl of Personal Injury Law* 5.

[9] The six Inspectorates are: Factories, Agricultural, Quarries, Mines, Nuclear Installations and Railways. Railways was transferred from the Department of Transport in 1990, and Off-Shore Safety from the Department of Environment in 1991.

[10] Nuclear Installations Act 1965, ss. 5 and 1(1)(d).

[11] Hutter and Lloyd-Bostock, *op. cit.*

[12] Rowan-Robinson, J., Watchman, P. and Barker, C., *Crime and Regulation* (1990), Chap. 5.

[13] Fire Precaution Act 1971 (as amended by the Health and Safety at Work Act 1974; general fire precautions at most places of work are dealt with by the fire authorities under the 1971 Act).

[14] Rowan-Robinson *et al, op. cit.*, p. 113.

of Sports Act 1987, itself the outcome of the Popplewell report
following the fire disaster at Bradford City football ground in 1985.
Fire certificates are required for certain hotels and boarding houses
and for certain factories, shops and railway premises.

An example of a body set up to regulate a specific area of activity
is the Football Licensing Authority (FLA) which oversees the certification of football grounds. Established in the wake of the Heysel
stadium deaths which were caused by stampeding fans, the FLA
was originally expected to supervise the football identity card
admission system.[15] The government's commitment to that
scheme soon evaporated in the light of Hillsborough and the
newly fledged FLA then found itself in charge of the transition to
all-seater stadia, which was the central recommendation of the
Taylor Inquiry Report.[16] It is an independent, non-departmental
public body now funded through the Department of National
Heritage (although its original sponsor department was the Home
Office). It is charged with operating a licensing system for grounds
at which designated football matches are played, with reviewing
the discharge by local authorities of their functions under the
Safety of Sports Grounds Act, 1975, with advising the Government
on the introduction of all-seated accommodation, and of ensuring
that any terracing retained in the second and third division clubs
meets required safety standards. In providing for the FLA to
oversee the safety responsibilities of local authorities the Football
Spectators Act thus introduces a three-tier scheme for safety
involving central and local government and a specialised body.

(2) Mitigation

Safety policy, as with other contributory aspects of disaster
mitigation, clearly involves a process of calculating costs against
benefits. So far, the discussion has been concerned with the impo-
sition of regulatory schemes which require those engaged in some
business activities or those who employ others in their enterprises
to observe particular standards. Levels of inspection, and the
amount of revenue devoted to these regulatory schemes are reflections of the acceptability of the various risks.[17] What, however,
about those areas of risk which fall less clearly within accepted
regulation? Should people whose homes are in high-risk areas for

---

[15] The FLA was established in July 1990 by the Football Spectators Act 1989, s. 8.
[16] See Chap. 2.4.
[17] Safety regulation is often dismissed as "red-tape"; see the debate as the Deregulation and Contracting Out Act 1994 was legislated.

landslip or for flooding be required, encouraged or given financial incentives to move elsewhere? Should farmers have to consider the wider impact of their land use systems such as long term soil erosion? As well as being public policy questions, in order for people to make decisions about such matters, they need to feel confident about the risk predictions that are available to them.

Communication of information about hazard and risk to the public may play a key role in the prevention and mitigation of disasters.[18] The more that is known about "choice in the face of adversity," the better. Engineering based approaches to mitigation emphasise protection, defence, constraint and control. Just as important, however, are the social processes of changing human attitudes and behaviour towards hazard. Communication is complex, and requires an understanding of the gap between "objective" and "subjective" risk perception.[19]

A contemporary example is that of the bush-fires which threatened the outskirts of Sydney in the early weeks of 1994. New South Wales' authorities had embarked on a fire management strategy in the 1970s, which involved burning selected forest areas in the cooler months. Protests about the polluting effects led to the abandonment of the plan. At the same time, builders continued to construct houses close to the forest areas. The Mississippi flooding in 1993 also demonstrated the difficulties of separating human from natural cause and of getting the right balance in safety measures. Efforts to control local flooding are thought to have exacerbated the damage caused when the river eventually did flood.[20]

Some of the factors which affect individual decision-making include prior experience with the hazard, material wealth, personality traits and the perceived role of the individual in the social group.[21] Four distinct behaviour patterns have been noted amongst people who live in hazardous places:

— risk denial, "it will never happen";
— passive acceptance of risk, "it doesn't matter what I do";
— taking action to reduce further losses, "I must be ready";
— drastic change in land use considered, "I will not let it happen".[22]

---

[18] Horlick-Jones, "Communicating Risks to Reduce Vulnerability" in Merriman and Browitt, eds, *Natural Disasters* (1993), from which the following discussion is drawn.

[19] *Ibid.*

[20] *The Higher*, 21 January 1994, p. 6.

[21] Burton, I., Kates, R. and White, G., *The Environment of Hazard* (1978).

[22] Horlick-Jones, *op. cit.*

There is a clear relevance in using these patterns when devising hazard reduction policies. Whereas in the past, variations like these were attributed to personality or psychological factors, more recently, cultural grid-group theory has added a different dimension. This associates risk-handling styles with different cultural forms.[23] Two key variables in this approach to cultural diversity are the continuums of social relationships and of social interactions. On the first scale, social identity runs from strong individualism to strong collectivism, while the second has extremes of restriction and independence.[24] Four institutionalised ways of responding emerge from the intersection of these two continuums: the entrepreneur, the egalitarian, the hierarchist and the fatalist. Where high levels of individualism and independence meet, the entrepreneur emerges. This style could be characterised in the prevailing political ideology of pursuit of personal profit. Egalitarians, who combine strong group membership with a high degree of independence, are squeezed out. Four different risk-handling styles have been identified as arising from these intersections:

> the hierarchical—in which risks are rejected and absorbed;
> the egalitarian—in which risks are rejected and deflected;
> the entrepreneur—where risks are accepted and deflected;
> and the fatalist—who accepts and absorbs.[25]

Although essentially subjective, this typology can be used both to account for seemingly "irrational" behaviour and to inform safety initiatives. In his study of the reaction of Cumbrian sheep farming communities to the advice of government scientists about radioactive fall-out as a result of Chernobyl, Wynne found barriers and resistance. The advice was perceived as coming from "outsiders" resulting in a process of "informal resistance by people in solitary sub-cultures to meanings, identities or rationalities imposed on them from 'outside'."[26] This confirmed the earlier thesis of Otway and Wynne that one of the paradoxes of risk communication, which they called the "information cultures paradox" is that the meaning of communications is shaped by existing and past relationships between the organisation disseminating the infor-

---

[23] See Douglas, M., *Natural Symbols* (1970), p. 104.
[24] Explained by Milton, "Interpreting Environmental Policy: A Social Scientific Approach" (1991) 18 *Journal of Law and Society* 4, p. 5. See also Chap. 7.3.
[25] Horlick-Jones, *op. cit.*, p. 28.
[26] Wynne, "Misunderstood Misunderstanding: Social Identities and Public Uptake of Science" (1992) 1 *Public Understanding of Science* 281–304.

mation and the targeted recipients.[27] The grid-group analysis gives a formal meaning to these findings, with the farmers exhibiting egalitarian and fatalist styles of behaviour within a broader climate in which the entrepreneur and the hierarchist find more sympathy.

Some of this is helpful too when looking at emergency planning and warning systems, when some specific issues related to communication also emerge, as indicated in the next section.

2. Planning for Disaster

Disaster relief and disaster preparedness are closely connected with wealth and living conditions. Disasters occur through interaction between natural forces and socio-technical systems.[28] Statistics of the largest natural disasters of the last 20 years show that high cost damage occurs in highly developed countries, while in less developed countries people lose lives and financial and economic consequences are more severe. The after affect to local and national economies following disaster is not inconsiderable. Rapid population growth, unlimited urbanisation, shrinking natural resources and newly-emerging technologies add together to form a powerful explosive brew.[29] The International Decade for Natural Disaster Reduction (IDNDR) is a call to all governments and the international community to work together to reduce these disaster effects, particularly in developing countries.

The United Nations has set a number of targets for the decade which include national assessments of risk due to various types of disasters (*e.g.* earthquakes, volcanoes, landslides, storms); national and/or local prevention and preparedness plans; and access to global, regional, national and local warning systems. Response at the European level is found in the Joint Research Centre on Civil Protection and on Climate and Natural Risks. The principle of subsidiarity informs much of the work, but the Maastricht treaty specifically mentions civil protection as an area for Community action.[30] Informing these missions is the notion of vulnerability, a concept described simply as "a community's capacity to suffer harm" or more sophisticatedly as "an erosion of a system's resili-

---

[27] Otway, H. and Wynne, B., "Risk Communication: Paradigm and Paradox" (1989) 9 *Risk Analysis* 141–145.

[28] Horlick-Jones and Amendola, "Towards a Common Framework for Natural and Technological Emergency Management" in Vincent, P. and Clementson, R., eds, *Emergency Planning '93*, (1993) 271 at 273.

[29] World Health Organisation, *Should Disaster Strike?* (1991).

[30] Horlick-Jones and Amendola, *op. cit.*, p. 272.

ence to perturbations generated by the interaction of the system with its socio-economic environment."[31]

An underlying paradox in talking about emergency planning arises from the fundamental nature of disaster—that it cannot be predicted, it is out of the run of things, a force beyond control. The one thing we know for sure is that disasters will happen. The dichotomy between preparedness and fatalism pulls perpetually. As one writer so disarmingly states, "There is hardly any subject which lends itself better to proposing the right answers to wrong questions than the topic of 'crisis management techniques'."[32]

Rosenthal suggests some words of warning. First, that crisis reality is not as homogeneous as is sometimes supposed; crises give rise to multiple, sometimes divergent perceptions and definitions of the situations. Various interested groups or "stakeholders" such as political authorities, administrative and operational agencies and private organisations pursue competitive or conflicting interests. Secondly, the tendency for clear-cut stories of success and failure following disasters should be avoided. A crisis for some may be an opportunity for others; the management of disasters is often more complex than appears and can be counter-productive. High degrees of uncertainty and time pressure are elements which need to be recognised in any attempt to "manage" crisis. Local rather than centralised decision-making may be more appropriate, and co-ordination may prove to be time-wasting, with bureaucratic politics still operating at times of crisis.

Rosenthal notes, however, that although crisis management is regarded as the prerogative of separate states, crises are increasingly trans-national. This seems to imply that while *planning* for disasters needs to be kick-started at an international level, the detail and the actual management of crises need to be considered as local concerns. Whatever plans are developed, they should recognise one extremely important truth, that at the time of strike, effective response to most disasters can *only* be implemented locally.

In the UK the term "civil defence" refers to preparing the civilian population to withstand external hostile attack, a task which has traditionally been carried out at local authority level.[33] Much

---

[31] *Ibid.*, p. 273.
[32] Rosenthal, "Crisis Management: Second Order Techniques" in Horlick-Jones, T., *Natural Risk and Civil Protection* (1995).
[33] Hilliard, "Local Government, Civil Defence and Emergency Planning: Heading for Disaster?" (1986) 49 *Mod. L.R.* 476. The provisions in Northern Ireland differ; see Topping, "Emergency Planning Law and Practice in Northern Ireland" (1988) *N.I.L.Q.* 39.

emergency planning for other contingencies such as environmental or technological disaster has emerged from this base.
Emergency planning also springs from the local basis of the police,
fire and ambulance emergency services.[34]

But while local authorities have always had some kind of duty
to provide for civil defence, for other emergencies there has been
no duty.[35] The Civil Defence Act 1948 imposes a duty on all local
authorities to "perform such functions as may be prescribed ...
by the designated Minister."[36] General in nature, the regulations
provide little in the way of obligation to keep plans up-to-date or
under regular revision. As a result of both understandable apathy
and resource prioritisation, by the 1970s, when nuclear weapons
became a politically volatile issue, many authorities had all but
abandoned any pretence at civil defence planning. Manchester
City Council's declaration that it was a Nuclear Free Zone in 1980
was followed eventually by 170 other councils. These authorities
refused to consider contingency planning for nuclear threat and
the Government was forced to cancel its "Operation Hardrock"
civil defence exercise in 1982 because over a third of authorities
refused to participate.[37] The Government was provoked into introducing regulations aimed at forcing authorities to take on civil
defence again.[38] These imposed a duty on county councils to draw
up, keep under review and revise their civil defence plans. In
addition, premises have to be established, equipped and maintained as control centres and training has to be undertaken. The
resources allocated centrally for implementation of these regulations have not been large and some have suggested both that
the motivation was political rather than practical and that there
was more concern with protecting government rather than the
public.[39] For example, the regulations only mention the public in
relation to the need for plans to utilise buildings for shelters, but
no resources were made available for this, unlike the provision of
protected control rooms for senior local government officers.

This then is the somewhat unfortunate background to the
development of systematic emergency planning in the UK. Instead
of having a well-documented and resource foundation on which

---

[34] Each of which has its own emergency procedures manual; see Home Office,
Dealing With Disasters (1992) Annex B.
[35] Civil Defence Act 1948.
[36] s. 2(1).
[37] Hilliard, *op. cit.*, p. 477.
[38] Civil Defence (General Local Authority Functions) Regulations 1983 (S.I. 1983 No.
1634).
[39] Hilliard, *op. cit.*, p. 478.

to build, the connotations and associations of the concept of civil protection were for many councils entirely negative. When the reality of the large scale technological or transport disasters hit the consciousness of public and government in the 1980s, a new interest in the need to plan for such contingencies emerged.

Unlike the duties in relation to civil defence in the wake of hostile attack, local authorities have no specific responsibilities for peacetime emergency planning. They do, however, have the power under the 1972 Local Government Act to incur expenditure to avert, alleviate or eradicate the actual or potential effect of any emergency or disaster involving destruction or danger to life or property in their area.[40] Since 1989 this has specifically included the power to include expenditure on contingency planning, which is defined as "making, keeping under review and revising of plans and the carrying out of training associated with the plans."[41] Further stimulus was added with the introduction in 1986 of a statutory power to divert civil defence resources for these purposes.[42] Many local authorities now use an "all hazards" approach, regarding the division between war and peacetime emergency planning as unnecessary.[43]

However, the pressure to establish a national disaster squad has so far been resisted.[44] Evidence of an emergent centralised strategy can be seen in the appointment, following the latest review of defence and civil emergency planning, of a Home Office civil emergencies adviser.[45] The Civil Defence College, re-named the Emergency Planning College, has taken on training in peacetime planning. A clear indication of central government's policy for disaster planning can be gleaned from the publication in 1992 of the adviser's report, *Dealing with Disaster*.[46] This confirms that responsibility for emergency planning rests at the local level. Authorities responsible for local services should undertake planning and providing the response to an emergency. The publication uses this working definition of disaster:

"an event (with or without warning) causing or threatening

---

[40] s. 138, as amended by Local Government Acts 1980 and 1989.
[41] Local Government Act 1972, s. 138 1(A) and (6), as amended by the Local Government and Housing Act 1989, s. 156.
[42] Civil Protection in Peacetime Act 1986, s. 2.
[43] Topping, *op. cit.*, p. 339.
[44] Wills, "Emergency" (1990) 6397 *Local Government Chronicle* 20–21.
[45] Home Office, *Review of Arrangements for Handling Major Civil Disasters in UK*, *Hansard*, 15 June 1989, col. 515–51.
[46] Home Office, *op. cit.*

death or injury, damage to property or the environment or disruption to the community, which because of the scale of effects cannot be dealt with by the emergency services and local authorities as part of their day to day activities."[47]

The sum of the report appears to be that there should be no alteration to the existing arrangements or budgets and that the numerous bodies involved should retain their autonomy. The central role is to give information and designate lead departments rather than actively coordinate any responses. Examples of lead departments are flooding (M.A.F.F.), radiation (D.T.I.), severe storms (Home Office) and earthquakes (Environment). This policy moves away from the "all hazards" approach previously endorsed to an emphasis on functional planning.

Electricity, gas and water utilities also have their own emergency plans. The combined response envisaged by the Home Office has the stated objectives of saving life, preventing escalation, relieving suffering, safeguarding the environment, protecting property, facilitating legal processes and restoring normality. A full-scale paper rehearsal for a non-nuclear accident in 1994, "Exercise Green Amanita", demonstrated some of the difficulties with the centralised but diffuse response structure which has developed. The need for central government to devolve emergency response strategy to the local level was confirmed.[48]

London provides an interesting example here with a unique range of hazard and planning problems.[49] Now that there is no political authority for the capital, how can disaster planning be effective across 33 boroughs, two separate police forces, one fire and one ambulance force? The pragmatic answer is through liaison arrangements such as the London Emergency Service Liaison Panel, but the formal, constitutional answer is wanting.[50] Civil defence planning for wartime is the responsibility of the London Fire and Civil Defence Authority. Peacetime planning is ad hoc, although the Hidden Report into the Clapham rail crash specifically mentioned the usefulness of Wandsworth's comprehensive local plan.[51] A report prepared by Epicentre, the London Emerg-

---

[47] *Ibid.*, para. 1.5.
[48] *The Independent*, 19 April 1994.
[49] Epicentre, *The Future of Emergency Planning in London* (1992), p. 9.
[50] New, B., *Too Many Cooks: The Response of the Health-related Services to Major Incidents in London* (1992) King's Fund Institute Research Report 15, Chap. 2.
[51] Hidden, *Investigation into the Clapham Junction Railway Accident* Dept. of Transport, Cm. 820 (1989).

ency Planning Information Centre, suggests five key elements in effective emergency planning: that public protection be given priority; that planning should be based on a critical evaluation of hazard; that planning should involve local communities; that wartime planning should be based on sound peacetime planning and that there should be a mechanism for recording lessons from past emergencies, such as a national disaster inspectorate.[52]

The absence of any statutory duty in relation to planning was highlighted in early 1994 when there was serious flooding in Chichester. The National Rivers Authority (NRA) which co-ordinates emergency procedures for flooding had not designated the Lavant a river. The NRA therefore had no contingency plan. It can also be noted that the NRA's responsibility for flood defence systems bestowed upon it by the Water Act 1989,[53] does not impose a duty to engage in emergency planning. However, public authorities appear to take seriously the potential for civil action against them if they exercise such powers negligently.[54]

The only statutory responsibilities for (non civil-defence) disaster planning are those in relation to specific hazardous industrial activities. These provide a good illustration of the argument that through disaster and the investigatory aftermath, come safety provisions. However, the process is not inexorable. One of the largest explosions to occur in peacetime UK destroyed the chemical works at Flixborough in 1974. Yet it was not until the Seveso chemical leak in northern Italy two years later, leading to increased European concern, that any specific regulations emerged. The Control of Industrial Major Accident Hazards (CIMAH) regulations implement the European Commission's "Seveso" directive.[55] The regulations are concerned with processing and storage of specific dangerous substances, mainly covering chemical and petro-chemical industries which use substances with flammable, explosive or toxic properties. For "top-tier" installations, of which there are more than 300, the manufacturer is statutorily obliged to submit to the Health and Safety Executive a written hazard assessment as well as provide those on the site with adequate information, training and equipment.[56] While on-site planning is

---

[52] Epicentre, *op. cit.*, p. 3.
[53] With flood warning empowered under the Water Resources Act 1991.
[54] See Barrett, "Common Law Liability for Flood Damage Caused by Storms" (1992) 142 *New Law Journal* 1608.
[55] S.I. 1984 No. 1902, implementing 85/510/EEC.
[56] For a detailed account, see Sefton, "The Enforcement of Article 8 of the Seveso Directive in Great Britain" in Gow, H. and Otway, H., eds, *Communication with the Public about Major Accident Hazards* (1990).

the responsibility of the manufacturer, the regulations impose on local authorities an obligation to make plans for off-site emergency. The costs of this can be recovered from the manufacturer by means of a civil debt.[57] The regulations do not require emergency planning for accidents while inflammable or toxic substances are in transit.

A similar approach to safety was advocated by the Cullen Report following Piper Alpha. On this occasion, the legislative response was somewhat keener. The Offshore Safety Act 1992, like the CIMAH regulations, demands a pro-active approach to hazard and safety. The major fault attributed to Occidental Petroleum in their attitude to safety on Piper Alpha was their failure to make a hazard assessment and to have in place a major emergency procedure.[58]

Radiation provides another specialised field, with the Radioactive Substances Act 1960 requiring the registration of persons keeping radioactive substances. The Radiological Protection Board, set up under statutory authority, has the function both of carrying out research and giving advice and information to relevant persons about protection from radiation.[59] In addition, under the Nuclear Installations Act 1965 licences are required for installation or operation of any nuclear reactor, the production of atomic energy, storage processing or disposal. Emergency planning requirements are built into the licensing system.

Disaster planning needs to consider a number of different phases of an emergency, including co-ordinating the roles of the emergency services, how to warn the public about any impending disaster and ensuring reparation and support services. It is to these that I now turn.

3. Disaster Response

Police, fire and ambulance emergency services are organised locally but separately.[60] The details of those different arrangements are less important than their implications for ensuring an appropriate and effective response at the scene of disaster. There is evidence that some lives are lost unnecessarily because of inad-

---

[57] (S.I. 1984 No. 1902), reg. 15.
[58] Offshore Installations (Prevention of Fire and Explosion, and Emergency Response) Regulations (Draft) 1993.
[59] Radiological Protection Act 1970, s. 1.
[60] Fire Services Act 1974; National Health Services Act 1977 and Police Act 1964.

equate medical care at the scene of the trauma.[61] Response mitigation is also important in relation to property and psychological
damage.

Similar problems arise in the less immediate aftermath when
numerous agencies, statutory and voluntary, may claim a role.
One of the vital aspects of planning is to ensure that there is a lead
agency and that it prevents convergence on victims of numerous
agencies, which occurs as much from intense inter agency rivalry
as through a desire to help.

Other aspects of disaster response have to be considered too,
such as shelter, food and clothing, which can often be provided by
voluntary agencies. This needs to be planned for. In addition,
recognition of the psychological trauma experienced both by survivors and rescuers has led to a growing literature on the need to
integrate mental health into disaster response schemes.[62] The
classic psychological phases—impact, heroism, honeymoon, dis-
illusionment and reconstruction—are often obscured by the practical effects of emotional numbness followed by the need to deal
with immediate problems of medical care, food, shelter and so
on.[63] Organisations get caught up in a euphoric desire to help but
are not always best able to target what they can offer.[64] Recent
disasters disclosed a "total lack of preparedness" by health, social
services and voluntary agencies in relation to the provision of
psychosocial help.[65]

It is usual for the police to assume the role of directing and
organising the other services at the scene of an emergency.[66] A
valuable study was made of the emergency care following a
number of high-profile disasters in London in the 1980s. The
Kings Cross fire, the Clapham and Purley rail crashes and the
sinking of the pleasure boat *Marchioness* all occurred in an
eighteen-month period. Although London has peculiar features
such as its large, dense population, its complex transport infra-
structure and its lack of metropolitan council, there is nothing
peculiar about the range of autonomous bodies to whom emergency calls will be made during a major incident. In fact, just the

---

[61] New, *op. cit.*, p. 10.
[62] Hodgkinson, P. and Stewart, M., eds, *Coping with Catastrophe* (1991); Lebedun and
Wilson, "Planning and Integrating Disaster Response" in Gist, R. and Lubin, B.,
eds, *Psychological Aspects of Disaster* (1989) p. 268.
[63] Lebedun and Wilson, *op. cit.*, p. 270.
[64] Hodgkinson and Stewart, *op. cit.*, Chap. 3.
[65] Hodgkinson and Stewart, *op. cit.*, p. 67.
[66] New, *op. cit.*

use of the term "major incident" has different meanings for the different services.[67]

There are five police forces in Greater London, of which the Metropolitan, the City of London and the British Transport Police are the most significant.[68] The Fire Brigade is organised by the London Fire and Civil Defence Authority (FCDA)—an umbrella body composed of nominated councillors.[69] In terms of statutory duty, fire brigades must act to save lives and prevent property damage caused by fire, but they attend and lend equipment where necessary even when there is no fire.[70] Health delivery is organised across four Regional Health Authorities with the London Ambulance Service the only London-wide organisation. There are more than thirty London Boroughs, each planning separately. Central planning, as we have seen, is the overall responsibility of the Home Office, with devolution to lead departments depending on the type of incident. Between them the Home Office and the Department of Health are responsible for hospital, ambulance, police and fire services.

The Civil Emergencies Adviser to the Home Secretary, first appointed in 1989, has no operational role in emergencies but is expected to work closely with senior officers of the emergency services, local authorities and others in order to draw out broad lessons from particular incidents.[71] Official guidance for the NHS response to a major incident is published in Department of Health circulars.[72] Regional Health Authorities are required to employ an emergency planning officer to deal with questions such as alerting procedures (the preferred terminology is "Major Incident-Stand-by" and "Major Incident Declared-Activate Plan"[73], pre-hospital care (through a Medical Incident Officer and a Mobile Medical team) and communications with receiving hospitals.

Mention has been made of the Liaison Panel (LESLP), a voluntary body, with members from the three main London police forces, the Ambulance Service, and the Fire and Civil Defence Authority. Since 1991, two borough representatives have also been included. There is no representation from any of the relevant

---

[67] See (the interesting discussion,) *ibid*. p. 10.
[68] The others are the Ministry of Defence Police and Parks Police.
[69] The FCDA is also the top tier planning authority for London's 20 or so sites covered by Control of Industrial Major Accidents Hazards Regulations.
[70] Fire Precautions Act 1971.
[71] Written Answer, *Hansard*, 15 June 1989.
[72] HC(90) 25 (Department of Health 1990).
[73] No doubt watchers of "Casualty" on BBC will be familiar with these.

health teams[74] As the report on the emergency responses to recent disasters in the capital concluded, the number of autonomous agencies is a key feature which "poses a major problem of co-ordination."[75] This resulted in an "implementation gap", with central plans failing to elicit the response expected. In some cases, hospital-based medical staff were used at the scene when their skills would have been more effective in their normal hospital setting. BASICS doctors (general practitioners who volunteer their services and experience at major accidents) may be more useful as a support to the increasingly para-medicalised ambulance teams who have replaced "scoop and run" with "stay and stabilise" systems. The message from this study was that central guidance needed to be clearer and that the liaison arrangements should include medical representatives as well as the traditional "uniformed" services.

Reflection on the nature of the emergency services as organisations (ESOs) points to distinguishing features. Rather than advertise for customers with a list of available products, they are demand driven.[76] Changes in organisational strategies which their commercial counterparts have been making have by-passed them. ESOs have difficulty in excluding uncertainty since they have little control over delivery times. Turner identifies primary tasks of two kinds possessed by ESOs: dealing routinely with other people's crises and coping with events which are crises for them also. Disasters fall into this second category. They require the implementation of special arrangements for dealing with large numbers of casualties, large numbers at risk, and large numbers of enquiries from the public and news media. "Responsive flexibility" is suggested as the organisational strategy. As Turner points out, a crisis is a challenge to

> "the meaning which would normally be attributed to the incident being dealt with. One portion of the world comes to be overturned, disrupted, shattered, transformed and even ideas about who has authority or control may be radically changed. Attempts to handle a complex and changing crisis situation in a routine manner may fail unexpectedly and inexplicably."[77]

---

[74] That is, accident and emergency consultants, health emergency planning officers (HEPOs) or immediate care volunteers (BASICS).

[75] New, *op. cit.*, p. 19.

[76] Turner, "The Role of Flexibility and Improvisation in Emergency Response" in Horlick-Jones (1995), *op. cit.*

[77] *Ibid.*

Evidence collected from recent disasters shows a high level of post traumatic stress. For example, twelve months after the *Herald* 90 per cent were displaying symptoms of PTSD.[78] While evidence suggests that those who can talk about the event have a better outcome, and that disaster survivors feel most at home with other survivors, people are often wary of accepting help. One aspect of disaster responses is to develop the most effective means of providing help to minimise the long term psychological effects. The Bradford fire was the first attempt to mount a pro-active social service outreach service and after the *Herald* the Herald Assistance Unit visited all those who did not actually refuse. This achieved a high level of acceptance. Nearly 72 per cent of survivors and 84 per cent of the bereaved accepted a visit.[79] Only 2 per cent declined to receive a newsletter in which feelings and experiences were exchanged.

4. Disaster Warning

Sometimes it is possible to issue a warning of an impending disaster. Meteorological forecasting allows prediction of storms, and flood levels can be monitored through the observation of tides and other phenomena. Escapes of toxic fumes or chemicals take time to spread, thus allowing for averting action. An example of how such warnings could be helpful is that of Bhopal; had people known that they should place wet cloths round their heads, cover their mouths and noses and stay indoors, many might have survived.[80] How should such warnings be given? What sort of preparation of the public, in case there is a need to warn, should take place? Most contingency plans in the UK rely on warnings to public being given by the police, with no education of the population in responding to warnings.[81] Extensive research exists on how best to disseminate warning messages and it is clear that for warnings to operate effectively in a crisis there must be adequate planning.[82]

---

[78] Hodgkinson and Stewart, *op. cit.,* Chap. 2.

[79] Hodgkinson, "Technological Disaster-Survival and Bereavement" (1989) 29 (3) *Social Science and Medicine* 351.

[80] Coggi, "The Commission of the European Communities Policy on Public Information on Major Accident Hazards" in Gow and Otway, *op. cit.,* p. 21.

[81] *C.f.* many other jurisdictions; see Horlick-Jones (1995), *op. cit.,* and particularly Quint, "Risk Communication on a National Scale: The Dutch Way" in that collection.

[82] Nigg, "Risk Communication and Warning Systems" in Horlick-Jones, *ibid.*

An underlying paradox, as Otway and Wynne point out, is that often the same populations who are being prepared for risk, have already been assured that the plan to build a chemical plant or whatever, carries only a slight risk.[83] They call this the "reassurance-arousal" paradox:

> "In siting, the authorities have tried to reassure people that they could *forget* about risks, but now, to be successful, the risk communication must create the opposite belief—that risks are not negligible and the message must be *remembered* (internalized) and acted upon where necessary."[84]

Even where the warnings are not preceded by acceptance of a hazardous enterprise in the locality, all sorts of difficulties still present themselves. Predictions are based on assessment of a number of risk factors; they are rarely capable of precision. When should forecasts be regarded as "safe"? Other issues concern the medium of communication. Scientific statements need to be transformed into something comprehensible yet authoritative. Resistance towards issuing warnings arises because of myths about public reaction to them.[85] Nigg observes two popular but contradictory myths: one is inaction, the other is panic flight. Research demonstrates that few people actually ignore warnings or exhibit true panic flight and that on hearing a warning people use sensory cues to assess whether they are in fact in danger, and in their absence turn to others around them for social cues. Local government, Nigg suggests, should have the major responsibility for advising citizens of risk and using its resources to help protect the community. The role of national or regional government is to plan how to use the media effectively, including guarding against the media's tendency to exaggerate and fuel panic.[86] The source of the message must have credibility (perhaps Mr Blobby would not be the best choice) and the more sources from which the message is heard, the more credible it will be and the more likely it will be received. Messages should be specific about the degree of the risk and give precise advice for action.

---

[83] Otway and Wynne, *op. cit.*, p. 142.
[84] *Ibid.* (emphasis in original).
[85] Nigg, *op. cit.*
[86] See Kelly, A., Gibson, R. and Horlick-Jones, T., *Local Authorities, the Media and Disasters*, Epicentre (1992).

5. Public Investigation of Disaster

(1) Inquiries

Major disasters are almost inevitably followed by some form of inquiry. Inquiries following disasters serve a number of purposes. As well as providing a forum in which those directly affected, whether bereaved or survivors, can transact their grief and anger or other emotions in a controlled and public manner, they can also furnish an opportunity to exert pressure for policy changes. For example, the resources of the Nuclear Installations Inspectorate were increased after Chernobyl, as were those of London Transport after the Kings Cross fire. The Sheen Inquiry into the *Herald* capsize led directly to the establishment of the Department of Transport's Marine Accident Investigation Branch.[87] The Offshore Safety Act 1992 implemented many of the recommendations contained in the Cullen Report into Piper Alpha. In addition, (arguably as a result of a number of recent inquiry reports) the resources devoted to health and safety have been increased since 1990.[88]

Not all recommendations made at inquiries are implemented. It has been argued that Hillsborough would not have happened if all the recommendations in the Popplewell report into the Bradford fire had been introduced.[89] It is also difficult not to feel a chilling sense of *déjà vu* when recalling that the opportunity to transfer responsibility for off-shore safety from the Department of Energy to the HSE was originally mooted in 1980, but was narrowly rejected by the Burgoyne Committee.[90] This, Miller notes, coincided with a government policy of regulation reduction as encapsulated in the White Papers *Lifting the Burden* and *Building Businesses not Barriers*.[91] Piper Alpha eventually underscored the necessity for the change, effected by the Offshore Safety Act 1992, but the Deregulation and Contracting Out Act two years later was heralded too by the government as releasing industry from the choking effects of too much regulation. Similar arguments may apply in relation to government interpretation of European safety directives.[92]

---

[87] Merchant Shipping Act 1988, s. 33.
[88] The HSC and HSE budget increased from £12 million in 1990–91 to £20 million in 1991–92, with a planned rise to £35 million in 1994–95.
[89] Fire Safety and Safety of Places of Sports Act 1987.
[90] Cmnd. 7866.
[91] Miller, "Piper Alpha and the Cullen Report" (1991) 20 *Ind. L.J.* 176, p. 179.
[92] Under the "Framework Directive" (S.I. 1989 No. 391); see Gifford, "Bilstthorpe

It could be argued that inquiries are merely ways of responding with hindsight to unavoidable accidents. Many inquiries do, however, reveal that there were warning signs if only they had been recognised as such, and the Disaster Prevention Unit at Bradford found in their study of over 1000 disasters since the nineteenth century that over 60 per cent could have been prevented.[93] Investigations following the *Herald*, *Piper Alpha* and the *Marchioness* disasters all disclosed previous incidents of disturbing similarity to those which led to the eventual tragedies.[94] Deregulation may exacerbate the tendency to ignore safety hazards until an accident confirms the presence of a risk of one occurring.

Although there is a tendency to refer to all inquiries following disasters generically as "public inquiries", the underlying legal structure is labyrinthine. Inquiries can be set up under a number of different statutory bases, although confusingly most of those concerned with disaster aftermath are not "statutory inquiries" within the terms of the Tribunal and Inquiries Act.[95] Inquiries into accidents are discretionary inquiries, either under powers laid down in a variety of statutes, for example, the Regulation of Railways Act 1871, s. 7 or the Civil Aviation Act 1982, s. 75, or, exceptionally, established under the 1921 Tribunals of Inquiry Act.[96] These Tribunals of Inquiry have the powers of a High Court and less than twenty have ever been set up, not all of which concerned major accidents. Of the disasters studied here, only the Aberfan inquiry was of this type.

As well as distinguishing different types of *public* inquiry, there are also inquiries or investigations which are not held in public. Inquiries in public are relatively common after railway and shipping accidents, but most investigations into air accidents are held in private. The Health and Safety at Work Act 1974, for example, gives the power to inspectors to investigate, but inquiries require the authority of the Secretary of State. Major incidents may lead to lengthy and detailed investigation by Health and Safety inspectorates. Although the evidence can be in public, they tend to favour private hearings.[97] Health and safety inquiries (as opposed to

Roof Fall Shows Mine Safety Deregulation has Gone Too Far", *The Guardian*, 25 January 1994.

[93] Cohen, D., *Aftershock* (1991), p. 218.

[94] See Chap. 2 for detailed accounts.

[95] 1992.

[96] The Lord Chancellor has powers to make regulations to bring discretionary inquiries within the scope of the Council of Tribunals; see Tribunals and Inquiries (Discretionary Inquiries) Order 1975 (S.I. 1975 No. 1379), as amended.

[97] HM Factory Inspectorate, *Report on a Petroleum Spillage at Micheldever 1983* HMSO (1984) and HSE, *The Abbeystead Explosion* HMSO (1985).

investigations) are normally held in public and the chair has powers to take evidence on oath, to require attendance of witnesses, production of documents and site inspections.[98]

The Railway Inspectorate, which now operates under the wing of the HSE, has the choice of conducting inquiries either under the 1974 Health and Safety Legislation or under the 1871 Regulation of Railways Act. The latter, which the inspectorate tends to favour, has two broad provisions. Section 7 states that the Secretary of State may direct an investigation where there has been an accident with loss of life, injury, collision or derailment or "which is of such a kind as to have caused or be likely to cause loss of life or personal injury". These investigations are conducted by an Inspecting officer, whose task is to determine the accident's causes and submit a report. It is not unusual for eight or ten such investigations to be held in a year. In addition, the 1871 Act provides for a more formal investigation, with assistance from a legally-qualified assessor or chair.[99] There is no prescribed procedure, but these inquiries may compel attendance of witnesses and require evidence on oath.[1] The inquiries into Clapham and Kings Cross were of this type. Reporting of railway accidents to the Department of Transport is, on the other hand, mandatory.[2]

Shipping accidents have had a different tradition. The Merchant Shipping Act 1894 mandates an inquiry following death on a non-fishing vessel.[3] Death caused by shipping accidents, "shipping casualties", are covered by the 1970 Merchant Shipping Act, section 55 of which gives the Secretary of State the power to order a Formal Investigation, which acts rather like an inquisitorial court, with power to impose penalties. This was the statutory base for the Sheen inquiry after the *Herald*.

Regulations dealing with civil aviation accidents state clearly that the "fundamental purpose of investigating accidents ... shall be to determine the circumstances and causes of the accident with a view to the preservation of life and the avoidance of accidents in the future; it is not the purpose to apportion blame or liability."[4] Investigations are held in private following a public appeal for representations. Alternatively, the Secretary of State can set up a public inquiry. An example from New Zealand is of interest here. After the New Zealand Airways crash on Mount Erebus, Ant-

---

[98] Health and Safety Inquiries (Procedure) Regulations 1975 (S.I. 1975 No. 335).
[99] 1871 Act, s. 7(1).
[1] s. 7(3).
[2] Railways (Notice of Accidents) Order 1986.
[3] s. 690.
[4] Civil Aviation (Investigation of Accidents) Regulations 1983 (S.I. 1983 No. 551).

arctica, the NZ Chief Inspector of Air Accidents held an immediate inquiry and found pilot error to be the probable cause. A judge was then appointed to conduct a Royal Commission to investigate the cause and circumstances. This exonerated the pilot and instead identified the actions of company executives and ground staff as the principal causes of the disaster and found, in addition, a pre-determined plan described as "an orchestrated litany of lies" to cover up these actions. To mark its disapproval the Commission ordered the airline to contribute £150,000 towards the costs. The airline successfully sought judicial review on the grounds that the Commissioner had acted in breach of the rules of natural justice, which required that any person represented at an inquiry who might be adversely affected by a finding should be warned of the possible criticism against him and given an opportunity to answer.[5]

There are also general statutory powers to appoint public inquiries into accidents occurring outside these spheres where there is an accepted occupational or transport risk. The 1921 Tribunals of Inquiry Act can also be used as an alternative. This occurred with Aberfan, which could have been investigated under the Mines and Quarries Act 1954. The reason for rejecting that particular course of action was that its "extreme horror and magnitude made this unthinkable."[6] The worst mining disaster in South Wales, at Senghennyd in 1914 when 440 miners were killed, gave rise to a Formal Inquiry under the then relevant statute, the Coal Mines Act 1911.[7] The Report notes that in 13 days of evidence, 21,837 questions were put to witnesses.

Because inquiries are set up under a plethora of auspices, their proceedings vary greatly. The Taylor inquiry following Hillsborough sat for 31 days, for example, in May and June 1989. During that time 174 witnesses gave oral evidence. Representation was accorded to nine categories including the bereaved and injured, the City Council, the police and fire services, the Football Association and Sheffield Wednesday Club and its insurers. Counsel made their submissions in writing a week after the oral evidence, followed by brief oral submissions.[8] The Investigation into the *Herald of Free Enterprise* capsize opened seven weeks after the event and reported two and a half months later. The terms of reference of an inquiry can obviously determine the range of conclusions

---

[5] *Mahon v. Air New Zealand Ltd* [1984] A.C. 808.

[6] Wraith, R. and Lamb, G., *Public Inquiries as an Instrument of Government* (1971) p. 154.

[7] s. 83: *Explosion at Senghennyd Colliery, Glamorganshire* Cd. 7346 (1914).

[8] *The Hillsborough Stadium Disaster Interim Report*, Cm. 765 (1989), para 12.

drawn.[9] Yet, although at the King's Cross Inquiry Desmond Fennell Q.C. emphasised that levels of funding were outside his terms of reference,[10] he then made a point in his report of stating that there was no evidence that the subsidy to London Regional Transport was inadequate to finance necessary safety standards.[11] In any case, the terms of reference of both the King's Cross and Clapham Inquiries were based on the Regulation of Railways Act 1871, section 7 of which provides that the investigation shall be in "such manner and under such conditions as [the persons holding the formal investigation] may think most effectual for ascertaining the causes and circumstances of the accident."[12] It is unlikely then that Fennell would have been procedurally constrained by such broad wording. Those in charge of public inquiries have considerable influence over the depth and breadth of their investigations, although the formal structure may hinder or enhance their discretion. Unlike those into shipping or air accidents, rail accident inquiries are not covered by the Tribunals and Inquiries Act 1992. They are neither governed by any statutory rules of procedure, nor give rights to legal representation or cross-examination.[13]

In a wide-ranging report *Justice* has reviewed criticisms of the inquiry system and noted that no procedure has yet been devised that satisfies the public or those involved as witnesses.[14] Terms of reference are either too wide or too narrow and *Justice* concluded that in some cases reports have been unrealistic of superficial. The issue of legal representation is a difficult one. It has the advantage of ensuring a more formal structure and providing a safeguard for witnesses, yet can lead to enormous duplication of effort. Without representation, the burden on the Chair is heavy, witnesses can more easily conceal important information and there is a danger that proceedings will degenerate into a formless discussion.

The public inquiry, or the formal investigation under statutory

---

[9] John Prescott, Shadow Transport Secretary, criticised both the Fennell Inquiry into King's Cross and the Hidden Inquiry into Clapham because wider questions of public subsidy were omitted; see *e.g. Hansard*, Vol. 143, Sixth Series, col. 647.

[10] *The Times*, 23 April 1988.

[11] *The Times*, 18 June 1988 and the Fennell Report, *Investigation into the King's Cross Underground Fire*, Dept. of Transport, Cm. 499 (1988), para. 19.6.

[12] In a Parliamentary question about the terms of reference for the Fennell Inquiry, David Mitchell's reply for the government that reference should be made to s. 7 was somewhat unhelpful: *Hansard*, Vol. 124, Sixth Series, 776w.

[13] Although the investigation has the powers of a summary court. See generally, Wade, H., *Administrative Law* (6th ed., 1988) p. 999 and Wraith, R. and Lamb, G., *Public Inquiries as an Instrument of Government* (1971) pp. 146–154.

[14] Justice, *All Souls Review of Administrative Law* (1988) para. 10.91.

powers, is actually overlaid on the normal, day to day, official processing of death. Death is a state event as well as a private concern, with numerous legal consequences. Death is officiated by a coroner, with the help of the medical profession. In the case of disaster, these proceedings are not replaced by inquiry, they are forced each to interact with the other with no necessary or clear co-ordination between them.

(2) Inquests

One thing disasters in England and Wales have in common is that each death will have been the subject of an inquest.[15] In Scotland there is a different system which is outlined below. The office of coroner dates back to medieval times,[16] and the coroner's role in respect of "sudden" or "unnatural" death was well established by the nineteenth century.[17] Gradually, the inquest has been subordinated to the medical profession, and more recently to the police and to the Director of Public Prosecutions. Sudden deaths can be dealt with by post-mortem without an inquest, unless the death was violent or unnatural.[18] The coroner has a discretion to hold an inquest in other cases in order to allay suspicion.

Overall, about one in eight deaths results in an inquest. Inquests have been pivotal in the move towards corporate manslaughter charges as the case studies in Chapter 2 demonstrate. The role of the inquest in relation to homicide has been curtailed formally in a number of significant ways in this century. The police can ask the coroner to adjourn for 28 days or longer if there are grounds for believing a person *may* be charged with the homicide.[19]

In order to bring in a verdict of unlawful killing, a jury needs to be convinced on the criminal standard of proof that the deaths

---

[15] Or, in the case of Lockerbie, the Scottish equivalent, a Fatal Accident Inquiry under the Fatal Accidents and Sudden Deaths Inquiry (Scotland) Act 1976; see "FAIs-After Lockerbie" (1991), *The Scots Law Times*, p. 225.

[16] The office was established in 1194, almost coinciding with the replacement of trial by ordeal by trial by jury in 1215; see Green, T., *Verdict According to Conscience* (1985), p. 51. See generally on the early years, Hunnisett, R., *The Medieval Coroner* (1961) and for a general history, McKeogh, "Origins of the Coronial Jurisdiction" (1983) 6 *University of New South Wales Law Journal*, p. 191.

[17] Warwick Inquest Group, "The Inquest as a Theatre for Police Tragedy: the Davey Case" (1985) 12 *Jnl of Law and Society*, p. 35, at 38.

[18] Now the Coroners Act 1988, s. 19. Various other statutes provide for a mandatory inquest following deaths in particular circumstances.

[19] And the D.P.P. can so request in relation to offences in "circumstances connected" with the deceased's death: Coroners rules 1984, rr. 26 and 27.

were caused unlawfully.[20] Before 1980 juries could add a "rider" to their verdict, but this was abolished on the recommendation of the Brodrick Committee.[21] However, this was at first ignored and the Bradford Fire inquest jury attached a list of 24 recommendations to their findings.[22] The Divisional Court has held that there is no such power and indeed that to make recommendations would contradict rule 36(2) that "Neither the coroner nor the jury shall express any opinion on any other matters" than who the deceased was, how, when and where she came by her death.[23]

The Coroners Act 1988 does not set down a list of possible verdicts for the jury. Section 11(3)(a) merely provides that they shall "give their verdict and certify it by an inquisition"; and subsection (5)(b) provides that "an inquisition ... shall set out so far as such particulars have been proved—

i who the deceased was and
ii how, when and where the deceased came by his death"

and under (c) the Lord Chancellor has power to prescribe its form by statutory instrument. The current rules provide a number of suggested verdicts, including accident/misadventure, unlawful killing and an open verdict.[24] The Hillsborough coroner took the unusual course of considering "who, when and where" in a series of mini-inquests, while the question of prosecution was being considered by the Director of Public Prosecutions.[25] Once the

---

[20] *i.e.* beyond reasonable doubt that the deaths were caused by another's gross negligence: *R. v. West London Coroner, ex p. Gray* [1987] 2 W.L.R. 1020.

[21] *Report of the Committee on Death Certification and Coroners* Cmnd. 4810 (1971). See, now, Coroners Rules 1984, r. 36(2). Coroners are entitled to make recommendations in writing to relevant authorities if thought necessary to prevent the recurrence of fatalities; r. 43.

[22] The Times, 30 July 1985. Some of these were more far-reaching than those of the Popplewell Inquiry, *Final Report of the Committee of Inquiry into Crowd Safety and Control at Sports Grounds* Cmnd. 9710 (1986).

[23] *R. v. Shrewsbury Coroner's Court, ex p. British Parachute Association* (1988) 152 J.P. 123.

[24] Coroners Rules 1984, Sched. 4, Form 22, note 4, (S.I. 1984 No. 552). Over half of verdicts record accident/misadventure, 10 per cent industrial diseases and 1.3 per cent unlawful killing: Home Office Statistical Bulletin, 5/91 (25 April 1991).

[25] The *Marchioness* inquests were also split in this way, but the first and second stages were adjourned pending the prosecution of the *Bowbelle*'s captain See Chap. 2.5

decision not to prosecute was announced, the inquests resumed to complete the "how" stage.[26]

This underlines the significance of the considerable procedural discretion bestowed on coroners, exercise of which can dramatically effect the extent to which these formal investigations are regarded as having served the interests of relatives, survivors or other interested parties. Coroners vary in the amount of detailed evidence they allow[27] and, with legal aid unavailable, much depends on whether relatives can afford legal representation.[28] The coroner is required to call all persons who tender evidence as to the facts of the death "whom he considers it expedient to examine."[29] As Bingham J. said in the judicial review taken during the *Herald* inquest, "[T]he coroner is by law an inquisitor; the witnesses called are those whom he ... thinks it expedient to examine, and he is very much master of his own procedure."[30] In neither that application nor the review taken from the Hillsborough inquest was the Divisional Court prepared to hold that the discretion had been exercised wrongly.[31]

Unlike the *Herald* review, which was taken during the inquest itself and involved both a point of law and the exercise of discretion, the Hillsborough case was brought after the inquest verdicts had been delivered. In such a case, a further question would arise as to whether, even if a coroner were found to have erred, it would be appropriate to order a fresh inquest. The main ground of complaint was that the coroner had been wrong to refuse to hear evidence of anything that occurred after 3.15 p.m. on the day of the disaster. Some of the victims may not yet have been dead by this time, it was argued. In order to succeed, the applicants would need to overcome the *Wednesbury* test of reasonableness, in other words that the coroner's discretion been exercised in a way no reasonable coroner would have done.[32] However, some guidance was given by McCowan L.J. as to the circumstances in which he might order a new inquest, if he had found any of the applicants' grounds made out. Those circumstances included questions

---

[26] There was a judicial review of both these stages: see Chap. 2.4.

[27] One complaint about the King's Cross inquest was that it lasted only one week. This can be compared with a month for Zeebrugge as against four minutes for Aberfan.

[28] The Legal Aid and Advice Act 1949 provided for legal aid to inquests, but this has never been implemented. See Justice, *Coroners Courts in England and Wales* (1986), p. 15.

[29] s. 11(2).

[30] *R. v. HM Coroner for East Kent, ex p. Spooner* (1989) 88 Cr. App. R. 10.

[31] *R. v. Coroner for South Yorkshire, ex p. Stringer and others* [1994] 17 BMLR 92.

[32] *Associated Picture Houses v. Wednesbury Corp.* [1948] 1 K.B. 223.

such as: what would the purpose of such an inquest be? If it were to obtain a verdict criticising the police, there was little point, given the Taylor report's reprimands. If it were to obtain a verdict criticising the emergency services, then the 3.15 cut off made no difference since the victims, if not legally dead, were brain dead by that time. Nothing would be gained from further examination of the last minutes of their lives. Nothing would be learned from a new inquest; it would be harrowing and potentially unreliable given that nearly five years had already elapsed.

For the *Marchioness* families, the protracted process of prosecution and inquiry led to a decision by the coroner not to resume the inquests when he was finally called upon to make the decision in July 1992. In exercising his discretion under the 1988 Act to resume an inquest after a criminal trial "if in his opinion there is sufficient cause to do so",[33] the coroner canvassed opinion from the bereaved. 19 families favoured a resumption against 17 who opposed it. 15 made no reply.[34] In giving reasons for his decision the coroner cited, *inter alia*, that fewer than half the relatives and other parties wanted a resumption, that he took into account that some witnesses had already given evidence in four different courts and that he had to consider whether the public interest would be served. However, the coroner's decision was set aside on other grounds in a later application for judicial review.[35]

Recent history reveals a new dynamism in relation to the inquest process. Beginning with the judicial review of the *Herald* inquest which paved the way for unlawful killing verdicts and the eventual prosecution of P & O for manslaughter, subsequent disasters have spawned other challenges.[36] Few of these have been successful, but they probably contribute to a wider awareness of the role of coroners and also encourage coroners themselves to attempt to reach agreement with relatives' groups as to the procedure to be adopted. Before considering proposals to streamline the inquest/inquiry process, the Scottish equivalent of the inquest is described.

---

[33] s. 16(3).
[34] *R. v. Dr Knapman and another, ex p. Dallaglio* Q.B.D. 7 July 1993, Lexis.
[35] *R v Inner West London Coroner, ex p. Dallaglio and others The Times* 16 June 1994, see Chap. 2.5.
[36] The basis of corporate manslaughter is considered in Chap. 7.1.3.

(3) The Scottish System: Fatal Accident Inquiries

A death in Scotland is dealt with differently. Under the Sudden Deaths and Fatal Accidents Inquiry Act 1976, a Fatal Accident Inquiry (FAI) is compulsory only in two circumstances: following a death in employment and following a death in legal custody.[37] This Act also abolished the use of juries. The procurator fiscal can also apply to the sheriff to hold an FAI where

> "it appears ... to be expedient in the public interest ... that an inquiry under [the] Act should be held into the circumstances of the death on the grounds that it was sudden, suspicious or unexplained, or has occurred in circumstances such as to give rise to serious public concern."

The 1976 Act specifically provided that it applied to deaths occurring on that part of the continental shelf to which Scots law applies and thus included the off-shore oil rigs such as Piper Alpha.[38] Inquiries have to be open to the public,[39] and at the conclusion the sheriff is required to issue a "determination" in writing, setting out where and when death occurred, and the cause; any reasonable precautions whereby death might have been avoided and the defects in any system of working and any other relevant facts should also be set out.[40] This is in striking contrast with the inquest protocol which forbids such recommendations.

As to how far the determination can cover the question of fault or blame, the sheriff conducting the Lockerbie Inquiry stated that it would be inappropriate to make a judgment on whether there was any basis for a civil action. However, the Lockerbie FAI confirmed the practice of appending a note to the formal determination dealing with matters falling strictly outside the statutorily mandated findings.

One weakness with the FAI procedure was revealed when five key managers of two oil companies refused to testify at an inquiry and could not be compelled because they lived outside the UK.[41]

---

[37] Fatal Accidents and Sudden Deaths Inquiry (Scotland) Act 1976, s. 1(1)(a).
[38] s. 9.
[39] s. 4(3).
[40] s. 6(1)(a)–(e).
[41] Miller, *op. cit.*

(4) A New System?

Coroners at inquests into recent disasters have been vocal in their attempts to explicate the different roles of inquiry and the inquest. In defending their separate roles, the *Herald* coroner suggested that the inquiry looks for the causes, including whether anyone is to blame and the inquest asks in what way or how did a person come to die?[42] Whereas the Sheen inquiry examined factors which led to capsize of the vessel and who was to blame for it, the *Herald* coroner asked a totally different question—in what way, or how did each person die? It is not clear that the difference is so obvious nor that it is particularly helpful. At the end of the Hillsborough inquest a newspaper editorial commented:

> "There is clearly something wrong with the way the English legal system handles such disasters . . . Given that the Director of Public Prosecutions had already stated that there would be no prosecutions for manslaughter whatever the verdict, there was no need to hold this inquest except to satisfy the law. A comprehensive inquiry under Lord Justice Taylor had already explored every avenue, commented robustly on causes and fault, and made recommendations designed to prevent such a tragedy occurring again . . . Something like the Scottish FAI, which would combine an English inquest with an English public enquiry, a "one-stop" system . . . would be kinder to relatives. The Hillsborough coroner said that the entire relationship between coroners' inquests and public enquiries was a nettle that had to be grasped."[43]

While this reveals a possible overlap in function between inquiry and inquest, a common complaint is that neither is satisfactory. There is a perception amongst bereaved families that the inquest should function as a procedure to address their particular, individual, grief. The view of bereaved families after the Hillsborough inquest was that "their interests, their needs and their assumed right to a full and thorough hearing have been marginalised and subordinated to professional interest and legal interpretation."[44]

---

[42] Sturt, "The Role of the Coroner with Special Reference to Major Disasters" (1988) 28 *Med. Sci. and Law* 275.

[43] *The Times*, 29 March 1991.

[44] Coleman and Scraton, "Unanswered Questions" (1990) *Legal Action* 8 November, p. 8.

Inquiries on the other hand, although also important to those directly affected, seem to be regarded as having longer term, forward-looking and more collective aims. Because inquests are held regularly outside the context of disasters there may be a cultural expectation that deaths out of the ordinary deserve the attention of this public institution. However, disasters clearly raise particular problems for the inquest process. Families want to know both something about the general cause of the disaster as well as something particular about each death.[45]

Problems, too, arise over who will bear the costs. While families have no right to have their costs met in public inquiries, the Government does usually meet the reasonable costs of interested parties. The inequity is more likely to emerge at the inquest, where there is no legal aid. Corporate interested parties are then at a significant advantage.

One of the reasons why inquests appear to duplicate inquiries is that the inquest is usually delayed until both the inquiry, and the decision with respect to prosecution, have been dealt with. By this time, relatives may well feel that their individual bereavement has not been fully explained. The inquest jury is expected both to determine the cause of death, which relatives hope will be a vehicle for ascribing accountability for the death, and yet refrain from attributing fault. Only if they are convinced beyond all reasonable doubt that there has been a criminal offence can an unlawful killing verdict be returned by the jury, a conclusion from which they are discouraged when the D.P.P. has already decided not to proceed. Although technically possible under the 1988 Coroners Act, no opportunity is usually given to the jury to record something reflecting carelessness. Recommendations for safety precautions are also outlawed. Inherent in the current procedure is vast scope for misunderstanding, bitterness and dissatisfaction. A lurking suspicion that the D.P.P. holds the strings in relation to criminal charges is hard to refute.

The inquest into the *Marchioness* collision was held up for almost three years because, although corporate charges had been ruled out early on, the D.P.P. had prosecuted the captain of the dredger *Bowbelle* under the Merchant Shipping Act 1988. When those issues had been settled, the coroner decided not to resume the inquest, a decision which was overturned because the Coroner made an unguarded reference to the relatives and laid himself open to a charge of bias.[46]

---

[45] *Ibid.*
[46] *R. v. Inner West London Coroner, ex p. Dallaglio* Q.B.D. *The Times* 16 June 1994.

The difficult question is how to accommodate these different requirements. The goal is to develop an institution which combines positives aspects of both public inquiries, inquests and FAIs. These are not, it might be noted, new problems. In 1961 a committee considered possible changes in air accident investigation;[47] although of course at that time, coroner's inquests were less restricted than they are now. The committee took the view that it would be difficult for an inquiry to antedate prosecution because of the potential for prejudicing a fair trial. Problems of evidence becoming stale were also acknowledged. Establishing cause might be urgent and might therefore need to take precedence over any prosecution. One answer to this would be to hold a preliminary, technical inquiry into cause. It is interesting to note that the reports into both the *Marchioness* disaster and the Manchester air fire were not released to the public for some time after their completion. In the former case the trial of the dredger captain was cited as the reason for its being withheld from public scrutiny.[48] The report into the Manchester air fire was not published until three and a half years after the disaster, and long after the inquest.[49]

The aftermath of the *Marchioness* highlights also the absence of any right even to a *public* inquiry, let alone how it might relate to an inquest. Mr Justice Sheen, who had conducted the *Herald* inquiry, took the step of writing to *The Times* to ask why there had been no public inquiry. The judge who heard the application for judicial review of the D.P.P.'s prosecution decisions added his voice: "The sinking of the *Marchioness* was an appalling tragedy. It is entirely understandable that the survivors and the other relatives and friends of those who died, and all who are concerned in the safe passage of vessels on the Thames, should seek a full public inquiry into its causes."[50] It would be a minimum requirement in any reform of the post-disaster inquiry system that the criteria for holding a public inquiry be rationalised. A second step would be to acknowledge that the rationale behind the provisions in the inquest legislation which require adjournment pending criminal investigation and forbid any finding of individual culpability have

---

[47] Committee on Civil Aircraft Accident Investigation and Licence Control (Cairns) 1961.

[48] *The Guardian*, 17 August 1990. The Marchioness Action Group unsuccessfully sought leave to challenge the D.P.P.'s decision not to pursue manslaughter charges: *The Guardian*, 30 October 1990. After two trial juries failed to agree on this, the Crown offered no further evidence: *The Independent*, 1 August 1991.

[49] The fire was on 22 August 1985, the inquest returned verdicts of accidental death on 22 September 1986 and the Air Accident Investigation Board published an Interim Report in July 1987 and a Final Report on 12 March 1989.

[50] Nolan, J., *R. v. D.P.P. ex p. Langlands-Pearse* Q.B.D. 30 October 1990, Lexis.

less persuasive force when corporate or governmental institutions are in the frame.

Secrecy still tends to plague safety campaigners. Despite the Sheen Inquiry's openness, and the recommendation that more stringent requirements for ferries be introduced, the Department of Transport was wary of revealing the names of ferries which failed the new stability standards.[51] Research conducted by the Campaign for Freedom of Information suggests that the Department of Transport is particularly prone to secrecy, and that shipping is one of its most closely guarded spheres. Reports, even following loss of life, are only shown to those with a "legitimate interest" which does not include the travelling public.[52] Taken together with the Lloyd's register's assessment that there will be one ferry collision a year, a rapid capsize every five years, a fire or explosion every two or three years, and a Zeebrugge disaster every 200 years, it might be thought that giving the public information was a major responsibility of the government department which oversees shipping safety.[53] Similarly, British Rail does not disclose details of the majority of accident inquiries, since these are internal. It is only the reports of the extremely rare bird, the formal accident investigation by the Railway Inspectorate, which come to public notice.

It is salutary to remind oneself that the office of coroner developed in a period characterised by the state attempting to centralize control of a conquered people through the appointment of a small number of administrators.[54] Perhaps this helps to explain the frustrations experienced in endeavouring to manipulate institutions of the state towards a self-critical stance.

---

[51] March 1989.
[52] *The Guardian*, 7 January 1991. See the criticism of the government by Christian L. "The Bereaved Deserve Better" *The Independent* 13 March 1995.
[53] "More Lives at Risk From Bigger Ferries" *Sunday Times*, 15 April 1990.
[54] Rosen, L., "Intentionality and the Concept of the Person" in Pennock, J. and Chapman, J., *Criminal Justice* (1985) Nomos XXVII p. 66.

4. Disasters: Groups, Funds, and Benefits

The three major sources of compensation for those injured or bereaved by disaster are charitable or trust funds, statutory schemes and civil law claims. In terms of chronology it makes sense to deal with them in that order, for payments may be made from the first two sources within hours or days of the disaster occurring, whereas legal settlements will often take years. Civil compensation, outlined in later chapters, differs in requiring proof of more than injury and may not in the end be payable at all. In terms of entitlement, there are of course distinctive characteristics within and between funds and the various statutory schemes and they are dealt with in this chapter.[1]

First, however, as part of the essential background, I introduce two features of disaster aftermath which are of immense significance to the legal processes and practices described throughout the book. The role of the media in informing, commenting upon and interpreting events is undisputed, and support groups for survivors and relatives are of great importance also. There is an interplay between the two, with groups pursuing campaigns on behalf of their own members or of others, through newspaper and television channels. The theme of groups, their impact and utility, which reflects the essential collective aspect of disasters (compared with individual tragedy), crops up throughout this chapter. It ends with a discussion of personal injury litigation, the growth of phenomena such as the disaster lawyer, and lawyers' groups and the nascent recognition of group actions by the courts. The roles played by the media, and by support and lawyer groups, are pivotal in providing a platform for compensation claims, the legal basis of which is pursued in chapters five and six.

---

[1] A discussion of the Criminal Injuries Compensation and Legal Aid schemes is also included.

1. The Media

Amongst professional groups, journalists and lawyers are central to the whole process of disaster response. Modern communication systems have undoubtedly contributed to public perceptions of disasters. Few can gainsay the power of the contemporaneous transmission of pictures of the *Herald of Free Enterprise* on its side in Zeebrugge harbour or of Pan Am 103's nose, with the words "Maid of the Seas" painfully intact, in a field outside Lockerbie. Images and representations are bounced around the globe, reinforcing dramatically the impact of catastrophe previously filtered through the medium of print. It is not just that the pictures get there more quickly. As a result of increased travel, more people can identify with events outside their own community. Having said that, there is still an intensely local facet of disasters which is reflected in the media.[2] In a fascinating and detailed study of the media reactions to the Lockerbie crash, Deppa shows the different concerns of the national and local networks.[3] 35 journalism students from Syracuse University died in the crash, something unlikely to have been forgotten in that city or in New York State. Yet how many people in the UK could recall that fact? As pointed out in a libel case in 1984 "Aberfan" is part of our accepted vocabulary, but it probably has no meaning outside the UK.[4]

One of the overlooked points about media portrayals of disaster is that they are not merely self-serving; people involved in disasters do gain benefits from the publicity in a number of ways. First, it confirms the importance of their experience. People have seen the failure to report an event as a denial of their trauma.[5] Secondly, it enables people to convert for the benefit of others their loved one from a statistic into a person who had a personality and a personal history. Thirdly, the media can help promote financial appeals and fourthly, the publicity can help to fuel campaigns for safety improvements, inquiries, compensation and so on, all of which are regarded by many of those involved as important ways of bringing good from tragedy.[6] These emotions need to be taken seriously. Conventional, disembodied accounts of legal processes can be based on assumptions which either deny emotions or

---

[2] See Kelly, A., Gibson, R. and Horlick-Jones, R., *Local authorities, the Media and Disasters* (1992).

[3] Deppa, J., *The Media and Disasters* (1993).

[4] *Kerria Developments Ltd and another v. The Reporter Ltd*, 31 July 1984, Lexis.

[5] Deppa, *op. cit.* p. 64.

[6] Kelly *et al., op cit.* p. 7.

invariably attribute unworthy motivations to campaigners. Nonetheless, it is also true that, especially in the immediate aftermath, some media professionals display a remarkable lack of concern for the privacy of ordinary people.

Deppa spends some time discussing the US networks' various answers to a dilemma presented to them by the Lockerbie disaster. It was only as parents arrived at Kennedy airport to meet their student sons and daughters from the plane, that some of them first heard of the crash. Some journalists had already arrived. By all accounts, Pan Am either had no emergency plan, or an inadequate one. As a result, one woman heard that her daughter had died while in the public area of the airport. Her reaction was to lose control. This was then recorded both in still and moving photographic form. Some newspapers and TV networks recognised that it would be an unreasonable intrusion into this woman's privacy to use the pictures; others did not. Quite where the line between acceptable and unacceptable use of such material should be drawn is difficult, but the argument here is reasonably straightforward. If a person chooses to receive bad news in a public place and have their reaction recorded and publicised, then no-one should prevent them. Equally, anybody is entitled to have the opportunity to learn of the death of a member of their family in as private a place as they choose. If, as here, that opportunity is denied them, then the next best step is to ensure that their privacy is not invaded any more than the circumstances dictate.

In a study of media reporting of recent UK disasters, Shearer found a high degree of satisfaction amongst a sample of 1050 adults.[7] In her study, least satisfaction was recorded for the reporting of Hillsborough with 22 per cent believing it was poorly handled and 66 per cent well-handled. This compared with the *Herald* tragedy where only 10 per cent gave a negative response against 79 per cent giving the media a favourable verdict. Hillsborough gave rise to criticism, because aside from the Liverpool local press, many reports relied on official sources which tended to blame the fans, alleging drunkenness, and at the same time to praise the police as heroes. Because the press was already at the scene in order to cover the football match, the potential for intrusive photography was much amplified, compared with disasters whose occurrence is the initial magnet for the media's interest.

Public responses to disasters are dependant on media portrayals

---

[7] Shearer, A., *Survivors and the Media* (1991); the demographically representative sample disclosed one fifth who had survived an act of violence or national disaster.

which both inform on and reconstruct the event. This helps survivors and relatives, especially where they are geographically
dispersed, to co-ordinate a support group. Another frequent reaction is to set up a fund with appeals for contributions made
through print and television. These two aspects of disaster aftermath are dealt with next.

2. Support Groups

A significant feature of disaster aftermath in the UK in the last
ten years has been the development of support groups.[8] Such
groups are noteworthy because they underline what marks out a
disaster from an individual tragedy. The survivors and bereaved
relatives following a motorway accident will experience many of
the same physical and emotional traumas as those involved in
disasters. But disasters, precisely for the reasons that they become
classified as such, bring forth an entirely different scale of
response. Disaster funds are one manifestation of that difference.
Support groups and the pressure they bring to bear on a number
of areas of the legal process are another.

Support groups have, it seems, two major roles. Internally, they
provide a forum in which those affected can share their experiences amongst a group of people who have some comprehension
of the kinds of feelings they are suffering. The group is both a
source of information and a means of communication. Externally,
the group can act on behalf of members in negotiating the various
legal structures, and as an important part of that process, provide
a channel for communication with the media. Support groups can
exploit the intense media interest in disasters by campaigning for
public inquiries, by lobbying for better levels of compensation and
for safety changes. This lobbying is often conducted in association
with legal representatives.[9]

The therapeutic and campaigning functions, although often
interactive for the group's members, are serviced and sometimes
initiated by different professionals. Groups are often a by-product
of efforts made by health and social services personnel to make
people aware of the range of help they can offer. Hodgkinson and
Stewart describe the mechanisms which are adopted to encourage
those affected by disaster to acknowledge their need for support.
As a matter of broad cultural generalisation, most people have

---

[8] And of groups of lawyers acting on their behalf; see below.
[9] Allen, P., "Plaintiffs and the Media" (1990) 140 *New Law Journal* 1530, 1531.

defences and barriers which prevent their looking to others for help, and resistance is particularly strong amongst men and older people.

The use of leaflets and newsletters has proved one of the most successful means of informing people of such services without alienating or intimidating them. Following the Bradford Stadium fire, the Mayor was sent copies of a pamphlet prepared by doctors in response to a bushfire in Australia in 1983. Its four main functions were:

(i) to provide information about the sorts of physical and emotional sensations likely to be experienced

(ii) to list "Do's" and "Don'ts"

(iii) to suggest when it may be appropriate to seek professional help

(iv) indicate where that can be obtained.[10]

The Red cross has now produced its own booklet, *Coping with a Major Personal Crisis.*[11] It appears then that, although survivor groups often flourish without professional support, the lessons from Bradford have supplied key lessons in how to promote groups amongst reluctant populations.

Campaigning generally involves lawyers and the legal process, but it is important to appreciate that support groups often precede any compensation or safety campaign. Yet, these latter functions can co-exist with a therapeutic role. Some commentators have attributed the formation of the Herald Families Association to the sense of symbolic deprivation felt by those who lost adult children for whom no bereavement damages are legally available.[12] The concentration of that group's energies on demands for a manslaughter prosecution is thus partly explained in terms of their search for some legal recognition of their bereavement. A similar point can be inferred from the campaigns of the *Marchioness* relatives.

Cultural changes have also played a part in moves towards criminal blame of collective bodies such as P&O.[13] Translating their reactions into legal claims is manifestly complex, involving many aspects of legal process, from representation at inquiries, to

---

[10] Hodgkinson, P. and Steward, M., eds, *Coping with Catastrophe* (1991), p. 118.

[11] 1989.

[12] Hodgkinson and Stewart, p. 28. Bereavement damages are discussed in Chap. 5.4.1

[13] This theme is explored further in Chap. 7.2.

challenging coroners' discretion, to civil claims and to pressure for corporate criminal liability. Few of these would be possible without a group to orchestrate them.

As well as campaigning by individual support groups, mass tort litigation has led to its own campaigning group, Citcom, (Citizen's Action Compensation Campaign), a group which aims to reform the tort system.[14] Disaster lawyers themselves lobby through membership of the American Trial Lawyers Association, itself a pressure group which seeks to redress the imbalance between private citizens and corporate forces.[15] Disaster Action, another umbrella group formed in 1991 from a coalition of the separate disaster support groups, has the stated priorities of defining and establishing corporate responsibility and accountability. All these groups use media publicity to promulgate their ideas. Television, newspaper and book channels are all utilised. The Herald Families Association and its charitable sister the Herald Charitable Trust has been productive in this latter regard with a number of commissioned publications.[16]

Just as groups are easier to establish where there is media attention, funds to compensate those damaged by disasters also depend on media involvement. Disaster funds are one of a variety of forms of financial assistance which disaster survivors and bereaved relatives might obtain.

3. Disaster Funds

The launch of an appeal for funds to assist survivors could almost be regarded as one of the necessary definitional requirements of a disaster.[17] The amount raised by such appeals varies greatly and not necessarily in any obvious relation to the numbers or needs of those affected. The fund for the 28 victims of the explosion at the Flixborough chemical works came to £50,000 while the *Herald* fund raised nearly £4 million. Two funds became well-known in their own right because of difficulties encountered in distributing the vast sums; the Aberfan Fund and the Penlee lifeboat Fund 1981.

The Mayor of Merthyr Tydfil launched an appeal on the evening

---

[14] Developed from the Opren litigation, see below.
[15] Harlow and Rawlings, *Pressure Through Law* (1992) p. 189.
[16] Crainer, S., *Zeebrugge: Learning from Disaster* (1993) and Bergman, D., *Disasters: Where the Law Fails* (1993).
[17] For a history of such appeals, see Luxton, P., *Charity Fund-Raising and the Public Interest* (1990) p. 120.

of the disaster at Aberfan with the purposes of relieving hardship and rehabilitating the village.[18] It faced the difficulty that, as they were mainly children, few of the victims left dependant relatives. The response was overwhelming and when the Fund closed it had reached £1.75 million. The first report of the Disaster Fund Management Committee ascribed the response to the unprecedented coverage by press, radio and television. It has also been suggested that the scale of response reflected a sense of responsibility deriving from the enjoyment most people in Britain had gained from the availability of cheap coal.[19] Another explanation is that the victims were not only children, but they were suffocated in their schoolroom, thus doubly amplifying the horror. As one journalist wrote, Aberfan was victim of two disasters: the landslide and then the avalanche of money. His explanation for the extraordinary level of donations was this: "We have always known that miners died; it was part of the price of coal, we accepted it. It was the miners' choice. But the children up in the schoolroom, saying their morning prayers, had no such choice".[20]

The money was far in excess of that needed to alleviate hardship, which gave rise to opportunities for dispute within the village as to how the remainder should be spent. The disputes themselves have been regarded by some as a form of scapegoat for the anger which the village might otherwise have directed at the National Coal Board, held by the Tribunal of Inquiry to be partly responsible for the disaster. This anger was further fuelled by the government's decision to claim £150,000 from the Fund to pay towards the cost of clearing the remaining tips round the village. The surplus money was used eventually to build various community leisure facilities and a Garden of Remembrance.

Aberfan was a community which had a collective sense of loss (almost two in every five residents was directly bereaved). In contrast the Penlee lifeboat fund was a response to the deaths of eight lifeboatmen while attempting to rescue a stricken tanker, the *Union Star*, in 1981. It raised an astonishing £4 million. The confusion as to the purposes for which the money was given, and the eventual decision to treat it as non-charitable thus allowing distribution amongst the families concerned, led to the publication of Guidelines by the Attorney-General. Legally, funds raise difficult questions.

So what is the legal background to appeals such as these? The

---

[18] Miller, J., *Aberfan: A Disaster and its Aftermath* (1974) on which this section draws.
[19] *Op cit.*, p. 31.
[20] Watkins, *The Times*, 17 October 1986.

natural legal machinery for a fund held on behalf of others is the trust, a mechanism which can come in charitable or non-charitable form. The legal, and consequential tax, implications of the distinction between charitable and non-charitable purposes are these. While charitable funds attract tax exemption on their investment income, the hands of their trustees are tied in terms of the beneficiaries and the amounts payable to them. To be charitable a fund needs to come broadly within the spirit of the preamble to the Charitable Uses Act 1601. This covers four broad heads: relief of poverty, advancement of education, advancement of religion and other purposes beneficial to the community. In each case the charity has also to satisfy a requirement that it is directed to the benefit of the public or a section of the public.[21] If a fund is limited to the alleviation of particular need of individuals affected, it is relatively easy to satisfy this even though only a specific group will benefit. But that rarely answers the difficulties. The fund is often much larger than necessary for that purpose and it is often felt inappropriate to administer a means test. If the fund also has purposes relating to the general "purposes beneficial to the community" then the community has to be drawn somewhat more widely. In other words, it may be possible to have a group of 10 people who are in need and they would satisfy the section of the public. But once their need was dealt with (which would generally reflect their particular circumstances), any surplus distributed under the "purpose to the community" would have to benefit a much larger group.

At one time it was assumed that a disaster fund would necessarily be charitable, but judicial doubt began to emerge as to whether a fund would satisfy the criterion of benefiting the public or a section of it, essential to a charitable trust.[22] Two cases can be contrasted: an appeal launched to relieve those affected by flooding in the south west in 1953 was regarded as having public benefit,[23] while a fund established in response to a bus crash which killed 24 marine cadets was not.[24] Thus, a disaster fund is not automatically charitable; to be charitable there should be an expression that it will only be distributed to individuals (who form a section of the public) on grounds of need, or it has to be devised in a way which brings it under the head of beneficial purposes which envisages a broader section of the public. It is

---

[21] *Income Tax Special Purposes Commissioners v. Pemsel* (1891) A.C. 531.
[22] Chesterman (1979).
[23] *Re North Devon and West Somerset Relief Fund Trusts* [1953] 1 W.L.R. 1260.
[24] *Re Gillingham Bus Disaster Fund* [1959] Ch. 62.

often wise for the terms of a fund to include both these purposes so that money surplus to need can be used for the wider public benefit.

Charitable funds have tax advantages (for both donors and the investment income of the fund) and there is a further mechanism for distributing any surplus, the *cy-près* application of the funds.[25] This can be invoked if the appeal fails to raise sufficient funds for the purpose, but this is less likely to occur with disaster funds. (It is more likely where a fund is launched for a specific project.) A non-charitable fund which accumulates a surplus has no alternative but to attempt to return it to the donors. Weighed against these advantages are the limitations that the definitions of charitable purposes may bring.

Armed with this background, it is now possible to demonstrate the difficulties to which they led with regard to the Aberfan and Penlee Funds. The Aberfan Fund was registered as a charity under the following formulation of objects:

1. for the relief of all persons who have suffered as a result of the said disaster and are thereby in need; and
2. subject as aforesaid for any charitable purpose for the benefit of persons who were inhabitants of Aberfan and its immediate neighbourhood (... called the "area of benefit") on [the day of the disaster] or who now or hereafter become inhabitants of the area of benefit and in particular (but without prejudice to the generality of the last foregoing trust) for any charitable purpose for the benefit of children who were [on the day of the disaster] or who now are or hereafter may become resident in the area of benefit.

The wording of the second purpose was deliberately adopted to allow expenditure beyond the needs of the specific bereaved families. Even so, the reality of what actually occurred somewhat strained the "charitable" terms of the fund. There was so much opposition to the idea that the payments under the first purpose should be means tested that permission was sought from the Charity Commissioners to allow distribution of a fixed sum of £5,000 to each bereaved family. This ran the risk of being a technical breach of trust and in theory any "person interested" could have challenged it.[26] When it came to spending the surplus under the second of the trust's terms, the request to contribute to the removal

---

[25] Charities Act 1993, s. 13.
[26] Under powers now found in the Charities Act 1993, ss. 32 and 33.

of tips divided both the community and donors. About 100 of the latter gave their views of this when asked and they were split. As Chesterman comments, the benefits of charitable status for the Fund turned out paradoxically to be mixed: "While charitable status undoubtedly increased the fund's resources by attracting exemption from tax on investment income, the ultimate effect of this was simply to augment by several thousand pounds the surplus for which modes of expenditure had to be found."[27] Yet without charitable status the secondary rules might have been void for uncertainty, thus giving rise to a resulting trust for the donors.

The Penlee disaster occurred in the week before Christmas. Almost immediately, Penwith District Council announced the appointment of trustees to deal with donations. There were eight bereaved families and the press release emphasised that the "total fund will be used directly for the benefit of the dependants and all money received will be distributed directly to families of the lifeboat crew."

By December 23 a second press release was issued referring to the magnificent response and informing readers that counsel's advice had been sought. That advice was that the fund was held on charitable trust and therefore could only meet reasonable needs. The surplus income would have to be used for other charitable purposes. However, this advice ran counter to the wording of the appeal because the persons receiving the money would have needed to execute a trust deed declaring a precise charitable trust.[28] The appeal made clear that it was destined for the private benefit of the dependants of the deceased lifeboatmen and not for another more widely dispersed benefit. The confusion was a matter of concern both for the individuals affected and for the government. Eventually the Attorney-General let it be known that he did not consider the main fund to be charitable.[29] The fund was treated as a private trust with the whole amount distributed amongst the families. Newspaper correspondence revealed that this was felt by some donors to be in accordance with their intentions, but others said they had given to relieve suffering, not to transform the beneficiaries into wealthy people.[30]

As a result of this muddle, the Attorney-General issued guidelines for disaster appeals from which subsequent funds have

---

[27] *Op. cit.*, p. 345.
[28] *Att.-Gen. v. Mathieson* [1907] 2 Ch. 383.
[29] Cairns, E., "Disaster Appeals" (1991) *Sol. J.* 46.
[30] Luxton, *op. cit.*, p. 123.

been able to benefit. Further practical guidance can be found in the more recent British Red Cross Disaster Appeal Scheme announced in 1991. All these have led to a move towards the use of private discretionary trusts for disaster appeals. Emphasis is given in the Attorney-General's Guidelines on the need to consider at the outset whether the appeal is going to be charitable or not. It is pointed out that non-charitable funds allow unlimited payments to individuals, but that they must ensure that they are sufficiently clearly worded as to the beneficiaries so that they do not risk being void for uncertainty. They should use a form of words such as this: "This appeal is to set up a fund, the entire benefit of which will be used for those injured or bereaved in the disaster ... or their families and dependants as the trustees think fit. This fund will not be a charity."[31] If the fund is going to aim to be charitable then certain things have to be provided. The form of appeal should include both relief of distress of those in need of help and, importantly, a statement that any surplus will be used for charitable purposes designed to help those who suffer in similar tragedies, to benefit charities with related purposes and to help the locality. This avoids the problem of a surplus having to be repaid to donors, yet retains the charitable benefits. Of course, it is always open to have two funds, one charitable and the other not. Both the Bradford and the *Herald* funds were split in this way enabling the charitable arm to engage in educational and safety promotion functions with the benefit of tax relief, while the payments to individuals were unfettered by the charitable purpose limitations.[32] Scotland does not have the Charity Commission but is subject to the same tax rules as England and Wales. The Lord Advocate has issued similar guidelines to those of the Attorney-General.[33]

Legal provision is necessary to deal with fraudulently based funds or with fraudulent mismanagement of funds. Because the donors are usually anonymous there are difficulties in returning donations, which is the only legal avenue for dealing with the undistributed sums from non-charitable trusts. Luxton proposes that the Crown, as the only possible claimant, should establish the practice of allowing use of the funds for a charitable purpose. As a general safeguard he also suggests that all public appeals for funds, whether charitable or not, should carry a duty to supply through the press basic information about the terms of the trust, the amounts raised, and the expenses incurred.[34]

---

[31] The Attorney-General's Guidelines (1982).
[32] See Suddards, R., *Administration of Appeal Funds* (1991) for an account of the Bradford Fire fund.
[33] *Scots Law Times*, 7 January 1983, pp. 1–3.
[34] Luxton, *op. cit.*, p. 126.

There have also been proposals for a national disaster fund, echoing one set up in the wake of the *Titanic* in 1912. The main argument is that different disasters raise grossly disproportionate amounts depending on factors such as timing (Penlee was just before Christmas), age of victims (young children were killed or bereaved at Aberfan and Penlee) and circumstances (lifeboats carry a volunteer-hero association). The Bradford Fire, the *Herald*, and Hillsborough funds all approached £4 million within four weeks, while the King's Cross underground fire brought in £628,000 and the *Marchioness* £55,000 in the same period.[35]

4. Benefits

(1) Statutory Benefits

In numerical terms, statutory benefit claims are the most significant source of financial assistance for victims of accidents. However, in monetary terms, the amounts paid are tiny in comparison with those gained as a result of tortious action. Less than 10 per cent of accident victims overall receive tort damages, yet their total value amounts to half the total paid to recipients of statutory benefit.[36] Amongst accident victims, it is already known that the two groups most likely to sue in tort are those injured at work and in traffic accidents, for the simple reason that both types of activity are subject to schemes of compulsory insurance. For those injured in disasters, the proportion receiving some form of compensation in addition to statutory benefits is undoubtedly higher than for accident victims generally.

Contributory schemes such as invalidity benefit, widow's benefit and unemployment benefit as well as non-contributory benefits such as disability living allowance, income support or family credit have been subject to a major overhaul.[37] The "earnings related" principle introduced in the 1960s has been eroded as part of the current philosophy of shifting responsibility from the state to private pensions systems. Statutory benefits, even the contributory ones, now provide only basic income support. Injuries sustained at work which were previously the subject of a

---

[35] *Op. cit.*, 127.

[36] Cane, P., *Atiyah's Accidents, Compensation and the Law* (5th ed., 1993), p. 17.

[37] Consolidated in the Social Security Contributions and Benefits Act 1992 and the Social Security Administration Act 1992. See generally Matthewman *et al. Tolley's Social Security and State Benefits Handbook* 193–4 (1993).

separate scheme are now subsumed within the social security system.[38] For injuries incurred after 1990, only disablement benefit remains. Short term benefit for injuries at work are brought within the ordinary sick pay scheme.[39]

(2) Criminal Injuries Compensation

One particular group of victims is treated exceptionally and can make a claim on the state for a payment based on civil compensation principles. Under the Criminal Injuries Compensation Scheme, set up in 1964, a claim can be made by anyone injured (physically or mentally) as a result of a crime of violence or while trying to prevent a crime or trying to apprehend a criminal.[40] The scheme was radically revised in 1994 as a result of the implementation of the 1993 White Paper.

Injuries from road traffic offences are excluded, not unreasonably, given the provision for compulsory insurance backed by the Motor Insurers' Bureau where the offender cannot be traced. The main restriction on the scheme is the discretion bestowed on the administrators of the scheme, the Criminal Injuries Compensation Board (from April 1994 the CIC Authority), to refuse a payment if the police were not immediately notified of the offence or if the applicant failed to cooperate with the police or they are regarded as being of bad character.

The scheme as a whole has been subject to devastating criticism,[41] but particular objection can be taken both to the notion of a "crime of violence" and to the "character" discretion. As to the restriction to crimes of "violence",[42] this is intended to exclude injuries resulting from regulatory offences such as pollution, health and safety and food safety. This serves to perpetuate the notion that individual miscreants, collectively comprising the deviant classes, are more a threat to the well being of the populace than deviant business enterprises. Another problem arises when this image of "violent crime" interacts with the requirement that a successful claim depends on prompt reporting. Manslaughter is quintessentially a crime of violence, but corporate manslaughter is a social construction only just emerging into public perception. A victim of corporate negligence might be forgiven for failing to report a case of corporate manslaughter, given that its official

---

[38] Social Security Contributions and Benefits Act 1992, Pt. 5.
[39] Social Security Contributions and Benefits Act 1992, s. 31.
[40] See Miers, D., *Compensation for Criminal Injuries* (2nd ed., 1990).
[41] Cane, *op. cit.*, pp. 251–256.
[42] Now formally embodied in the scheme, but originally introduced by the Board.

reception, which has been opaque to say the least, has lagged behind its popular recognition.

Assessment of the claimant's character as a criterion of qualification also serves to embed a "them and us" paradigm of criminal behaviour. This goes much further than the limitations on civil claims imposed by contributory negligence, for example.

A tariff scheme was introduced in 1994 to replace the system whereby the level of compensation was assessed in the same way as a court would assess damages if a person were to sue the assailant.[43] Under the new scheme there is a set sum for different types of injury. Calculations based on loss of earnings are no longer used and with medical and other expenses now excluded, lower levels of compensation are bound to result. There is a £250,000 limit on awards, which can be compared with the £834,000 highest award given by the CICB under the old scheme.[44] The time limit of three years from the injury, which was comparable to the limitation period for personal injury claims, has been reduced to one year.[45] As before, the minimum award is £1,000 and claims are reduced by the full value of present and future D.S.S. benefits, pension payments and some insurance payments. The combined effect of these set-offs and the removal of special damages for loss of earnings will further erode the value of the awards. In fatal cases, it seems that a bereavement award of £10,000 will replace those previously based on loss of dependency. An additional reform is that appeals will be heard by a panel no longer solely drawn from the legal profession.

Because the Criminal Injuries Compensation scheme has never been placed on a statutory footing, these changes have been made by the exercise of executive powers. Although the Criminal Justice Act 1988 makes provision for a statutory scheme, the relevant section has never been brought into force.[46] When the wide-ranging alterations to the system of assessing levels of compensation referred to were announced, a challenge by way of judicial review was brought arguing that making changes in this way was contrary to the 1988 Act. The House of Lords upheld an argument that it was an abuse of power for the Home Secretary to ignore the statutory provisions, even though they were not in force, by seeking to impose the tariff scheme.[47]

---

[43] As from 1 April 1994. The controversy caused by this is discussed further below.

[44] Walker, "Criminal Injuries Compensation: A Government Betrayal?" [1994] *J. of Personal Injury Litigation* 47, 49.

[45] *Ibid*. For limitation for civil actions for personal injuries, see Limitation Act 1980, ss. 11–14.

[46] Criminal Justice Act 1988, s. 181(1).

[47] *R. v. Secretary of State for the Home Department, ex p. the Fire Brigades Union and others*, *The Times*, 6 Apr 1995. The old scheme will revive until new legislation is passed.

(3) Legal Aid

A further form of state benefit which ought to be of practical significance is the Legal Aid system. Unfortunately, the impact of this has been greatly reduced over the last decade, with the number of people qualifying for it ever decreasing. Whereas in 1979 it was estimated that 80 per cent of households were eligible, the Lord Chancellor's Department suggests now a figure of 48 per cent.[48] Administered by the Legal Aid Board, the scheme has three main types of assistance: advice, representation and reimbursement of costs.[49] In addition, it is still possible to obtain a half-hour of legal advice for £5.00. Under the "green form" scheme, those entitled to full legal aid can obtain free legal advice and representation. The Law Society oversees the Accident Legal Advice Service, in which a free initial interview is offered to accident victims by about 2,500 solicitors.

Assistance with costs can be met in full or on a contribution basis, assessed according to a sliding means test. To qualify, it has to be demonstrated that the case has reasonable merit. An idea of the limited scope of the scheme can be seen by examining the upper limit for eligibility for any contribution, which in the case of personal injuries means no legal aid at all for a person with a disposable income of more than £7,500. The lower limit, below which no contribution is required, is £2,294. Disposable capital of more than £8,560 would also disqualify a claimant. How legal aid provision and personal injury litigation affect each other is considered in the section on group action below.

This account of benefits compensation through charitable funds and benefits obtainable through statutory and other schemes is, as we have seen, unpredictable, uneven and largely outside the control of their recipients. Legal actions, whether in the form of civil liability claims, or pressure for criminal prosecution, are, on the other hand, driven more directly by the survivors and the families of the victims of disasters themselves. As described above, the support group, amongst other things, provides one mechanism through which these campaigns are conducted. Co-ordinated action by lawyers is the next aspect to be considered.

---

[48] Fennell, "Access to Justice for Personal Injury Litigants" [1994] *J. of Personal Injury Litigation* 30.
[49] The Board was established by the Legal Aid Act 1988, taking over a role formerly undertaken by the Law Society.

5. Disaster Lawyers

Reflecting the cultural significance of disasters, a new vocabulary has emerged, which includes phrases such as "corporate manslaughter" and "disaster lawyers." This latter term describes firms of solicitors who have responded to the difficulties associated with mounting compensation claims in tort. The existence of lawyers specialising in personal injury litigation is of course not a new phenomenon, but disaster lawyers belong to a subspecialism with an expertise going beyond the traditional territory of personal injury claims. A natural progression from this has been the formation of groups of solicitors to handle the negotiations between plaintiffs and defendants after a disaster. Because the law involved can be a complex mixture of negligence, product liability, personal injury and fatal cases, co-ordinated action between solicitors is used to enable multiple claims to maximise success.[50] Some of the early groups were prompted by the difficulties of establishing claims in the United States where that would be an option because of the nature of the disaster. Lockerbie and Piper Alpha both gave rise to questions of jurisdiction and to "ambulance-chasing" by lawyers from the United States, a critical issue for local solicitors. Establish-ing a steering committee was an obvious defensive response by local lawyers.[51] In addition, if it does not already exist, lawyers will encourage the development of a disaster support group.

Some of the advantages of groups of solicitors acting on behalf of the multiple victims of a single incident are that the victims can benefit from others' experience, they can take advice from specialists more cost-effectively, information can be shared, and pressure through the media can be co-ordinated, resulting in the more efficient conduct of negotiations.[52] Disadvantages emerge if the group does not represent the majority of claimants or if it is difficult to identify the claimants, because defendants are understandably anxious to know the extent of potential claims. McBryde and Barker also point to various pitfalls to be avoided by those involved in group representation, including the importance of limiting the size of the steering committee and devising a formal constitution.[53]

What happens in practical terms is that the "lead firms", who

---

[50] McCool, G., "Disaster Co-ordination" (1991) 16 *Intl. Leg. Practitioner* 23.
[51] McBryde and Barker, "Solicitors' Groups in Mass Disaster Claims" (1991) 141 *New Law Journal* 484.
[52] *Ibid.*
[53] *Ibid.*

are specialists in personal injury, form the steering committee which negotiates with the defendant on behalf of all claimants in relation to matters common to the whole group.[54] The "feeder firms" handle their own clients' personal matters.[55] For example, following the *Herald*, a steering committee of six firms acted as co-ordinator for 120 firms representing 318 claimants. The Law Society now provides, through its Disaster Co-ordination Service, an initial contact point for solicitors acting in personal injury claims. Arising originally from the *Herald* case, it has been used in a number of subsequent mass cases, including King's Cross, Clapham Rail, Hillsborough and *Marchioness*. After the initial press release, factsheets for solicitors, victims and families are produced. Solicitors register with the service, which compiles a central register and initiates a meeting where a steering committee is elected.[56] Disaster lawyers "play an exceptionally creative role" according to Harlow and Rawlings, and their impact is reinforced by the fact that they are "repeat players who camouflage the fact that the plaintiffs are one-shotters".[57]

6. Group Actions

Group litigation functions partly to make law accessible to individuals, as a counterbalance to corporate weight.[58] However, the legal aid system reflects the underlying individualistic ideology in legal structures, and is unsympathetic to the use of courts for campaigning. Additionally, significant parts of the legal process, such as inquests, do not attract legal aid support. In the United States, where there is no legal aid, campaigning is often funded by charitable institutions. One of the paradoxes produced by a system of publicly-funded legal aid is that the state may be "cast in a dual role of wrongdoer and benevolent source of funds".[59]

Groups of solicitors handling claims are not, however, the same as group action. One firm in particular, Pannone Napier, was the pioneer in developing a multiple claims strategy in personal injury actions. It is testimony to the pragmatic, even accidental, development of much English law that, without that firm's direction, much of the pressure exerted on the range of legal institutions would

---

[54] Legal Aid Act 1988, ss. 4(5) and 15(4) contemplates group actions.
[55] Cane, *op. cit.*, p. 228.
[56] Harlow and Rawlings, *op. cit.*, p. 123.
[57] *Ibid.*
[58] *Ibid.*, p. 112.
[59] *Ibid.*, p. 121.

not have occurred. Legal innovation does not generate itself.

Although informal networks can be used effectively, English developments towards more formal arrangements have their antecedents in US lawyers networking over the anti–cholesterol drug MER/29, where plaintiffs groups formed a committee to act as clearing house and for negotiating discovery of documents.[60]

The development of procedures to deal with group actions is one of the remarkable features of the last decade and is something to which it can be said that disasters have contributed. Most defendants are traditionally corporate bodies, of course, with insurance companies often standing behind them. Group plaintiffs are numerically insignificant, but the impact of their cases in terms of public awareness through media attention gives them a disproportionate profile.[61] "Mass torts", as some writers call them, arise both in the context of disasters as understood in this book and in relation to drug and product liability claims.[62] It was in the actions against the pharmaceutical company, Eli Lilley, as a result of side effects from the use of the arthritis drug, Opren, that the new group procedures began to evolve.[63] It was the largest example of personal injury litigation hitherto seen in England.[64]

English courts have never recognised the class action which is a characteristic of the American legal system, but even there it is not used extensively for group personal injury actions and its main use has been for injunctive relief in public law, particularly the civil rights sphere.

US Federal Rules of Civil Procedure authorise class action as do many individual states. Under the federal rules, class action is allowed where

a. the class is so numerous that joinder is impossible
b. there are common questions of law or fact and
c. the representatives will "fairly and adequately protect" the interests of the class.

In addition, a class action has to be "superior to other available

---

[60] *Ibid.*, p. 126.
[61] Hedley, "Group Personal Injury Litigation and Public Opinion" (1994) 14 *Legal Studies* 70, 71.
[62] Which are likely to increase as a result of the Consumer Protection Act 1987, although commentators differ in their assessment of how "strict" is the liability imposed: see Cane (1993) p. 88.
[63] *Davies v. Eli Lilley* [1987] 3 All E.R. 94.
[64] Harlow and Rawlings, *op. cit.*, p. 131.

methods for the fair and efficient adjudication of controversy."[65] However, class action has been described as an American concept "which is often misunderstood and even idealised in England."[66] One reason that class actions have been used less for mass torts is that in the United States, the contingency fee system (where the lawyer gets nothing if the case is lost but a percentage of damages if it is won) gives more incentive to establish liability in individual cases first. This is especially so where punitive as well as compensatory damages are available.[67] In these cases, the class action tends to be used to "hoover up" lesser claims once the initial case is determined.[68]

Essentially, a class action results in a global sum of damages which is then divided amongst claimants. The English "representative action" allows one party to sue as a representative of a group, with the decision binding all the represented parties.[69] The stumbling block is that such an action can only determine issues common to all the represented parties, but assessment of damages will generally be an individual question. Representative actions have thus been limited to cases brought by members of a club or association, where the damages are of equal value to each member.[70] A pragmatic solution to the needs of groups of personal injury claimants has been the development of a second type of group action, where claims are co-ordinated and a "lead" case is taken to trial, with the result used as a basis for settling similar cases.[71] In the Opren litigation, for example, 700 claims of the 1,500 claims were co-ordinated by six firms of solicitors. Separate writs were issued, but the statement of claims referred to a master statement of claim running to over 100 pages.[72] The High Court facilitated the action by appointing one judge to take charge of the preliminary procedural steps.[73] There has been considerable judicial support for the scheme devised for the Opren litigation,

---

[65] US Federal Rules, R. 23.
[66] Harlow and Rawlings, *op cit.*, p. 124.
[67] Discussed further in Chap.6.7.
[68] Harlow and Rawlings, *op. cit.*, p. 126.
[69] R.S.C., Ord. 15, r. 12(1).
[70] R.S.C., Ord. 15, r. 12(1); see Uff, "Class, Representative and Shareholders' Derivative Actions in English Law" (1986) *Civil Justice Quarterly* 50, p. 51.
[71] R.S.C., Ord. 4, r. 9(1); see Supreme Court Procedure Committee, *Guide for Use in Group Actions* (1991) which also lists some variants such as joint plaintiffs issuing one writ; R.S.C., Ord. 15, rr. 4–7.
[72] Uff, "Recent Developments in Representative Actions" (1987) 6 *Civil J Qu.* 15, p. 17.
[73] R.S.C. Ord. 4, r. 9(1).

reflecting a willingness to accommodate multi-plaintiff cases.[74]

However, there are still difficulties. The success of any group action depends on the co-operation of the defendants. Because there are no formal rules of court, defendants can engage in delaying tactics and wear down the patience of the claimants, or they can "buy off" lead claimants with out-of-court settlements. This then leaves other claimants without a decision on the common issue.[75]

The second major hurdle is that of costs. In the *Opren* case, the Court of Appeal approved the procedure adopted by Hirst J. that the costs should be distributed pro rata amongst all the claimants.[76] This frustrated the motives of the lawyers, who had selected as the "lead actions" those claimants who were fully legally aided.[77] The effect of the judge's order was to make all the plaintiffs liable, irrespective of their legal aid status, for a percentage of the costs. It amounted to something like 66p for every £1,000 of costs. Otherwise, the lead plaintiffs would effectively be forfeiting their own damages, for the amount they would receive in compensation would not be sufficient to meet the costs of bringing the case. However, the effect of the order was, of course, to put pressure on the non legally-aided plaintiffs, even in respect of their own costs.

It was estimated that, if the case had gone to trial, the costs would be £3–6 million, yet most of the plaintiffs expected to receive only a few thousand pounds. If they had won, and been legally aided, the legal aid fund would have recouped its own costs from their award. If they had lost, both sets of costs would be borne by the plaintiffs. For the legally aided (about two-thirds of the group) their liability would be limited to any contribution required under the regulations, plus the amount of any order for costs made under the Legal Aid Act 1988, s. 17. Although this section provides for an order for costs against an assisted party, it is not usually invoked where the defendant is insured. However, that would not help the non-funded plaintiff, who is also subject to more pressure from a payment into court; failure to accept a payment into court which is larger than the final damages awarded can lead to an order to pay the defendant's costs. Where payments into court are made, which is probably in less than half of cases, the vast majority are accepted, which testifies to the pressure the costs provision

---

[74] See *Chrzanowska v. Glaxo Laboratories* (Q.B.D.) *The Independent* 13 March 1990 and *Horrocks v. Ford Motor Co.* (C.A.) *The Times,* 15 February 1990; *AB v. John Wyeth and Brother Ltd* (1993) 12 *Butterworths Medico-Legal Reports* 50.

[75] Hepple, B. and Matthews, M., *Tort: Cases and Materials* (4th ed., 1991), p. 30.

[76] *Davies v. Eli Lilley* [1987] 1 W.L.R. 1136.

[77] See Civil Legal Aid (General) Regulations 1989 (S.I. 1989 No. 339).

exerts.[78] Legal aid is both means tested and merit tested, (requiring demonstration of reasonable prospects of success and the benefit to be gained proportionate to the cost of obtaining them). The Courts and Legal Services Act 1990 authorises the making of conditional fees agreements in certain proceedings.[79] This allows for the "speculative" or "conditional" fee; the lawyer is paid nothing if there is no recovery and normal fees and a small premium if successful. The incentive is less great than would be provided by a contingency fee system, which, it is suggested, is resisted because of concerns about any conflict of interest between client and lawyer and because it may encourage unnecessary litigation.[80]

The Opren litigation underlined explicitly the economic calculation which a personal injury litigant has to make. As Donaldson M.R. candidly admitted:

> The real problem here is that in relation to any claim it can happen that it will cost too much to enforce it: the costs will be out of proportion to any benefit which is likely to be obtained ... Trying 1,500 cases together is much cheaper than trying 1,500 cases separately, so the plaintiffs as a group can spend more before they reach the economic limit ... [T]hese cases are no exception to the general rule that settling genuine disputes by agreement between the parties is almost always in the interests of *all* parties.[81]

The case was rescued only when a benefactor underwrote the costs of the non legally-aided to the tune of £2 million. Settlements are generally confidential, but the amount was reported to be in the region of £2.25 million, amounting to £1,800 per plaintiff.[82]

Obviously, an arrangement has to be made with respect to the costs of the solicitors handling the individual claims and those of the steering group dealing with matters common to them all. The Practice Note issued in relation to the Marchioness group reads as follows:

> "Unless the Court otherwise orders, the costs of the Steering Committee of the *Marchioness* Disaster Solicitors Group incurred up to the date of this order and hereafter shall be

---

[78] Cane, *op. cit.*, p. 232.
[79] s. 58, brought into force in 1993.
[80] Harlow and Rawlings, *op. cit.*, p. 115.
[81] *Ibid.*, p. 100.
[82] *Ibid.*, p. 133.

apportioned equally between all plaintiffs or claimants who issue and serve writs against the defendants and/or file claims in the Admiralty Registry in Action 1990 Folio 483 if and to the extent (if any) that such costs do not relate solely to matters affecting any particular plaintiff or claimant alone."[83]

It has been argued that reducing entitlement to legal aid is an inefficient method of response to personal injury litigation.[84] The Government actually benefits from personal injury ligation, because it raises money from other sources, largely insurance, which allows sums paid out in statutory benefits to be recouped.[85] Court fees and VAT on legal costs also contribute to public funds. In a civil action "costs follow the event"; in other words, the winner can claim costs from the loser. However, the winner does not necessarily cover all his and her costs, since the loser is only liable to pay reasonable costs incurred.[86] The winner may have incurred costs with his or her own solicitor which do not qualify as reasonable and yet the solicitor is still entitled to be indemnified.[87] Where the defendant has to pay the plaintiff, the case is therefore "self-financing", because under the legal aid scheme there is a charge on the plaintiff's recoveries. This takes priority and if the costs recovered from the defendant do not cover the legal aid paid out, the sum is recovered from the plaintiff's damages.[88] In his survey of personal injury solicitors, Fennell found that in over 90 per cent of legally aided cases costs or damages were paid to plaintiffs and that in all those cases the total paid exceeded the plaintiff's legal costs.[89] The legal aid fund thus recovered its costs, yet in the process, incurred high administrative costs of its own in operating the scheme. There is also an argument that the low rates of legal aid work deter entry into the specialism by talented lawyers. Fennell argues that further research is needed, which considers whether overall public expenditure might be reduced by more generous provision of legal aid.

Research appears to confirm that specialist personal injury lawyers achieve a higher success rate for their clients,[90] and also

---

[83] Order of Sheen J., Admiralty Court, 8 May 1990.
[84] Fennell, *op. cit.*
[85] The recoupment rules are described in Chap. 5.4.4.
[86] R.S.C., Ord. 62, r. 12(1).
[87] R.S.C., Ord. 62, r. 12(2).
[88] Legal Aid Act 1988, s. 16(6).
[89] *Op. cit.*, p. 41.
[90] Genn, H., *Hard Bargaining: Out of Court Settlement in Personal Injury Actions* (1987).

that the most significant factor in determining whether a person brings a claim is the availability of advice to see a solicitor.[91] Disaster claimants are well-placed in both these regards. Advice will be forthcoming either from pre-existing sources such as unions or from support groups. Group claimants are often buffered by payments from appeal funds, which are not offset against any eventual damages and they may also benefit from the willingness of defendants to make interim payments. In addition, the findings of any public inquiry also assist in bolstering the negotiation process. Thus, although through their leverage on the media, disaster claimants publicise their frustrations in achieving satisfactory compensation, in many ways they are better placed than victims or more individualised misfortune.[92]

For all accidents, less than 12 per cent of those injured institute claims. Ignorance, uncertainty, problems of evidence, delays in the legal process and lack of resources all deter people from making legal claims.[93] Only delays in the legal process and lack of reasons present real obstacles to victims of disaster. In the "lottery" that personal injury law has been accused of representing,[94] disaster victims, who may already have received payments from an appeal fund, probably fare better than many. However, the stress which is brought by the unpredictability of both sources of compensation compounds the stress which the event has already visited upon them. This then is an appropriate point at which to unravel further the nature of the claims which disaster victims can bring.

---

[91] Harris *et al.*, *Compensation and Support for Illness and Injury* (1984), p. 49–77.
[92] Harlow and Rawlings, *op. cit.*
[93] Genn, *op. cit.*
[94] Ison, T., *The Forensic Lottery* (1967).

5. Tragic Negotiations: An Outline of Civil Liability

"But acts or omissions which any moral code would censure cannot in a practical world be treated so as to give a right to any person injured by them to demand relief."[1]

1. Introduction

One view of disaster victims is that they see themselves as entirely innocent and free of blame; that their only concerns are to get at the truth of what caused the disaster so that it does not happen again and to obtain compensation for their losses. Another view, and a perhaps more complicated one, is that the process of seeking compensation diverts their attention at a time of severe psychological distress, part of which may involve an element of self-blame. Survivors may blame themselves for failing to rescue others, or merely for having been one of the "lucky" ones,[2] at the same time as feeling anger towards some person or body of persons whom they regard as to blame for the disaster. Bereaved relatives may also feel guilty for things left unsaid, for still being alive, for escaping the horror of the event, as well as feeling angry at those whom they have targeted as responsible for the catastrophe.

The search for causes and for ways of ensuring future prevention is conducted mainly through the institutions of inquiry and inquest already described. Blame and accountability are steered through various legal channels, involving civil or criminal liability or both. The next two chapters concentrate on issues of civil liab-

---

[1] Lord Atkin in *Donoghue v. Stevenson* [1932] A.C. 562, 580.
[2] Hodgkinson and Stewart report that this was particularly problematic for the elderly men who survived the Bradford Fire when so many young men died: *Coping with Catastrophe* (1992), p. 122.

ility leading to claims for damages to compensate individuals. The motivation for such actions are often expressed, not in terms of the need for financial compensation, but in terms of justice and fairness. To that extent, the line between civil and criminal legal mechanisms is more fluid than formal pronouncements of their respective roles might indicate. Traditionally, civil law is perceived as compensatory, with an underlying deterrent function, while criminal law is a state-enforced system of punishment, again with an underlying deterrent purpose. These questions, together with the apparent increased tendency to blame through use of criminal laws are discussed in Chapter seven. They serve to underline the multiple motivations of casualties of disaster (using that phrase to comprise both survivors of and those bereaved by disasters) in their use of the legal process.

Disasters can kill, injure and otherwise transform people's lives. Some of the emotional reactions commonly experienced after close encounters with death and untoward events such as disasters were rehearsed in the first chapter. Shock, denial, distress, a sense of helplessness, and images of death and destruction are common features. Different people will be affected in different ways by the same event, even where there is an apparently similar relationship, for example, where both have spouses who have been killed. Also, the same event may affect people differently because the victims are in differing relationships to them; the loss of a child is not the same as the loss of a sibling, for example. Following a disaster, there will almost certainly be a number of bereaved relatives, some of whom may also have been economically dependent on the victim; there may also be survivors who have been physically or psychologically damaged or both; there may be rescuers, either professional or passersby, who have been injured, again physically or psychologically, or both. The legal basis for compensation claims against the person or organisation which is alleged to have caused the disaster from which these different types of damage flow is often complex, although in practice many claims are settled long before they reach trial.

Many of the issues discussed below are not peculiar to disasters. When someone is killed or injured as the result of an accident (in the broad sense of the term) they may be able to sue for compensation. Their success in doing so does not, as a matter of law, depend on whether they were alone or in the company of hundreds when the injury occurred. However, in practical terms, the context of the injury is highly significant. Many accidents do not give rise to damages claims because there is no suitably wealthy or insured person to sue. Many others do not give rise to claims because they are not perceived as compensatable. Domestic accidents, which proportionally account for a large share of personal injuries, rarely result in legal actions. One of the defining qualities of disasters is that they involve large numbers of victims. This has several results. It increases the likelihood that the injuries or losses incurred will be perceived as compensatable. It also means that there may be large numbers of actions against only one, or possibly a couple of defendants. Furthermore, those defendants are likely to be corporate bodies insulated either by insurance or through their own assets or often both. Their "sue-ability" itself contributes to the idea that there is someone to blame and that compensation should be sought. The different elements overlap and reinforce each other, but the important point to note is that the group identity which disasters foster informs and affects the legal process. However, this is not something reflected in legal principles, which rest on core assumptions of individual plaintiffs seeking redress from individual defendants, albeit with implicit recognition that the real defendants are often the insurance companies.

As the case studies in Chapter two revealed, few disasters result in fully litigated cases and a significant factor in that process is the use of co-ordinated claims, where the co-ordination consists both in solicitors' groups and the use of test cases. However, as with any practices, they cannot be easily understood unless there is also an understanding of their relationship with theory. Whereas many of the legal processes dealt with in this book may not be particularly familiar, most lawyers will be conversant with the account given here. However, my hope is that many other readers will find this exposition assists in their quest to make sense of the legal responses to disasters.

A number of different points have to be clarified, and these are reflected in the structure of this and the following chapter. The key question of when one person is expected to compensate another for damage they have caused is explored. Civil liability to compensate another for injuries (whether physical, psychological or financial) is largely based on the tort of negligence and that will be the main focus. Preceding the section on negligence in this chapter is an introduction to a number of types of civil liability which might also be relevant to the disaster context. These derive from both statutory provisions and common law, and can be divided into generic liability, such as employer's liability, *Rylands v. Fletcher* liability, product liability and breach of statutory duty on the one hand and specific liability, such as that contained in the Nuclear Installations Act 1965, on the other.

Account has to be taken, too, of the different kinds of damage for which compensation can be sought. Death, physical injury, and psychological trauma are all variables here, giving rise to legally distinct outcomes. There are also special groups, such as rescuers, for whom the law reserves special treatment. While compensation for death and physical injury of disaster victims are discussed here, psychological damage and special groups such as rescuers are dealt with in Chapter six. Also covered there are a number of questions on determining levels of compensation, such as which law applies where disasters occur outside the territorial jurisdiction (of particular relevance for air and sea disasters such as Piper Alpha); how payments are made (lump sum and structured settlements are discussed); and what principles do or should guide the level of compensation (should there be exemplary in addition to compensatory damages)? The purpose of these two chapters is to give an account of the legal framework relevant to claims for civil compensation following disasters; a broader debate about the appropriate roles of state, tortious and criminal systems of response can be found in Chapter seven.

2. Specific Areas of Tortious Liability

(1) Employer's Liability

In a disaster, some or all of the victims may be employees who qualify under the industrial injuries system which provides a system of no-fault compensation.[3] The scheme covers only employed earners in respect of accidental injuries "arising out of and in the course of employment". This does not exclude the possibility of bringing an action in tort as well and employers are subjected to compulsory insurance provisions.[4] Claims made as a result of injury at work account for almost half of all tortious actions. However, awards of damages and settlements are subject to claw-back where industrial injury benefits have already been paid.[5]

The common law provides employers with specific duties towards their employees. Two types of duty have emerged, personal and vicarious, although the abolition of the doctrine of

---

[3] Social Security (Contribution and Benefits) Act 1992.
[4] Employers' Liability (Compulsory Insurance) Act 1969.
[5] Social Security Act 1989, s. 22; see Chap. 5.4.4.

111

common employment has tended to blur the distinction.[6] Retreat from the effect of this doctrine, under which an employer was not liable to an employee for injury negligently caused by another employee, explains much about the development of liability in tort, thus justifying and explaining the insertion of discussion of this species of negligence liability here.

Employers owe a personal duty to provide a competent staff, adequate material and equipment and a proper system and effective supervision.[7] This is often re-expressed as "a duty to take reasonable care so as to carry on operations as not to subject the persons employed to unnecessary risk".[8] In order to cover the situation where the employee uses equipment which has a latent defect undiscoverable by the exercise of reasonable care by the employer, the employer has been made statutorily liable for any third party fault in producing or supplying it.[9]

Vicarious liability makes an employer liable for torts committed by an employee in the course of employment. Deciding whether a person is an employee or an independent contractor (distinguishing between a contract of service and a contract for services) is of significance in a number of areas of law and has spawned quantities of case law. A combination of tests is used, comprising: control of the work (or its organisation), method of payment, risk of loss and provision of materials and so on.[10] The employer is only liable for torts committed within the course of employment, which includes acts expressly or impliedly authorised by the employer, or authorised acts done in an unauthorised manner.

(2) The Rule in Rylands v. Fletcher

Compensation for damage caused by another usually involves demonstrating some negligence or failure to conform to an objective standard of reasonable behaviour. Yet, at the same time as the tort of negligence developed, so did the principle that in some circumstances liability would be strict. Developed from liability in nuisance, the rule in *Rylands v. Fletcher*[11] is probably the best known, but least understood, of heads of claim. Although less

---

[6] Eventually abolished by Law Reform (Personal Injuries Act 1948, s. 1(1).

[7] *Wilsons Clyde Coal v. English* [1938] A.C. 57.

[8] Winfield and Jolowicz, *On Tort*, (14th ed. 1994), p. 214.

[9] Employer's Liability (Defective Equipment) Act 1969.

[10] See *Stevenson, Jordan, Harrison Ltd v. MacDonald* [1952] 1 T.L.R. 101; *Ready Mixed Concrete (South East) Ltd v. Minister of Pensions and National Insurance* [1968] 2 Q.B. 497.

[11] (1868) L.R. 3 H.L. 330.

strictly marked out from negligence liability now, the emergence of the rule is of particular contextual significance, since the case concerned a burst dam. Reservoirs and their containing dams are important features of British agricultural and industrial development.[12] Dams do fail, and along with accidents resulting from shipping, mining, explosives and railway operations, reservoir bursts were not uncommon in the last century. Simpson describes two such disasters which might have influenced the litigation in *Rylands v. Fletcher*, each causing large loss of life.[13] A relatively recent French dam burst reminds us that, like earthquakes, dam breaks will happen.[14] *Rylands v. Fletcher* arose from the flooding of Fletcher's mine when a newly excavated reservoir was filled. Unlike the Holmfirth and Sheffield bursts described by Simpson, this was a private work, not one constructed under the powers of a private Act of Parliament. By the second half of the nineteenth century, there were two or three hundred private bills passed annually, many of them setting up schemes for waterworks and other industrial and transport developments. There were specimen bills (precedents) for the different types of enterprise and the one dealing with waterworks laid out the terms of liability for failure. As one might expect, the proposers of the bill ensured that their liability was limited. After the Holmfirth burst, compensation was paid from a special charitable fund; no litigation was begun.[15]

Hence the significance of a common law action such as that in *Rylands v. Fletcher* was that it concerned an event hitherto dealt with as a matter of statutory construction. However, unlike public statutes, these private Acts did not lay down the law for anyone else. There were factual points of difference as well. Rylands' reservoir was excavated rather than held in by a retaining dam. The leak of water was downwards, not over the top, and the property it damaged, Fletcher's mine, had hidden underground workings whose geological link with the reservoir was hitherto unknown. After protracted litigation, the case was decided in Fletcher's favour, and the now well-rehearsed principle first formulated:

[A] person who, for his own purposes, brings on his land and collects

---

[12] See Simpson, "Legal Liability for Bursting Reservoirs: The historical Context of *Rylands v. Fletcher*" (1984) XIII *Journal of Legal Studies* 209, 216 and references therein.

[13] *Ibid.*, p. 219.

[14] 300 people died when the Malpasset dam burst in 1959, devastating the town of Frejus.

[15] Simpson, *op. cit.*, p. 223.

and keeps there anything likely to do mischief if it escapes must keep it at his peril, and if he does not do so he is *prima facie* answerable for all the damage which is the natural consequence of its escape. He can excuse himself by showing that the escape was owing to the plaintiff's default; or perhaps that the escape was the consequence of *vis major*, or the Act of God.[16]

Easy to state, the rule has proved difficult to apply. Liability is based on a bringing onto land and an escape from land. A gloss on it added in the House of Lords was that the use of the land must be "non-natural". In subsequent cases it has become clear that "natural" is not contrasted with artificial or man-made but with unusual or out of the ordinary. "It must be some special use bringing with it increased danger to others and must not merely be the ordinary use of the land or such a use as is proper for the general benefit of the community."[17] This definition began to undermine the original strictness of the liability, so that "natural" use excluded application of the rule. It also makes the categories of activity for which liability will follow under the rule somewhat unstable, and subject to social and land use change. A factory is unlikely to be regarded as non-natural;[18] dams might be non-natural, domestic water tanks are not. The boundary which the "non-natural" test reinforces is that there is some conduct which creates an abnormal risk which in the view of the courts ought not be borne by the public. By introducing a defence of Act of God, the courts limited the impact of the rule considerably, which reflects, along with other cases at the time, as Simpson comments, "the inability of the English judicial system of the period to produce any coherent scheme of civil liability for dangerous and private works."[19]

But is liability under *Rylands v Fletcher* strict, or does it require proof of some kind of fault? A recent appeal led the House of Lords to reconsider the separate basis of liability under the rule.[20] At the same time as confirming foreseeability of the damage as a prerequisite, the House of Lords expressed the view that as a general rule it is more appropriate for strict liability in respect of operations of high risk to be imposed by Parliament. Thus, the gap between liability for negligence and the apparently stricter

---

[16] *per* Blackburn J. and approved by the House of Lords in dismissing the defendant's appeal.

[17] *Rickards v. Lothian* [1913] A.C. 263.

[18] *British Celanese v. Hunt* [1969] 1 W.L.R. 959.

[19] *Op. cit.*, p. 255. It can be noted that Scots law does not recognise the rule in *Rylands v. Fletcher* at all.

[20] *Cambridge Water Co Ltd v Eastern Counties Leather plc* [1994] 1 All ER 53.

rule in *Rylands* appears, where hazardous use is involved, to have been narrowed.

(3) Product Liability

In practical, as opposed to moral, terms the difference between strict and fault liability is often one of evidence and proof. It is not always possible to show why something has gone wrong and in relation to one-off events such as reservoir escapes, the evidence will often have been destroyed.[21] One area where it has emerged explicitly is in product liability, with the Consumer Protection Act 1987 introducing a "strict" liability for personal injury, actionable against not only the producer but also an own-brand supplier or importer, or sometimes an ordinary distributor.[22] None of these may have been responsible for the defective nature of the product, but since "defective" means that the product is not as safe as people are generally entitled to expect,[23] inviting a balancing of risks against benefits, the liability may be similar to a negligence test.[24] The defences also bring liability close to that of negligence; the "state of the art" or "development risk" defence is essentially a plea of no negligence in the design, development and testing of a product.[25]

(4) Action for Breach of Statutory Duty

We have already seen in Chapter three that there are numerous statutes which establish regulatory schemes aimed at improving safety in particular areas of activity. These regulatory schemes generally set up an inspectorate which then enforces a number of criminal offences in respect of breach of the provisions of the Act or of regulations made under it. Civil courts have sometimes, but not always, interpreted the breach of such statutory duties as giving rise to an action in tort. The criterion for imposing liability has been the intention of Parliament, which, or course, is a thin disguise for judicial gap-filling in areas of perceived compensation deficit. One stated principle has been that if the statute were passed to protect the public as a whole (all road users, for example) no separate tortious action for breach is likely to be implied, but if it

---

[21] Simpson, *op. cit.*, p. 259.
[22] s. 2.
[23] s. 3.
[24] Cane, P., *Atiyah's Accidents, Compensation and the Law*, (5th ed., 1993), p. 88–90.
[25] s. 4(1)(e).

had been passed to protect a particular class of persons (school-children or pedestrians, for example) it will. However, to go into the detail and extract a predictive principle would be doomed to failure and in many of the cases whether there is a class or the public as a whole in the frame really depends on where the frame is placed. As was pointed out long ago, the logic is an odd one even if it were workable: "[I]t would be strange if a less important duty, which is owed to a section of the public, may be enforced by an action, while a more important duty owed to the public at large cannot."[26] Other considerations judicially taken into account in determining Parliamentary "intention" include whether the harm suffered was the "mischief" the Act was designed to prevent and whether the remedy provided by the Act is adequate,[27] but neither of these is particularly helpful, except in supplying *ex post facto* reasons. Lord Denning suggested that the distinction was so blurred that "you might as well toss a coin to decide it."[28] Some statutes specifically exclude a civil remedy for breach of a duty.[29]

One important area in which the courts have been consistent has been in relation to industrial safety legislation, which can be explained by the need at one time to compensate for the harshness of the common employment rule. The Health and Safety at Work Act 1974 now provides a presumption that breaches of regulations will give rise to the liability to pay damages unless the contrary is stated,[30] but the wording of the Act's general duties and also of many of the regulations which are gradually replacing the earlier industry specific legislations (such as the Factories Act), is much less likely to give rise to actions for breach of duty. The general duties in the 1974 Act are phrased in terms of "so far as is reasonably practicable", which is clearly not susceptible of action in the same way as the duty to fence contained in the Factories Act 1961: "[E]very dangerous part of any machinery ... shall be securely fenced."[31] Employers are obliged to insure against liability for injury sustained by their employees in the course of their employment.[32] Failure to do so is itself a criminal offence.[33] It has been held that failure to comply with the Act does not give rise to a

---

[26] Atkin L.J. in *Phillips v. Britannia Hygienic Laundry* [1923] 2 K.B. 832.

[27] *Groves v. Wimborne* [1898] 2 Q.B. 402, *cf. Atkinson v. Newcastle Waterworks Co.* (1877) 2 Ex D. 441.

[28] *Ex parte Island Records* [1978] Ch. 132.

[29] Fire Safety and Safety of Places of Sport Act 1987, s. 12.

[30] s. 47(2).

[31] s. 14(1).

[32] Employers' Liability (Compulsory Insurance) Act 1969, s.1.

[33] s.5. If the employer is a corporation, individual directors also commit the offence if done with their consent or connivance.

civil claim for breach of statutory duty against the employer.[34]

In disasters, then, where there have been breaches of certain health and safety regulations, breach of statutory duty may be added to the grounds of legal claim. As it does not require proof of fault, this type of action can succeed where negligence might fail. In practice, however, the two are likely to reinforce rather than compete with each other. Breach of statutory duty has been described as "a special common law right which is not be confused with a claim for negligence ... the particular remedy for an action for damages is given by the common law in order to make effective for the benefit of the injured plaintiff his right to the performance by the defendant of the defendant's statutory duty."[35] This underlines the point that not everyone injured through non-compliance with a duty can recover for the breach. The widow of a fireman killed fighting a fire in a factory could not recover in respect of an alleged breach of safety regulations because they were intended to protect "those employed" there.[36]

It is also important to establish that it was the defendant's breach which caused the damage. This becomes complicated in the industrial sphere, for the employee injured may also be the person responsible for the breach. If the employer can show that the only act or default of anyone causing the non-compliance was that of the plaintiff, that is a good defence.[37] If the non-compliance was that of another employee, then the employer will be liable vicariously. As Lord Diplock explained, "For the legal concept of vicarious liability requires three parties: the injured person, a person whose act or default caused the injury and a person vicariously liable for the latter's act or default. To say 'You are liable to me for my own wrongdoing' is neither good morals nor good law."[38]

(5) Strict Liability Provisions

There are numerous statutes providing strict liability for exceptional risks, including those covering nuclear hazards and oil pol-

---

[34] *Richardson v Pitt–Stanley* [1995] 1 All ER 460. This leaves an injured employee without redress where the employer company has gone into liquidation. The company's directors, although potentially criminally liable under s.5, cannot be sued for breach of statutory duty.

[35] Lord Wright in *London Passenger Transport Board v. Upson* [1949] 1 All E.R. 60.

[36] *Hartley v. Mayoh & Co.* [1954] 1 Q.B. 383.

[37] *Boyle v. Kodak Ltd* [1969] 2 All E.R. 439.

[38] At p. 673.

lution.[39] Under the Nuclear Installations Act 1965 only the UK Atomic Energy Authority or licensed operators can operate nuclear plants. Those approved operators are under a statutory duty to ensure that no nuclear incident causes injury to any person or damage to property and imposes upon them strict liability in respect of such damage.[40] the only defence concerns hostile action.[41] Incidents caused by unforeseeable natural disasters such an earthquake still give rise to liability.[42] The major advantage for claimants is that the normal period of limitation does not apply; a claim will be entertained up to 30 years after the act which caused the incident, although after 10 years claims are payable by the government rather than the licensee.[43] In one of the few cases to be argued under the Act, it was held that the contamination of a house at Sellafield which reduced its value and increased the risk of developing cancer to the occupants did not amount to injury or damage to property within the meaning of the Act.[44] In some circumstances occurrences outside the UK are covered: s. 13(1).

Another example of special legislative liability is found in relation to off-shore drilling and was passed in response to the Sea Gem rig collapse which killed 13 in 1965. The Mineral Workings (Offshore Installations) Act 1971 provides that breach of the Act's provisions or regulations made under it is actionable so far as it causes personal injury.[45] Damage caused by pollution in the form of poisonous, noxious or polluting waste, also give rise to civil liability.[46] With regard to oil pollution, which is less likely to give cause for action in relation to personal injury, the Merchant Shipping (Oil Pollution) Act 1971 imposes liability on the owner of a ship carrying a cargo of persistent oil in bulk for escape or discharge of the oil from the ship.

It might seem from the above account that a comprehensive scheme of liability exists in relation to the kinds of hazards with which this book is concerned. However, outside negligence, there are still gaps. For example, chemical explosions are not covered

---

[39] See also the Gas Act 1965, s. 14, the Water Resources Act 1991, s. 208, and the Water Act 1989, ss 30, 45(7), 58(7).

[40] Nuclear Installations Act 1965, ss 7,12.

[41] Nuclear Installations Act 1965, s. 13(4)(a).

[42] Nuclear Installations Act 1965, s. 13(4)(b).

[43] s. 16. The amount of compensation payable by an operator is £140 million per incident. For prescribed sites the limit is £10 million; Nuclear Installations (Prescribed Sites) Regulations 1983 (S.I. 1983 No. 919) covers small installations like research reactors.

[44] *Merlin v. British Nuclear Fuels plc* [1990] 3 All E.R. 711; [1990] 3 W.L.R. 383.

[45] s. 11.

[46] Control of Pollution Act 1974, s. 88.

by any special legislation and one commentator speculates that had litigation ensued following the Flixborough explosion, it might not have been covered absent proof of negligence. However, the views expressed by the House of Lords in the *Cambridge Water* case suggest that a chemical factory might well come within *Rylands v. Fletcher*.[47] The new emphasis on foreseeability of the risk does, on the other hand, make *Rylands* closer to negligence than some had previously thought. The *Cambridge Water* decision is a clear indication that any strict liability for hazardous activities, including those which involve environmental pollution, will in future mainly derive from specific statutory provisions such as those discussed here. It is thus to the generic tort of negligence that I now turn.

3. Negligence

The tort, or civil wrong, of negligence, although a potentially unwieldy beast, is the most common basis of claims for personal injury and death. These actions account for a large proportion of all civil litigation, but only a tiny minority, estimated at one per cent, actually go to trial. Disasters constitute events which often push the legal system to its limits through a combination of heightened media interest and sheer force of the extent of damage and the number of potential claimants. It should not surprise us if a disproportionate number of those going to trial is formed from disaster cases, especially with the somewhat easier attitude to group litigation recently displayed. The main area of interest has clearly been that of psychological injury discussed fully in the next chapter, but other aspects such as bereavement payments have also caused concern.

When does negligence liability arise? An allegation of negligence involves a judgment on another's behaviour, *i.e.* that they have acted outside the bounds of reasonable conduct, that they could have been expected to act differently. The following statement, taken from the case of *Donoghue v. Stevenson*,[48] has been described as "the most influential in any decision on any subject in the history of the common law"[49]

"You must take reasonable care to avoid acts or omissions

---

[47] Winfield and Jolowicz, 12th ed. *on Tort*, p. 457, n. 30.
[48] And comes shortly after the quotation above, n. 18.
[49] Rogers, W.V.H., *The Law of Tort* (1988), p. 39.

which you can reasonably foresee would be likely to injure your neighbour. Who, then in law is my neighbour? The answer seems to be—persons who are so closely and directly affected by my act that I ought reasonably to have them in my contemplation as being so affected when I am directing my mind to the acts or omissions which are called in question."[50]

Three elements can be distilled from this: a duty to take care, breach of that duty and damage caused by the breach. In other words, there must be a "neighbourly" relationship between plaintiff and defendant, the defendant must have failed to take reasonable care and as a result, the defendant's actions or omissions must have caused reasonably foreseeable damage to the plaintiff.

(1) The Duty of Care

Often the duty to take care is obvious and well-established, as in the case of vehicle drivers to other road users, or public transport operators to their passengers or sports clubs to their spectators. In other cases, either the duty itself or its extent can be less easy to determine. For example, the extent of the duty to those not actually injured in an accident but suffering what the law calls "nervous shock" but more recognisable as Post Traumatic Stress Disorder (PTSD), is still somewhat fluid. Establishing a duty of care involves concepts of foreseeability, proximity and policy, but in the end they tend to implode into one another, such that it has been said that the concept of foreseeability signifies little more than that liability will be imposed if the court thinks it is fair that the defendant should bear responsibility for the damage.[51] In relation to personal injury (except nervous shock), the accepted position is that foreseeability is the sole criterion for establishing the existence of a duty of care. It has been noted also that while the neighbour principle originally operated as a means of expanding liability for negligence, it is most commonly used now as a means of justifying a refusal to impose liability. Cane is brutally honest: "To say that a person owes a duty of care in a particular situation means (and means only) that the person will be liable for causing damage by negligence in that situation."[52] In relation to the subject matter of

---

[50] Lord Atkin in *Donoghue v. Stevenson* [1932] A.C. 562.

[51] Cane, *op. cit.*, p. 60.

[52] *Ibid*. p. 61.

this book, the main area of doubt arises over PTSD liability.[53]

(2) Reasonable Care and Foreseeability

Establishing a duty of care is necessary, but it is not a sufficient condition of liability; the duty has to be shown to have been breached. This can only be done by asserting a failure to observe a "proper" standard of care, and thus the fault which lies at the core of tortious liability for personal injuries is upheld. Knowing that the standard to be observed is that of the "reasonable man" does not take the inquiry very much further and it is accepted by most people, including judges themselves, that the reasonable man is more a shorthand for "justice" or "policy" in the sense that a finding that the defendant's conduct fell below the standard of the reasonable man is a necessary step towards a finding of liability. Foreseeability often features here as well in the sense that whether the event was foreseeable is an important consideration in determining whether the defendant observed a reasonable standard of care. However, it is not the only consideration, for the taking of some risks is inevitable part of life, including, therefore, the "reasonable" conduct of life.[54] A case which has important resonances for many of the disaster scenarios already discussed arose when, through its engineer's carelessness, a tanker, *The Wagon Mound*, discharged oil into Sydney harbour. The oil drifted into a wharf and was set alight, damaging both the wharf and other ships. One of the issues which arose was what was meant by "reasonable foreseeability" in relation to the oil's being set alight. The oil had ignited as a result of welding being undertaken on ships in the wharf. It was regarded as extremely unusual for furnace oil, which this was, to ignite on water, and the welders had been assured by the wharf owners that it was safe to continue. However, that did not exonerate the tanker owners: their engineers had no justification for discharging the oil; they knew or ought to have known that there was a risk, albeit remote, that oil could ignite on water; that if it did, serious damage to other ships was very likely; and that the precautions required to avoid that risk were relatively simple.[55]

---

[53] See Chap. 6.2.

[54] *Bolton v. Stone* [1951] 1 All E.R. 1078.

[55] *Overseas Tankship (UK) Ltd v. The Miller Steamship Co. Pty Ltd (The Wagon Mound (No. 2)* [1967] 1 A.C. 388. This amplified the decision in a suit brought by the wharf owners, that liability is determined on grounds of reasonable foreseeability: *Overseas Tankship (UK) Ltd v. Morts Dock and Engineering Co. Ltd* [1961] A.C. 388.

Although foreseeability is dominant, it comprises elements of probability, magnitude of damage and the level of precautions required to avoid the damage.

It is clear that professionals, particularly doctors, find sympathy when they argue that they observed the care customarily practised by their colleagues,[56] while drivers who say that everyone ignores the speed limit do not. In many disasters, there is no doubt about the negligence of one or more employees, and the principle of vicarious liability automatically brings the employing company into the reckoning.

It is easier to establish negligent operation rather than negligent design. An interesting case, both in relation to foreseeability and to the design/operation divide, is that of the Abbeystead explosion in 1984. Residents of a village downstream of an underground water pumping system were taken on a tour of the station to reassure them that there was nothing to fear. 36 people left the village on that summer's evening to meet eight people from the Water Board. Less than an hour after setting out, all 44 were either dead or injured.[57] A build-up of methane gas while the water was not being pumped exploded, killing 16 and seriously injuring 20 others. Although the HSE's official inquiry exonerated the designers, constructors and operators of the tunnel in finding that the presence of methane was not foreseeable,[58] this was subjected to the criticism that a criminal standard of proof was allowed to influence the initial question of foreseeability.[59] As with many disasters, it could not be shown as a matter of undisputed fact that the particular circumstances which gave rise to the explosion had indeed been foreseen. That, however, is to ask the wrong question. Foreseeability depends on the construction of a range of scientific knowledge, some of which is highly specialised and specific, in order to determine whether that which occurred fitted into a class of previously observed incidents. Here, scientific evidence crossing a number of sub-specialities of geology was involved.[60] The crucial question is not whether there was previous knowledge, but whose knowledge and expertise would count.

When the civil action came to trial, foreseeability was treated differently and the civil engineers who designed the project were

---

[56] *Sidaway v. Governors of Bethlem Royal Hospital* [1985] A.C. 871.

[57] Greaves, W., *The Times*, 10 October 1988.

[58] H.S.E. *The Abbeystead Explosion* (1985).

[59] Wynne, B., "Establishing the rules of laws: constructing expert authority" in Smith, R. and Wynne, B., eds, *Expert Evidence* (1989), Chap. 1.

[60] *Ibid.*

held liable.[61] At the design stage they failed to take reasonable care in assessing the risk of encountering methane, the presence of which in significant, though not necessarily dangerous, quantities was held to be reasonably foreseeable as a matter of probability. The reasonableness of their care was measured against the standard of an ordinarily competent civil engineer in their position. Although the trial judge had apportioned blame between the engineers (55% liable), the contractors (15%) and the water authority (30%), the Court of Appeal took the view that neither the contractors nor the water authority should be held responsible.[62]

(3) Causation

Causation has been left to the last in describing the three elements in establishing negligence liability, although logically it might have been regarded as the first. The plaintiff needs to show that the injury or damage was "more probably than not" caused by the defendant's negligence. That is not enough, however, for the damage itself has also to be of a foreseeable kind; it must, in other words, not be too remote. To some extent, the tests of foreseeability in relation to duty, standard of care and remoteness collapse into each other.[63] If it is thought that the defendant "caused" the damage, then a willingness to imply fault is more likely to be forthcoming. Another case arising from *The Wagon Mound* oil spillage tends to confirm this.[64] In the earlier action fire damage to the *wharf* was conceded not to have been foreseeable. Previous authority suggested that so long as the damage was a direct consequence of a foreseeable harm (the oil spillage), the defendants would be liable.[65] When the owners of a *ship* also damaged in the harbour fire sued, no such concession was made.[66] However, as with other analytical uses of foreseeability, weaving a clear and consistent path between its applications is an impossible task.

---

[61] *Eckersley v. Binnie and Partners* (1988) 18 *Construction Law* 1.

[62] The contractors were absolved, for their duty extended to the detection of methane during construction, and the water authority were not liable, for they had no reason to suspect that the design was defective.

[63] Harlow, C., *Understanding Tort Law* (1987) p. 55.

[64] *Overseas Tankship (UK) Ltd v. Morts Dock and Engineering Co. Ltd* [1961] A.C. 388.

[65] *Re Polemis* [1921] 3 K.B. 560.

[66] One reason for the concession was that the plaintiffs would otherwise have been held bound by that foreseeability themselves and, therefore, held contributorily negligent. At the time this would have wiped out their action in Australia; England had already introduced a proportional system: Law Reform (Contributory Negligence) Act 1945.

When it is remembered that relatively few cases of accidental injury are litigated, and that few of those which are go to trial, it has to be concluded that the tort of negligence is founded on fairly shifting sands.

Of the disaster cases which have gone to trial, the problems have not related to negligence liability for death or physical injury, but for psychological stress disorder, and the foregoing attempt to summarise the tort is intended to provide a reference point for the ensuing discussion of these three types of injury.

4. Damages

It should be emphasised, however, that whether the action is founded in negligence or on one of the other types of tortious liability mentioned earlier, the principles of recovery for the different types of loss are the same. Here, I am concerned with damages paid as a result of death or injury to those involved in a disaster. The question of damages for psychological injury to victims, or their relatives, is discussed in Chapter six. The point about psychological damage is that, on its own, it mainly arises as a compensatable cause of action in negligence.[67]

(1) Damages for Bereavement

Tortious damages aim to restore the plaintiff to the *status quo ante*, the position in which they were before the injury. This principle, *restitutio in integrum*, is a somewhat hollow aspiration where the victim has died. If I am killed by your negligence there are two ways in which the loss might be characterised. My death could be regarded as a personal loss such that my estate might expect to be reimbursed on account of it. Or, those people who are dependent on me, such as my partner and children, could regard the loss of my income as recoverable. As far as the first is concerned, the common law was harsh and subsequent statute helps little. Although the Law Reform (Miscellaneous Provisions) Act 1934 allows actions in tort to survive death for the benefit of the deceased's estate, its main motivation is to ensure that others can claim on the estate, rather than the other way round.

It is not death itself which is compensated, but losses suffered between the injury and death. Thus, in a case brought after the

---

[67] It can arise intentionally, too, *e.g. Wilkinson v. Downton* [1895–99] All E.R. Rep 267.

Hillsborough disaster, a claim was made on behalf of the victims' estates for their pain and suffering in the immediate period before death.[68] Two sisters, aged 15 and 19, were crushed to death. Because they had no dependants, apart from a bereavement payment for the 15-year-old (see below), the only possible action was one directly by their estate. As the defendant Chief Constable did not contest his liability to persons who suffered damage in the disaster, the sole question for decision in the courts was whether any damage had been suffered. Lord Bridge in the House of Lords specifically noted that "the action was not brought for the sake of the money … but rather to mark the anger of these parents and other bereaved relatives at what occurred."[69] The argument was that there must have been a gradual build up of pressure, causing increasing breathlessness, discomfort and pain before they lost consciousness, and that compensation for that pain and suffering should be awarded. The House of Lords, however, affirmed the view of both the High Court and the Court of Appeal that the evidence did not establish that there had been any physical injury or suffering before the loss of consciousness. The fear of injury or death was not itself recoverable: "fear of impending death felt by the victim of a fatal injury before that injury is inflicted cannot by itself give rise to a cause of action which survives for the benefit of the victim's estate."[70]

This is a fine line both in terms of fact and in terms of relevant loss. If the injury preceded loss of consciousness, there would presumably be grounds for recovery in this type of case. However, even if it did not, the refusal to rate fear alongside physical injury is a critical difference between the legal and cultural assessment of events.

The loss of a person's income is recoverable by those who were dependent on it. This helps to explain the crucial difference between those bereaved by disasters such as Piper Alpha, where the victims were employed men, often with dependent families, and the *Marchioness*, where they were young adults. (Hillsborough and the *Herald* affected a mixture of young and old.)

Statute defines the class of persons which comprises dependants.[71] Included are spouse and former spouse, or a person living as spouse for at least two years and still doing so immediately before death; a parent of ascendant;[72] any child or descendant or someone treated as a child of the family; and brother, sister, uncle

[68] *Hicks v. C.C. S. Yorks.* [1992] 2 All E.R. 65.
[69] At. p. 68.
[70] At p. 69.
[71] Fatal Accidents Act 1976, S. 1.
[72] Or a person treated as a parent.

or aunt or their issue.[73] Claims under the Fatal Accidents Act have to show that the death resulted from a tortious act or omission, that the deceased would have been able to sue for the injury had it not been fatal, and that there is a resulting loss of financial support. The calculations involved in assessing the loss of dependants are not unlike those in personal injury cases, outlined below.

What about the death itself—should this give ground for recovery by dependants? Compensation via the fault-based tort system is, in general, subject to a variety of criticisms, with many pointing out that victims of negligent accidents are at an advantage *vis-à-vis* other accident victims, and that victims of negligent accidents are better provided for than those of negligently caused chronic illness. Payments for bereavement attract particularly polarised positions.

The common law never gave damages solely for bereavement; bereaved relatives who were financially dependent could recover for loss of support; otherwise, there was nothing until the introduction of a fixed sum in 1982.[74] Originally £3,500 but later increased to £7,500,[75] the sum is paid for a limited class of dependant (narrower than that which can claim for loss of financial support). Covered are spouses (not cohabitants, except in Scotland[76]) in respect of the other's death, and parents in respect of minor child.[77] The parents of young adult children, unless there was some dependency, are entitled to nothing. It was this which led to the claim on behalf of his daughters' estates in the *Hicks* case; it has been said to account for much of the drive behind the *Herald* support group, and was also a source of much anguish for the parents of the *Marchioness* victims.

On the other side, however, the payments have been described as "highly objectionable."[78] Cane questions both the motives of the claimants and the arbitrariness of compensating relatives for death, but not for suffering caused by injury. Such payments, he concludes, ought to be a low priority in any legal system which denies adequate compensation to so many injured in accidents or suffering disabling illness. There would seem to be answers to all

---

[73] Adoption and half-blood relationships are included throughout, as are step and illegitimate children.

[74] Administration of Justice Act 1982, s. 3(1), by insertion of s. 1A in the Fatal Accidents Act 1976.

[75] Damages for Bereavement (Variation of Sum) (England and Wales) Order 1990 (S.I. 1990 No.1575).

[76] Damages (Scotland) Act 1976.

[77] The same Act abolished a deceased's estate's right to award of a conventional sum for loss of expectation of life.

[78] Cane, *op. cit.*, p. 76.

of these points. Any examination of personal injury claims would disclose a mixture of motives both within and amongst claimants, and it seems somewhat odd to pick out this particular group and ascribe "poor" motivation without specifying the criteria by which such motivation is judged. While lingering life, in a state of unconsciousness or dependency, is, of course, distressing to relatives, the comparison between death and injury is a poor one. Compensation will be payable to the injured person, which will often benefit relevant close relatives, if only by allowing them to feel that an acceptable exchange has taken place, even if they do not directly benefit. More than that, however, death is of a different order, as all legal systems recognise in all sorts of different ways. Lastly, while it might not be disputed that as a matter of priority, such payments should not be high, it can hardly be said that a fixed sum of £7,500 to an extremely limited class of relatives, is unduly generous.

An example illustrating how the various payments payable in a fatal case inter-relate is seen in the claim of the mother and grandparents of a *Marchioness* victim, a 20-year-old self-employed fitness instructor who lived with her mother at the time of death.[79] The defendants admitted liability but argued quantum. Clearly, no-one qualified for a bereavement payment because the deceased was neither a minor nor married. A claim was made both on behalf of the estate under the 1934 Act and on the mother's and grandparents' behalf under the 1976 Act. For the estate, funeral expenses are payable under the 1934 Act, but the defendants disputed the sum of £400 spent on a reception for 300 people. A master of the High Court held that since the social obligation attendant on a funeral service could not be ignored, the full amount claimed was allowed. The claim based on loss of financial support under the 1976 Act was based on the deceased's estimated annual earning of £11,520 per annum, leaving a net income of £6,500, which would have been £7,500 by the time of trial. Her mother had lost a contribution to household expenses worth £30 per week. For how long would this have lasted? A multiplier of two years was allowed. Because of her loving and close relationship with her grandparents the deceased was accustomed to giving presents worth £300. This was offset by the £30 value of presents from them. Total damages awarded: £15,424.

---

[79] *Smith v. Marchioness/Bowbelle* (1994) 144 *New Law Journal* p. 199.

(2) Damages for Physical Injury

Damages are awarded for both pecuniary and non-pecuniary loss. Pecuniary losses are calculated on the basis of lost earnings, and expenses arising from medical or other care. The assessment of such damages is a complex and difficult task which is beyond the scope of this book. The complexity and difficulty arises from the need to make future predictions. Some of those predictions are inevitably hypothetical, because, in relation to lost earnings, no-one can know how long the person would have remained in employment, or in good health had the injury not occurred. As to other aspects of prediction, the difficulty is caused more by the need to settle the issue of the defendant's obligation at a fixed point. Then, an additional area of uncertainty enters the picture, because rates of interest and inflation have a bearing upon the value of any capital sum paid, yet these are inherently unstable (even if related to each other). However, some of these latter problems have been partly met by the introduction of structured settlements (as to which, see further below). All this can be summed up in Lord Scarman's phrase: "There is really only one certainty: the future will prove the award to be either too high or too low..."[80]

Some points of principle can be elucidated. The defendant takes the victim as found, such that high earners are entitled to recompense for their higher losses. Although medical care is available without cost, if private care is engaged this can be claimed. This principle derives from a provision passed shortly after the national Health Service was established to the effect that in determining the reasonableness of expenses, the possibility of avoiding them by taking advantage of the public health service shall be disregarded.[81] A Law Commission proposal to replace this by a requirement that private medical expenses should be recoverable only if it were reasonable on medical grounds to incur them has not been implemented.[82] Since at the time that any acute medical attention is required, the outcome of the negligence claim will not be known, this can hardly act as an inducement to victims to be spendthrift. On the other hand, the benefits of long term medical care provided at public expense are set off against any damages paid.[83]

---

[80] *Lim Poh Choo v. Camden and Islington Area Health Authority* [1980] A.C. 174, at 183.

[81] Law Reform (Personal Injuries) Act 1948, s. 2(4).

[82] Law Commission, *Report on Personal Injury Litigation—Assessment of Damages* No. 56 (1973).

[83] Administration of Justice Act 1982, s. 5.

A difficult area is that of services rendered by a relative or friend which, in the absence of provision by such a person, would have to be bought in. One argument is that since the services have been provided free, there is no loss to compensate. The other argument is that it is the need for such services which is compensated, and the fact that they have fortuitously been available without cost is irrelevant. The second of these arguments has prevailed.

Non-pecuniary losses are paid for pain, suffering and loss of amenity. Pain and suffering include distress from the injury itself as well as worries about its effect on the plaintiff's way of life. Thus, compensation for psychological effects presents no problem when they accompany physical injury. Although loss of expectation of life is no longer recoverable as a conventional sum,[84] anguish caused by awareness of that loss is compensatable. Loss of amenity or function is a more objective aspect of loss and is subject to compensation even where the plaintiff is unconscious.[85] In terms of loss of function, limb or sensory or whatever, a tariff system has developed. Precision cannot be expected, but types of injury are fitted into an appropriate bracket of upper and lower limit, arbitrated ultimately by the appellate process. Tables of awards are compiled and consulted by lawyers in settling cases, and by courts in disputed cases.

(3) Structured Settlements

Traditionally, damages awards and settlements have been paid in the form of a once-for-all lump sum. This form of payment has two major disadvantages. One is that assessment has to be based on an unpredictable future in terms of the plaintiff's needs. Indeed, this is the explanation for the campaign currently being waged by those affected by thalidomide. Predictions of life expectancy and fertility of those born limbless following their mothers' use of the thalidomide drug in pregnancy have proved wildly pessimistic. The second disadvantage is that few people have the financial skills to spread their award over a large number of years. Evidence of spending patterns following personal injures awards is not altogether reliable. Many commentators quote a study which suggested that most recipients spend their lump sums within three years of receipt, but its original source is obscure.[86] What people

---

[84] Administration of Justice Act 1982, s. 1(1)(a).
[85] H. West and Son Ltd v. Shephard [1964] A.C. 326.
[86] See Lewis, "The Merits of a Structured Settlement: the Plaintiff's Perspective" (1993) 13 Oxford J.L.S. 530.

do with a small lump sum may be very different from their hand-ling of a large amount intended to pay for care and other essentials dictated by their injuries.

However, the use instead of structured settlements in large personal injury actions has become increasingly common since they became a realistic possibility in July 1987, following an agree-ment negotiated between the Inland Revenue and the Association of British Insurers. Structured settlements address the second of the disadvantages attached to lump sum payments.[87] A structured settlement effectively provides a pension brought about by the defendant's insurer purchasing an annuity on the plaintiff's life with part of the capital lump sum award.[88] Tax is one distinct advantage. Whereas income from capital sums is taxed, the Inland Revenue treats the periodic payments in structured settlement as instalments of capital.[89] A major advantage is that the damages cannot run out, as Lewis puts it, because the "life expectancy risk can be transferred from the plaintiff and defendant to a life insurer."[90] Structured settlements may also reduce stress and encourage earlier case resolution.

They cannot be seen as a universal panacea, however.[91] A con-comitant disadvantage will, of course, be the lack of access to a large capital sum nor can structured settlements address the changing needs of accident victims.

(4) Relationship with Statutory Benefits

Damages settlements or awards do not generally flow into people's bank accounts for some months or years after the disaster, if at all. Many survivors and relatives will have also received assistance via social security benefits and fund payments as out-lined in Chapter 4. The relationship between these different forms of payment is complex and tends to defy rational explanation. Payments from disaster funds have no effect on damages paid. Social security benefits are another matter. A new system, intro-duced in 1989, sought to recoup from defendants payments made under statutory schemes, based on the idea that double recovery

---

[87] Guidelines were laid down in *Kelly v. Dawes*, *The Times*, 27 September 1990.
[88] Lewis, *op. cit.*
[89] Relying on *Dott v. Brown* [1936] 154 L.T. 484.
[90] Lewis, *op. cit.*
[91] See Lewis, R., "Legal Limits on the Structured Settlement of Damages" (1993) 52 *Camb L.J.* 470 for an account of circumstances where structures cannot apply.

was unacceptable.[92] Under the previous scheme, which had operated since 1948, defendants could deduct from loss of earnings damages 50 per cent of some benefits and the full value of others. The amount deducted benefited the defendant, for it was not repayable to the state.[93] The Recoupment Regulations now modify these provisions by ensuring full deduction of statutory benefits and their re-channelling to the Department of Social Security.[94] Unlike the 1948 system, the deduction is made from the award as a whole, and is not confined to the loss of earnings part of it. No account is taken of contributory negligence, either. If the damages are reduced by 50 per cent, the Department claws back the full 100 per cent.[95] The clawback scheme applies to settlements of more than £2,500 where the plaintiff has received a relevant benefit. Exempt are payments under the Fatal Accidents Act 1976, Criminal Injuries Compensation awards and redundancy payments taken into account in assessment of damages.[96] Criminal injuries awards have to be repaid to the CICB, however.[97] The Department of Social Security administers the scheme through its Compensation Recovery Unit, which requires defendants to notify any claims and to obtain a certificate of the total amount of benefit paid. This must be deducted from the award and paid over.

Tort compensation, since it includes loss of faculty, is, of course, assessed on a wider basis than the statutory benefits to which recoupment applies, whose sole concern is income loss.

This chapter has attempted to give an outline of the principles of civil liability which will apply after a disaster. The next explores what might be called complications of the civil process, with some but not all of those complications being peculiar to the disaster scenario. It continues the account of assessment of damages before moving onto matters affecting the process of claiming, such as whether, whom and where to sue.

---

[92] Social Security Act 1989, s. 22, Sched. 4 and the Social Security Act 1990, s. 7 and Sched. 1, consolidated in the Social Security Administration Act 1992, Pt. IV, ss. 81–100.

[93] s. 2, Law Reform (Personal Injuries) Act 1948.

[94] S.I. 1990 No. 332.

[95] Antoniw, "New System for Deductions of Social Security Benefits: A Tax on Accident Victims" (1991) 10 *Litigation* 103.

[96] And some others, see 1989 Act, s. 22(4).

[97] Criminal Justice Act 1988, s. 108.

6. Tragic Negotiations: Complications

Many of the issues discussed so far are reasonably straightforward applications of standard civil liability principles. The numbers of claims resulting from a disaster make a difference but do not necessarily challenge the substantive law or procedures to a significant degree. Of course, law and its processes are not unitary, separate institutions, and the impact of these claims on the legal system as a whole should not be underestimated. In this chapter I deal with "complications" of the civil process. First, consideration is given to two groups of claimants whose experiences derive closely from the fact of the disaster itself: those involved in rescuing the primary victims, and those who suffer psychiatric stress from their perceptions of the effect of the disaster on their relatives. They are both particularly pertinent examples of the ways in which the tort of negligence has adapted (not always satisfactorily) to some of the consequences of disaster. A second area of interest revolves around questions of whether to sue, whom to sue, and where to sue. And lastly, I consider extraneous factors affecting the level of payable damages to plaintiffs. This covers complications of the settlement process arising from the location and type of disaster. Air and sea accidents are covered by international conventions limiting the amount payable. I conclude with a consideration of the arguments in favour of the award of exemplary damages.

1. Rescuers

Thus far, an account of compensation for death and injury based on the primary victims and their dependants has been given. It now falls to consider one other group, those who go to the rescue of the victims of an accident. Assuming that the victims themselves are owed a duty of care by the defendant, the question arises whether that duty extends to the rescuer. Three potential qualifications might affect the defendant's liability and form the basis of a defence: *volenti non fit injuria*, remoteness of damage and contributory negligence. As to *volenti* (the voluntary assumption of risk), the courts have long held that it does not apply to rescue cases.[1] The reasoning seems to be that since the claim is made on the basis of a duty owed to the rescuer directly (if the emergency itself was foreseeable, therefore it is also foreseeable that a person effecting a rescue will be exposed to danger), it would be a contradiction to deny relief on grounds of *volenti*. In a situation of rescue, freedom of choice is compromised and thus to speak of "volunteering" is inappropriate. A further point is that the defendant's negligence precedes the plaintiff's decision to run the risk.[2]

Remoteness of damage challenges the nexus between the defendant's negligence and the rescuer's injury, but courts have dismissed such arguments and held the rescuer's intervention to be both a direct and foreseeable consequence of the defendant's wrong. The duty to the rescuer is independent of that, if any, owed to the rescued.[3] Contributory negligence would be difficult to establish as a means of liability avoidance or mitigation. The burden of proof would be on the defendant and it would have to be shown that the rescuer's conduct was "so foolhardy as to amount to a wholly unreasonable disregard for his own safety."[4] Willmer L.J. continued, "Bearing in mind that danger invites rescue, the court should not be astute to accept criticism of the rescuer's conduct from the wrongdoer who created the danger."[5]

The other side of the rescue coin is whether there are circumstances in which there may be liability because of a failure to rescue or because the rescue was in some way carried out negligently. English law imposes no general duty to rescue, either as a civil or criminal matter,[6] but there may be a duty under statute or common law. Local authorities who provide policing, fire and other related services are under statutory duties and may be sued for breach of those, or in negligence as explained in the preceding chapter. In addition to specific duties, public authorities are often

---

[1] *Haynes v. Harwood* [1935] 1 K.B. 146.
[2] Winfield and Jolowicz, *On Tort* (14th ed. 1994), p. 737.
[3] *Videan v. British Transport Commission* [1963] 2 All E.R. 860.
[4] *Baker v. T. E. Hopkins and Son Ltd* [1959] 1 W.L.R. 966, at p. 984, *per* Willmer L.J.
[5] *Ibid.*
[6] *cf.* Some European jurisdictions and four US states; see generally Handmer and Behrens, "Rescuers and the Law: The Legal Rights and Responsibilities of Rescuers in Australia" (1992) 4 *Disaster Management* 138 at 483.

given powers which they can choose to exercise. Emergency planning powers, discussed in Chapter three, are an example. If they choose to exercise such powers, authorities will be liable if they do so negligently. The standard of care expected of a professional rescuer will be higher than that of a bystander and, indeed, in relation to the voluntary good samaritan, courts would be most reluctant to entertain a suit based on negligence in pursuit of heroism.[7] In some jurisdictions, the fear of being sued which is thought to act as a deterrent to the would-be rescuer is allayed by legislation conferring some immunity to good samaritan rescuers.[8]

2. Psychological Injury

Another difficult issue arises with regard to those who suffer psychologically from the results of disaster. Psychological stress accompanied by physical injury causes no difficulty, so long as the injuries fall within the scope of the duty of care. However, the net of psychological effect will often fall much wider, including those involved but uninjured, rescuers, and friends and relatives not actually present at the scene. Some but not all of these may be able to recover.

Two recent trends are noticeable. One is the development of a fuller understanding of the potential disasters have for causing severe psychological damage. The other, perhaps not unconnected tendency has been a restrictive attitude from the appellate courts.

(1) The Emergence of PTSD

There is now wide acceptance that the psychological effects of disaster extend beyond the immediate aftermath and affect not only survivors but those engaged in rescue and relief work or involved through kinship.[9] Recognition of Post Traumatic Stress Disorder (PTSD) came about as a result of studies of Vietnam veterans, which revealed the behavioural patterns now well-documented amongst disaster survivors: flashbacks, over-alertness and avoidance of memory-triggers of the incident. PTSD received confirmation as a respected psychiatric disorder in 1980 when it first appeared in the American Psychiatric Association's Diagnostic

---

[7] *Watt v. Hertfordshire C.C.* [1954] 1 W.L.R. 835.
[8] Handmer and Behrens, *op. cit.*, at 140.
[9] Gleser, G., Green, B., and Winget, C., *Prolonged Psychosocial Effects of Disaster* (1981) p. 2.

and Statistical Manual. Post-traumatic neuroses are classified as anxiety disorders and the latest version, DSM-IIIR, issued in 1987, lists the symptoms and findings necessary for an operational diagnosis. Ewalt and Crawford define PTSD in this way:

> "PTS syndrome ... is the popular name currently given to anxiety neuroses resulting from severe external stress that is beyond what is usual and tolerable for most people. Such neurotic reactions can occur after any unusually stressful event such as explosion, hurricane, flood, major fire or aeroplane accident."[10]

In contrast with many other neuroses, in PTSD the external source of the stress is real.[11] Although a large proportion of those affected by disaster will have PTSD symptoms, in most cases they will gradually fade. For perhaps 10 per cent, however, the symptoms persist and effectively disable the sufferer. The symptoms may not emerge for some weeks after the event, and are not always obvious unless health workers have some relevant training.[12] Traditional medical treatment methods are inappropriate, especially as disaster victims usually display reluctance in seeking help.[13]

A detailed study was made of the survivors of the Buffalo Creek dam disaster as part of the preparation of data for the litigation which ensued.[14] All the litigants displayed to a substantial degree symptoms of anxiety, depression, somatic concerns, belligerence, agitation, social isolation and changes in routine and leisure activities. In addition, there was evidence of considerable alcohol abuse amongst males. Based on two sets of interviews by different mental health professionals, it was concluded that the psychic distress was crippling to the extent of interfering with effective daily functioning after two years. Only one in six was asymptomatic and 35 per cent were moderately to severely disturbed.[15] This may not have been a typical disaster since the relative isolation of the community and the severity of the environmental

---

[10] Ewalt and Crawford, "Post-traumatic Stress Syndrome" (1981) *Current Psychiatric Therapies*, 148, 146. See generally Morgan, "Relatively Late Payments" in Lee, R. and Morgan, D., *Death Rites* (1993) p. 223.

[11] Ewalt and Crawford, *op. cit.*, p. 147.

[12] McFarlane, "Post-traumatic Morbidity of a Disaster" (1986) 174 *Jnl of Nervous and Mental Disease* 4, p. 13.

[13] Hodgkinson, "Technological Disaster-Survival and Bereavement" (1989) 29 *Soc. Sci. Med.* 351, p. 356.

[14] Gleser, G., *et al*, *op. cit.*

[15] *Ibid.*, p. 138.

change were particular features here. However, this would affect the incidence and spread of the reaction; numerous studies testify to the widespread similarity of symptoms amongst disaster survivors. It appears that loss of life leads to more traumatic symptoms than loss of material possessions, more severe impairment was evidenced by children of school age than younger and that there was a connection between the degree of the children's impairment and that of their parents.

At any disaster the majority of professional and other helpers will probably have never encountered death, suffering and devastation, on such a scale.[16] Of the 399 police involved in operational duties at the Bradford Stadium fire in 1985, 59 per cent completed a questionnaire about the after-effects. The five particular problem areas most often mentioned were: performance guilt (doubts about the correctness of their actions); reconstruction anxiety (repeatedly thinking about what might have happened); focused resentment (resentful about specific events and actions taking place around the time of the fire); generalised irritability and motivational changes (their values, goals, plans, etc. thrown into disarray).[17]

(2) Legal Recognition of PTSD

Legal recovery for psychological damage, quaintly termed "nervous shock", pre-dates the naming and syndromising of PTSD and this phrase still has currency in legal claims of this type. At first, courts were reluctant to acknowledge psychological damage.[18] By the beginning of the century, recovery was allowed where the "shock" was a direct result of fear for one's own personal safety at the scene of an accident.[19] This was extended to fear for the safety of one's immediate family,[20] but not to a mere bystander who came upon the aftermath.[21]

The test for recoverability was reasonable foreseeability of harm from shock, but only in cases where the plaintiff was intimately involved in the accident itself, covering, for example, fellow workers and survivors. Trauma resulting from fear for one's own life is one clearly recognised category. Rescuers can recover too,

---

[16] Duckworth, "Disaster Work and Psychological Trauma" (1988) 1 *Disaster Management*, p. 25.

[17] *Ibid.*

[18] *Baker v. Bolton* [1808] 1 Camp. 493; *Victorian Railway Commissioners v. Coultas* (1888) 13 App. Cas. 222.

[19] *Dulieu v. White* [1901] K.B. 141.

[20] *Hambrook v. Stokes* [1925] 1 K.B. 141.

[21] *Bourhill v. Young* [1943] A.C. 92.

including volunteers, even though the shock was not induced by fear for themselves or even for others, but by the sight of the accident and involvement in salvaging casualties.[22] They can be regarded as a special case.[23] A recent award of damages amounted to £144,390 to a fireman who attempted to continue to work for three years after the King's Cross fire but was forced to retire.[24] Claims by police officers at Hillsborough who were not in the front-line have been rejected, however.[25] A similar settlement was reached in the Scottish courts on behalf of a painter who witnessed the Piper Alpha explosion and unsuccessful rescue attempts from a support vessel.[26]

The category which has caused the most soul-searching has undoubtedly been that where the trauma arises not from fear of one's own safety, but from fear for others. Here the courts originally required presence at the scene and sight of the accident as well as a clear and close relationship with those for whom the fear was felt. That type of relationship appeared confined to spouse, parent or child.[27] This was extended to cover cases where the accident was within earshot and the plaintiff witnessed the immediate aftermath.[28] It was probably at this point that the difficulties which later emerged as to where to draw the line for recovery of this type of damage began to develop. Had the courts stuck rigidly to categories of fear for oneself or fear for others through witnessing an accident, the scope of liability would have been capable of both prediction and justification. However, in 1983 the House of Lords in *McLoughlin v. O'Brian* allowed the "immediate aftermath" category to spill over and left open a potentially vast area of liability.[29] The plaintiff was two miles away at home when she was told that her family had been involved in a car crash an hour earlier. She was taken to the hospital where she saw her husband and surviving children in various states of distress and disarray. Her 3-year-old daughter was dead, her 17-year-old son seriously injured and her husband and 11-year-old daughter still covered in oil but not seriously hurt.

The duty of care revolves in this and subsequent cases around three questions: foreseeability, proximity and an assessment of

---

[22] *Chadwick v. British Transport Commission* [1967] 1 W.L.R. 912.
[23] *McFarlane v. E.E. Caledonia Ltd* [1994] 2 All E.R. 1 C.A.
[24] *Hale v. London Underground* [1993] P.I.Q.R. Q30.
[25] *The Times* 11 April 1995, High Court, Sheffield.
[26] *Dalziel, The Scotsman,* 29 June 1994.
[27] And possibly covering the witnessing of property destruction, *Attia v. British Gas* [1987] 3 All E.R. 455.
[28] *Boardman v. Sanderson* [1964] 1 W.L.R. 1317.   [29] [1982] 2 All E.R. 298.

what the court considers "fair, just and reasonable" to impose on one party for the benefit of the other.[30] Lord Wilberforce admitted candidly in *McLoughlin* that allowing her claim was "on the margin of what the logical progression would allow".[31] To draw the line above her case would not be as harsh as in some cases, but to so draw it "would not appeal to most people's sense of justice."[32] Arguing partly by analogy with the rescue cases, the House allowed Mrs McLoughlin to recover. Although she was not in sight or hearing, nor did she arrive at the immediate aftermath, it was as though she had so arrived because her family were still in the state they had been in at the scene of the accident. "[A] person of whom it could be said that one could expect nothing else than that he or she would come immediately to the scene (normally a parent or a spouse) could be regarded as being within the scope of foresight and duty."[33]

It was against this background that many of the disaster settlements included amounts for psychological stress for those affected by recent disasters. In most of these cases, there was little difficulty in establishing that people were either clearly within the accepted category because they feared for themselves or their close relatives or clearly outside because they did not come upon the immediate aftermath, even though that concept had been stretched in *McLoughlin*. Hillsborough proved to be the breaking point, where two different groups of claimants sought to use this new elasticity to recover damages for psychological stress. The first group were present at the ground but were not in danger themselves. They were witnesses to an event which, they correctly feared, would result in the deaths of their close relative–(brother and/or brother-in-law). The other group were close relatives who witnessed the unfolding tragedy on television or radio and who later identified the bodies of their loved-ones in the mortuary.

In *Alcock v. Chief Constable of the South Yorkshire Police* both the Court of Appeal and the House of Lords reversed the trial judge's finding in favour of the two groups of plaintiffs.[34]

95 people were killed and 400 injured when South Yorkshire police, who were responsible for crowd control at an FA cup semi-final in 1989, allowed too many supporters into the terraces at one end of the pitch. As more entered the back of the standing area, those already there were pushed against the mesh barrier dividing

---

[30] Morgan, *op. cit.*, 233.
[31] At p. 303.
[32] p. 302.
[33] p. 305.
[34] [1991] 4 All E.R. 907.

them from the pitch. When the match started, the crowds surged causing those in this part of the terrace to be crushed. Scenes from the ground were broadcast live on television and recordings shown later. The Chief Constable of South Yorkshire admitted liability in negligence in respect of deaths and physical injuries. The 10 separate actions considered together in this case concerned people who were not present at the ground or were in other parts of the ground. They were selected as test actions in order to represent the full range of potential claims.[35] All were either related (or engaged) to those in the area of the disaster. In most cases the relative was killed, in others injured, and in one uninjured. They claimed damages for nervous shock resulting in psychiatric illness caused by the experience inflicted on them by the disaster. The defendant admitted that if he owed a duty of care, and if they could show causation, then he was in breach and would be liable to pay damages.

The cases of the ten claimants were as follows:

Plaintiff one was present at the ground, and knew that both his brothers would be in the pens; he saw the scenes; he knew people had been killed or seriously injured. He tried to find them when the match was abandoned after six minutes. At 11 a.m. the next day he was told they were both dead.

Plaintiffs two and three lost their son. They saw it on live TV. They were told at 6 a.m. that their son was dead.

Plaintiff four lost her brother. She saw scenes on TV. She thought her brother was in the stand seats. She learned from her sister-in-law at 5 p.m. that he was in the pen and at 6 p.m. learned he was dead.

Plaintiff five lost a brother who was 11 years younger and whom she had fostered. She knew he had a ticket for the pens. She was told by a friend that there had been trouble at the game. At 4.40 a.m. she learned that he was dead; she went with her mother two days later to identify him.

Plaintiff six lost his brother whom he knew was at the match. He saw TV and saw bodies. He went to the temporary mortuary and found his parents there in tears, and so learned of the death.

Plaintiff seven was in the stand with the son of the deceased, his brother-in-law, whom he believed to be in the stand also. In fact, he had gone to the terrace. Later he found him at the mortuary; the sight of the body appalled him.

---

[35] Thought to be about 300.

Plaintiff eight lost her brother; she knew he was at the match; she heard about the trouble at 3.30 p.m. and at 4.30 learned that there had been deaths. At 10 p.m. she saw recorded TV and thought mistakenly she saw him collapsed on the pitch. Later her parents told her he was dead.

Plaintiff nine lost his 14-year-old grandson. He did not know he had gone to the match. He heard of the disaster; and that his grandson was there; and at 3 a.m. he learned that he was dead.

Plaintiff 10 knew her fiancé was at the match; she saw TV and felt he was in trouble. She learned of his death at 11 p.m.

Of the five judges hearing the appeal in the House of Lords, four gave reasoned judgments.[36] It was the third time that the question of recovery for "nervous shock" had been considered at this level.[37] All four agreed that the mere fact that "nervous shock" to the plaintiff was reasonably foreseeable as a result of the defendant's negligence, which was not in dispute, would not usually be enough on its own to give rise to a duty of care. The key to the additional factor lay in the concept of proximity. Three variables were relevant to the notion of proximity: the closeness of the relationship of the plaintiff to the deceased or injured person; the closeness of the accident in time and space; and the means by which the shock was transmitted.

(a) Relationship

The possible range is between the closest of family ties (spouses, parent and child) and the ordinary bystander. The closer the tie (not merely in relationship but also in care) the greater the claim for consideration. Lords Keith and Oliver both held that any person who could factually establish the kind of relationship which involves close ties of love and affection would be within the class. This would be assumed in the case of parents, children and spouses. That presumption was rebuttable. For Lords Jauncey and Ackner the relationship of love and affection must be equivalent to that normally associated with parents and spouses.

Other ties of family or friendship may suffice if it is demonstrated that the relationship is comparable to that of a close

---

[36] Lords Keith, Ackner, Oliver and Jauncey. Lord Lowry concurred.
[37] The other two being *Bourhill v. Young* [1943] A.C. 92 and *McLoughlin v. O'Brian*.

family tie. Legislation specifying these necessary relationships would be desirable, as in Australia.[38]

Also, the judges admitted that in certain types of cases a "mere bystander" who had no relationship to the deceased other than physical propinquity would be within the class. One example would be a bystander actually involved as a rescuer. Another would be innocent involvement in action which led to death as in *Dooley v. Cammell Laird*.[39] (P was a crane driver whose load fell, through no fault of P, into the hold of a ship where a fellow employee was working) A further possibility would be a witness to a particularly horrendous accident. However, there is some difficulty in imagining an event more horrendous than witnessing 95 deaths by crushing, and it may be that this "super-horrific" category will evaporate. The Court of Appeal has already shown some reluctance with the notion of bystander recovery.[40]

(b) Time and space

The House was unanimous in holding that PTSD must arise in the immediate aftermath of the event. Viewing the body eight hours later in a mortuary was not close enough. The tension between the legal construction of death as a "normal" occurrence for which fortitude can be expected, and the development of greater knowledge of the psychology of the bereavement process, is again evident. The fact that some people do suffer severe psychological trauma while others do not is no different than the fact that some people have thick skulls and others thin. However, while the law copes with physical difference by holding defendants liable for the particular victim, psychological difference is translated into categories of liability.

(c) Medium of communication

The technology of communications means that even with the immediate aftermath limitation on liability, a person could be both miles away, and also contemporaneously witnessing the disastrous event. Again, the House of Lords was keen to keep a secure lid on the box it had been asked to investigate. Presence at the scene within sight or hearing brings a person within the frame. Those at the ground were counted as sufficiently proximate wit-

---

[38] Reference was made to the Law Reform (Miscellaneous Provisions) Act 1944 (NSW); see comment by Lynch, "A Victory for Pragmatism? Nervous Shock Reconsidered" (1992) 108 *Law Quarterly Review* 367, p. 371.
[39] [1951] 1 Lloyds Rep. 271.
[40] *McFarlane v. E.E. Caledonia Ltd* [1994] 2 All E.R. 1. And see supra n. 25.

nesses, but the television viewers and radio listeners were not. One reason given was that since broadcasting guidelines do not permit pictures of individualised suffering, the images were too generalised to give rise to recovery. Another connected reason was that had those guidelines been breached and the pictures shown specific people, then the chain would have been broken and the defendant would no longer have been causally responsible. Again, if there is ever to be recovery for PTSD, this seems an artificial line of reasoning. Is the trauma of actually seeing a loved one being crushed to death really so very different in kind from the trauma of wondering whether your loved one is amongst those whom you can see being crushed to death?[41] In the same way that people cope better with risk and danger when they feel they can exercise some control, uncertainty is as potent a cause of stress as sure knowledge.

The result was that none of the ten claims succeeded. They had presumably been chosen because they represented the range of circumstances the disaster threw up. Yet the claims either failed because the plaintiffs were not immediately present, although their relatives were closely related, or they were at the ground, but were not sufficiently closely related. In order to recover they would need not only to have been bereaved by the defendant's negligence and to have suffered PTSD, but they would also need to have had the right relationship with the deceased and to have been at the scene of the disaster. The two appellants present at the scene failed because their fear was for a brother or brother-in-law. In neither case was there evidence that there was an unusually close relationship between them.

They would have come within the range of foreseeability only if they had been on the terraces, and feared for their own safety, or if they had been involved in the rescue operation.

The appellants who feared for parents and fiancés were in a class of persons such that "in each of these cases the closest ties of love and affection fall to be presumed from the fact of the particular relationship." However, they were not at the ground and so failed on the "direct perception" aspect of the test.

The *Alcock* case can thus be summarised in this way—where P suffers nervous shock from seeing injuries inflicted on B by D, P's ability to recover from D is guided by the principle of reasonable foreseeability, which itself turns on relationship, proximity and perceptual immediacy. In a later case, the Court of Appeal has

---

[41] See Nasir, "Nervous Shock and *Alcock*: The Judicial Buck Stops Here" (1992) 55 *Modern Law Review* 705, 709, a view the Law Commission endorses, LCCP No 137 (1995).

distinguished between recovery for PTSD caused by witnessing the incident or its aftermath, and pathological grief disorder caused by events subsequent to the death.[42]

The limited extent of this type of liability was further underlined in a claim brought by an oil rig worker traumatised by the Piper Alpha explosion.[43] The plaintiff worked on the fated rig but was off-duty on a support vessel 550 metres away at the time of the explosion. At the original trial the judge found that he was a participant in the sense that he was in fear of his life and that fear caused the psychiatric damage. The Court of Appeal allowed the defendant's appeal on the ground that the judge had failed to apply foreseeability as an *objective* test. Should the reasonable owner and operator of an oil rig have foreseen that a person of ordinary fortitude in the position of the plaintiff would reasonably be in such fear of his life and safety as to suffer psychiatric shock. Such foresight would extend to participants fearing injury to themselves or to passive, unwilling witnesses. The plaintiff was not a participant because he was neither in the actual area of danger, nor could he reasonably think he was, nor was he a rescuer. In *Alcock* the passive witness category had been left deliberately open. However, as Stuart-Smith L.J. says in the Court's judgment:

"The whole basis of the decision in *Alcock's* case is that where the shock is caused by fear of injury to others as opposed to fear of injury to the participant, the test of proximity is not simply reasonable foreseeability. There must be a sufficiently close tie of love and affection between the plaintiff and the victim."[44]

If the duty extended to those with no such connection, then the test would be one of foreseeability. This would create practical problems since, he went on to say, reactions to horrific events are entirely subjective. Therefore, he concluded, as a matter of both principle and policy the duty should not extend to those who are mere witnesses unless there is a sufficient proximity of time, place and relationship between plaintiff and victim.

The Court of Appeal is more consistent in refusing to consider a claim outside the proximity tests applied in *Alcock*, but the reason given for doing so undermines the basic structure that *Alcock* built. For, if the reason for refusing to consider the bystander is that

[42] *Calascione v. Dixon* [1994] J.P.I.L. 82.
[43] *McFarlane v. E.E. Caledonia Ltd.*
[44] At p. 14.

reactions to calamitous events are subjective, then the same can be said for any PTSD claim. No-one suggests that it is *inevitable* that PTSD will develop however much a person feared for themselves or for their most dearly loved relatives. It is not an absolute certainty in the way that it is certain that a person whose skin is exposed to a flame will be burnt. No-one knows whether the plaintiffs in *Alcock* would have been able to satisfy the factual test as to the nature of their disorder, nor how many potential plaintiffs there might have been, for the case proceeded on the preliminary issue of liability in law based on assumed facts. The High Court in an earlier case accepted evidence that a small but significant proportion of the population is liable to suffer prolonged grief reaction and that there is no medical or diagnostic difference in an anxiety state caused through witnessing the accident itself or through being present at the aftermath or through learning about it later.[45] As one commentator perceptively notes "As far as nervous shock is concerned, English courts have never authoritatively decided whether the relevant form of injury is very rare (and therefore perhaps not foreseeable) or very common (with recovery therefore requiring to be limited)."[46] However, what is certain is that PTSD has real and disabling consequences for those who do suffer from it. If it is caused by an event which arose from another's negligence, then more adequate reasons for limiting liability claims need to be advanced. Or, alternatively, it could be decided that the categories should be further limited. At the extreme, no PTSD claims could be considered, or just those arising from fear for one's safety, or, in order not to deter altruism, include also those arising from involvement in rescue. Instead, the position arrived at is pragmatic and unsatisfactory, and it is one that is even more difficult to comprehend in the light of a reported settlement agreed in Scotland by another Piper Alpha painter, who like McFarlane was on the support vessel Tharos during the explosion and subsequent rescue operation.[47] The difference may be accounted for by the fact that there was evidence that McFarlane had previously suffered depressive illness, thus making it easier for the defendants to argue that PTSD in a person of reasonable fortitude was not foreseeable.

---

[45] *Ravenscroft v. Rederiaktiebolaget Transatlantic* [1991] 3 All E.R. 73, *per* Ward J., p. 79; the finding for the plaintiff was overruled as a result of *Alcock*, [1992] 2 All E.R. 470.

[46] Steele, "Two Cheers for *Caparo: Ravenscroft v. Rederiaktiebolaget Transatlantic* (1993) 56 *Modern Law Review* 244, 245 and see comment by plaintiff's counsel, Gore, A., "Correspondence" (1994) 57 *Modern Law Review* 174.

[47] *Dalziel, op. cit.*

Although the result in *Alcock* must appear to the appellants to be verging on the capricious, it makes certain sense in relation to the history of nervous shock cases. Its major failing is that it leaves open too many opportunities for litigation and too few guidelines for settling cases.[48] The reality of the civil claims process in the sphere of disasters is that it is easier to fend off a claim than to pursue one. Defendants are usually corporate bodies, backed by insurers, with much to gain from delay and dispute. Encouraging defendants to force psychiatrically damaged plaintiffs to provide evidence of a "particularly close tie" with a relative outside the presumed class is lamentable, and encouraging defendants to displace the presumption that a parent was emotionally close to their dead child, or doubting a wife's attraction for her dead husband, is deplorable.

3. Whether to Sue

While tortious awards account for only six and a half per cent of those injured each year, the total value paid equals half that paid out to accident victims in the form of social security.[49] We have already seen that tort plaintiffs also benefit because they can claim social security or occupational sick pay (although these are subject to clawback under the Social Security Act 1989[50]) and then they can be compensated not only for loss of income but also for loss of faculty.

There is no doubt that for those caught up in disasters the decision whether to sue is more straightforward than for those injured in an ordinary accident. Road and industrial accidents form the categories of accident victims most likely to sue because these are activities which are either subject to compulsory insurance or strict liability. If there is potential liability for a disaster it will almost certainly lie against a corporate body, which will either have insured against liability or act as self-insurer. Together with the benefits of publicity, solicitors' groups and group actions, this means that the question whether to sue is translated into how much to claim and whether to press for criminal prosecution. This does not mean that claimants are motivated solely by

---

[48] See Robertson, "Liability in Negligence for Nervous Shock" (1994) 57 *Mod. L.R.* 649, 662.

[49] Cane, P., *Atiyah's Accidents, Compensation and the Law*, (5th ed., 1993) p. 17.

[50] s. 22 and Sched. 4 which applies to settlements for claims of more than £2,500 after 1 January 1989. It does not apply to costs; Social Security Act 1990, s. 7, Sched 1.

the prospect of financial compensation. Ideas of corrective justice include the notion that the target of blame and therefore the source of compensation are as important as the compensation itself. These wider aspects of the claim and blame process are discussed in the next chapter. In terms of courts, recent civil justice changes have meant that all claims of less than £50,000 must start in the county court.[51]

4. Whom to Sue

Events usually have multiple causes. In relation to corporate activity in particular, from which disasters often arise, there will be a number of layers of responsibility, including those identified as the immediate cause through to the company itself. There may be more than one company involved in delivering the product or service or undertaking the activity leading to the disaster. One of the features of modern capitalism is the specialisation of tasks within and across organisations. Transport operators depend on others to build their vehicles or vessels, football clubs depend on others to construct their stands and to police their crowds and so on. Which of these bodies should be sued and what happens if the defendant wants to shift some or all of the blame onto a third party? Tort law invokes a principle of joint and several liability. Each person who has (legally) caused damage is liable and the injured person can choose whether to sue one or more of those who fall within this category. This does not mean, of course, that plaintiffs can recover compensation more than once. It does mean that defendants may well feel aggrieved that they have borne responsibility for injuries to which others have contributed. The harshness of the principle is somewhat mitigated for such aggrieved defendants and a contribution can be sought from another tortfeasor responsible for the same damage.[52] This is a battle fought out by the defendants which does not affect the plaintiff's position.

After Hillsborough, for example, the writ was issued against the Chief Constable for South Yorkshire alleging negligence in conducting the fans into the ground. He in turn sought contributions from two other potential tortfeasors, the football club who owned the ground and the civil engineers who had designed the relevant stand. The apportioning was settled out of court. As

---

[51] High Court and County Courts Jurisdiction Order 1991.
[52] Civil Liability (Contribution) Act 1978.

soon as a writ is issued, the defendant can seek to join others to it in order to reduce or even avoid altogether their own liability. Thus, following the Bradford fire, a writ was issued against the Football Club, who sought to blame the Health and Safety Executive (HSE) and the West Yorkshire County Council for their failures in relation to different statutory safety regimes. The HSE was responsible for making adequate arrangements for enforcement of the Health and Safety at Work Act 1974. The County Council had statutory duties under the Fire Precautions Act 1971 and under the Safety of Sports Grounds Act 1975. These two bodies then became joined in the original action as second and third defendants.[53] In the trial, liability was found to fall on the first and third defendants and it was apportioned between them in a ratio of two-thirds against the Club and one-third against the local authority.[54]

Another possibility is that a defendant might argue in defence of a claim that the plaintiff was partly responsible for the accident. Damages will be reduced "to such extent as the court thinks just and equitable having regard to the claimant's share in the responsibility for the damage."[55]

5. Where to Sue

Mid-air or sea disasters, and others involving products or machines designed or manufactured outside the UK raise different questions. The first is where to sue. It is well-known that some American states are far more favourable in terms of their damages awards than this country. Although the possibility of using one of the American states as the appropriate forum was not altogether straightforward,[56] the Piper Alpha settlement was thought to reflect a mid-Atlantic level of damages, in other words, it was a compromise between the level which could definitely have been obtained here and the rather more chancy, but possibly more lucrative, American potential.[57] The settlement was incidentally negotiated by a group of 142 solicitors, the Piper Disaster Group,

---

[53] Hepple, B. and Matthews, M., *Tort: Cases and Materials* (5th ed., 1991), Chap. 1.
[54] *Fletcher and Fletcher v. Bradford City Association Football Club (1983) Ltd* (H.C), Leeds, 23 February 1987.
[55] Law Reform (Contributory Negligence) Act 1945, s. 1.
[56] Kolman, "The Piper Alpha Oil Rig Disaster: Is There a Forum for Pursuers in the United States?" (1988) *Scots Law Times* 293.
[57] News (1989) 86 *Law Soc Gazette* 3; the Manchester air fire was also thought to have given rise to a "mid-Atlantic" settlement.

representing families of 135 men and 50 survivors. "Forum shopping" is inevitable where the differences in compensation levels are considerable, for, as Lord Denning gracefully put it, "As the moth is drawn to light so is the litigant to the United States."[58] European Community members are governed by the Brussels Convention which led to the Civil Jurisdiction and Judgments Act 1982.[59]

Although here I have concentrated on tortious recovery, it can be noted that contractual claims often arise as well or as a by-product of a tortious action. For example, the water authority responsible for the Abbeystead pumping station sued the civil engineers for both breach of contract and negligence following the finding that the engineers were fully responsible in negligence to the victims. This did not raise a jurisdictional question, but similarly, Occidental may have wanted to sue the manufacturer of part of the Piper Alpha rig in contract, as a means of spreading its loss. The Contracts (Applicable Law) Act 1990 gives world-wide effect to a Community convention and provides that in the absence of the parties' having specified a choice of law, the law of the country with which the contract is most closely connected applies.

6. Limitations on Damages

Some spheres of commercial activity, particularly shipping and air travel, are subject to international conventions, which impose a liability ceiling that can usually only be exceeded if something more than negligence is proved. Shipping accidents at sea are covered by the 1974 Athens Convention and the 1976 London Convention (which also applies inland).[60] The Athens convention applies when the ship is flying a British flag or the contract of carriage was made here or it is sailing to or from this country. Under the Athens agreement, the limit for personal injury and death is now £80,000 for a British carrier, £38,000 if not.[61] The burden of proof is reversed, with

---

[58] *Smith, Klein and French v. Bloch* [1993] 2 All E.R. 72.

[59] For details see Bissett-Johnson, "Major Disasters: Liability and the Conflict of Laws" [1991] 7 *Oil and Gas Law and Taxation Review* 220.

[60] Athens Convention on Carriage of Passengers and Luggage 1974, and the London Convention on Limitation of Liability for Maritime Claims 1976, both implemented by orders made under the Merchant Shipping Act 1979, s. 16.

[61] Carriage of Passengers and their Luggage by Sea (UK Carriers) Order 1987 (S.I. 855 and 1989/1880) (100,000 and 46,000 units of account respectively). The Convention does not apply to crew.

the carrier liable unless fault or neglect can be disproved.[62] However, the losses claimed still have to be proved.

The London Convention imposes a further overall limit for each ship involved, which is much reduced for non-passenger carrying ships. This meant that the much smaller *Marchioness* was subject to a total limit of £5.9 million (calculated on the number of passengers) while the *Bowbelle's* total potential liability amounted to £300,000.[63] The *Herald's* limit was £20 million, and under this convention the burden of proof is not reversed.

There are two possible ways of avoiding the "pincer movement" of these two Conventions.[64] The first would be to join other involved parties. For example, following the *Herald*, contemplation could have been given to joining the shipbuilders, the harbour authorities and possibly the government in any negligence action.[65] These defendants would not be protected by the Convention, but then the plaintiffs would again bear the burden of proving negligence. The other route for breaking through the ceilings would be to show recklessness. The limitations do not apply "if it is proved that the damage resulted from an act or omission ... done with intent to cause such damage, or recklessly and with knowledge that such damage would probably result."[66] The compensation agreement negotiated by the *Herald* steering group needs to be seen in this light. As well as exceeding the Athens Convention limits, the settlement also paid £5,000 to everybody whether injured or not and £10,000 in each and every fatal case, clearly going beyond the Fatal Accidents Act both in coverage and amount.

Most air crashes are covered by the Warsaw Convention 1929 with the major exception of flights to and from the US, where the Montreal Rules govern. Under Warsaw the limit is £14,000. The historical explanation for the Warsaw convention is that it was needed first, to avoid costs and delays in deciding which law applies and secondly, to protect an infant airline industry from crippling insurance costs. However, the liability is strict: fault does not have to be proved. For US flights, Montreal provides compensation limits of £36,700 exclusive of legal costs (£46,000

---

[62] Athens Convention, Art. 3(3).

[63] See Gaskell, "The Zeebrugge Disaster: Application of the Athens Convention 1974" (1987) 137 *New Law Journal* 285 and see *The Bowbelle* (1990) 1 W.L.R. 1330.

[64] Arnheim, "Zeebrugge: is it a good offer?" (1987) 131 *Solicitors' Journal* 606.

[65] Clark, "The Herald of Free Enterprise—A Defective Product?" (1987) 137 *New Law Journal* 891.

[66] Athens Convention, Art. 13 and London Convention cl. 4, which inserts the word "personal" before "act or omission", Arnheim, *op. cit.*

inclusive). These limits can again be broken if the airline was reckless in carrying out security arrangements. Hence, the significance after Lockerbie of suits for recklessness brought in the United States was threefold.[67] Success would enable the Convention limits to be overcome, US courts are more generous in the levels of compensation awarded and, additionally, they offer the possibility of punitive damages.

Compensation to those injured on the ground was not subject to these limits, for the Civil Aviation Act 1982 imposes strict liability on a carrier for injury or damage caused by objects falling from the sky. Thus, two brothers who lost their parents and sister when debris from PanAm Flight 103 destroyed their home at Lockerbie were reportedly awarded £2.1 million from the global settlement sum.[68]

7. Exemplary Damages

At present, tortious awards for personal injuries negligently caused are computed on a compensatory basis. Account is not taken of any potential risks inherent in the defendant's attitude to safety. Only those risks which are realised will be reflected, because the underlying basis of tortious awards is that they compensate the plaintiff's actual loss. Not only is the system of negligence liability a particularly inefficient instrument of compensation because many accident victims are precluded from benefiting, it is also clear that other goals inform the tort of negligence. An award of damages assessed on compensatory principles is the mechanism by which the tort of negligence seeks to deter people from engaging in risky activities.

However, there is a long history in English law of a recognition in limited circumstances of the principle of non-compensatory damages. By 1963 exemplary awards had been countenanced in a wide range of torts, including trespass to land and goods, assault, breach of copyright, defamation and private nuisance.[69] They have never, however, applied in the sphere of negligence, which is, of course, the basis of the majority of personal injury actions. The

---

[67] The first US court to find that PanAm was guilty of "wilful misconduct" awarded £4.8 million damages at a trial at Brooklyn federal court, New York, July 1992; confirmed by the Federal Appeal court, *The Times*, 2 February 1994.

[68] Witcomb, "An Outdated Justice" (1990) 140 *New Law Journal* 788.

[69] See Pipe, G., "Exemplary Damages after Camelford" (1994) 57 *Modern Law Review* 91, 92.

question arises whether they should be.[70] The possibility of a common law extension effectively disappeared after the House of Lords decision in *Rookes v. Barnard*,[71] which limited exemplary damages to three categories: oppressive, arbitrary and unconstitutional action by government servants, conduct calculated by the defendant to make a profit in excess of compensation payable to the plaintiff and those expressly authorised by statute.

The opinion of the House of Lords is contained in the single speech of Lord Devlin, which is characterised by a clear view that such damages are anomalous. At that time, it was not open to the House to overrule previous authorities and thus, the three categories can be seen as an exercise in damage limitation. In Devlin's view, exemplary damages confuse the civil and criminal functions of law. The decision, which was concerned with the tort of inducing breach of contract, was emphatic in its lack of sympathy with the notion that damages should ever perform a punitive function, but it was ambiguous in the restrictions it placed on the existing categories. One reading of the case is that it would allow exemplary damages in considering damages for any tort, so long as the defendant's behaviour fitted the categories. The other, inevitably more restrictive, interpretation was that such damages would be available only where the tort alleged had given rise to exemplary damages before *Rookes v. Barnard*. Subsequent cases confirmed the controversial nature of Lord Devlin's opinions on the fundamental issue of the appropriateness of exemplary damages. As a result, courts tended to veer between a restrictive and extensive interpretation according to their preference for a solely compensatory system of damages or not. When the House of Lords had the opportunity to express a view, it endorsed the view that *Rookes v. Barnard* had indeed restricted the categories for which exemplary damages might be awarded.[72]

This is the background to a recent Court of Appeal decision, which ensures that any extension of exemplary damages in negligence will have to be introduced by statute. To qualify for consideration for exemplary damages, the plaintiff's cause of action has to be one in respect of which there had been a claim prior to *Rookes v. Barnard*, which clearly excludes negligence.

That case, *AB v. South West Water*, is a good example for present purposes, because although the harm caused was not really

---

[70] Law Commission Consultation Paper No. 132 (1994).
[71] [1964] A.C. 1129.
[72] *Cassell v. Broome* [1972] A.C. 1027; this was a defamation case and the opinion on this was therefore *obiter*.

serious, potentially it might have been and it resulted from poor corporate operating procedures. The plaintiffs brought actions for nuisance, negligence and breach of statutory duty after they had suffered ill effects from drinking water contaminated when the water authority released 20 tonnes of aluminium sulphate into the system at Camelford water treatment works.[73] The claim for exemplary damages was based on the allegation that the water authority failed to inform them that the water had been contaminated. The defendants sought to have this part of their claim struck out and although the trial judge declined to do so, the Court of Appeal allowed their appeal. *Rookes v. Barnard* was regarded as having created a "cause of action" test; only torts which had attracted such damages prior to 1964 could qualify. None of the torts on which the claim was based fell into that category; private nuisance arguably qualified, but not public nuisance as claimed here. It was not felt that any of the three possible conditions for imposing such damages was satisfied: the fact that the defendant was a nationalised industry at the time did not qualify it under the category of action by government servants, there was no evidence of a liability-loss calculation and none of the statutory duties had founded pre-1964 claims. On these last two conditions, the arguments are interesting. To meet the loss calculation part the Court held that a plaintiff would have to do more than make a bare assertion in the hope that the hunch would prove right on discovery of documents. The deliberate decision by the defendants to continue the nuisance, coupled with their recognition that this might involve them in the payment of damages did not establish that they had knowingly committed the tort for the purpose of gaining some pecuniary or other advantage. Some evidential material would have to be available to the plaintiffs to back the claim from the start. This is a tall order in relation to corporate defendants. On breach of statutory duty, again a restrictive approach emerged. Prior to 1964 there were examples of breaches of statutory duty for which exemplary damages had been paid, but the court in the Camelford case apparently looked for examples of such damages arising from breaches of the specific statutory duties alleged, one of which, the Consumer Protection Act 1987, could not *ex hypothesi* have been such an example, and the other, the Water Act 1945, had not in fact given rise to any such claim.

The Court also took the view that exemplary damages awards in multi-plaintiff cases would be "peculiarly unsuitable":[74]

---

[73] [1993] 1 All E.R. 609.
[74] Stuart-Smith, L.J., p. 624.

"Unless all their claims are quantified by the court at the same time, how is the court to fix and apportion the punitive element of the damages? Should the court fix a global sum of £x and divide it by 180, equally among the plaintiffs? Or should it be divided according to the gravity of the personal injury suffered?"[75]

The present position then is that exemplary damages would only be available in respect of mass disaster claims resulting from product liability claims, breach of industrial safety requirements or transport accidents if a nominate tort for which there was a precedent for such damages, such as trespass to the person or private nuisance, can be established.

A number of states in the US have expressly codified availability of exemplary damages, mainly in cases involving aggravated misconduct. These have been used as a means of enhancing compliance with the law and giving the plaintiff a mechanism for recovery of costs not otherwise recouped in US procedure. In the Pinto case, concerning Ford's calculated gamble not to recall potentially dangerous cars and which went on to become a landmark corporate manslaughter indictment, a jury awarded $125 million.[76] It can be noted too that the Opren litigation in the US led to punitive damages of some $5 million in one case, yet the settlement of the civil actions in this country is thought to have amounted to only £2.25 million altogether.[77] The increase in exemplary awards against corporate defendants has prompted efforts in some states to restrict claims, including increasing the standard of proof, limiting the amount of the award and re-directing part of the award to state funds.[78]

In their recent review of exemplary damages the Law Commission of England and Wales pointed out that the range of views on this question is at heart a product of radically different perceptions of the role of the law of civil wrongs, in particular tort law, and its relationship with criminal proceedings.[79] At the core, these differing perceptions concern whether tort is exclusively about compensation, or do other goals, including punitive, deterrent and restitutionary functions, have a legitimate role.

Exemplary damages can be seen as having four possible pur-

---

[75] Ibid.

[76] Grimshaw v. Ford Motor Co. (1981) 174 Cal. Rptr 348.

[77] Harlow, C. and Rawlings, R., Pressure Through Law (1992) p. 131.

[78] See Law Commission Consultation Paper No. 132, Aggravated, Exemplary and Restitutionary Damages (H.M.S.O. 1993), paras. 4.15–18, 6.14 and Appendix.

[79] Op. cit.

poses: punishment, deterrence, pacification and shortfall.[80] The punishment function can be seen in terms of retribution leading to a proportionate penalty for the relevant transgression. Deterrence implies both specific and general deterrence. Pacification reflects the idea that victims should feel that they have been justly treated by the legal process and thus be deflected from private vengeance. Based on similar premises, the shortfall argument suggests that exemplary damages can rectify deficiencies in the compensatory system. Dealing with these two arguments together, an obvious response is that concentration would better be placed on improving compensation. If the premise underlying them were accepted, it would make more sense to adjust compensation principles accordingly. However, the arguments do raise a different point which concerns the nature of compensation. Compensation for financial losses have always been easier to justify and administer than for more intangible losses. Bereavement payments and pursuit of PTSD claims illustrate this in different ways. Bereavement payments have been resisted because of a particular view of the nature of loss. PTSD attracts pragmatic objections based on the evidential difficulties compared with claims based on physical injury. In addition, attitudes to psychiatric illness had to be transformed before PTSD could be seen as legitimate damage.

What both these heads of claim represent, however, is a sense of loss that traditional assessments, notwithstanding the intangible pain and suffering aspect, fail completely to capture, and that is a loss of faith or breach of trust, a feeling of injustice brought about by the failure to observe proper safety standards. This kind of loss is reflected in the separate category of aggravated damages identified in *Rookes v. Barnard* and was dismissed as inapplicable to negligence in the Camelford water case, where the plaintiffs claimed aggravated damages based on the intangible loss caused by their feelings of indignation aroused by the "high handed manner" in which the defendants dealt with the incident.[81] In other words, the claim was that they suffered loss over and above that of physical or psychological injury, from the mere fact of the way the defendants treated them. If accepted, this would have had fascinating implications for disaster claims where the alleged cause is poor corporate attitudes to safety. It would amount to saying that the loss of faith in the defendants' trustworthiness was

---

[80] Anderson, L., "An Exemplary Case for Reform" (1992) *Civil Justice Quarterly* 233, 234.

[81] [1964] A.C. 1129, and *AB v. South West Water* [1993] 1 All E.R. 609; see Law. Com., para. 3.2

a compensatable loss. It should also be pointed out, however, that the basis of aggravated damages, which is addressed to the nature of the plaintiff's loss, is conceptually different from that of punitive or exemplary damages, which addresses the defendant's wrong-doing. In the negotiations over the Opren claims one plaintiff resisted the settlement offered on the ground that she did not want money, she wanted the company "brought to justice, for justice's sake" and whereas pursuing the case to trial was a means of obtaining the truth about Opren, the settlement closed the "window on the company's files".[82]

Confusion of the boundary between criminal and civil liability is one of the main arguments against exemplary damages, damages should not be used as a form of penalty when defendants are deprived of the criminal standard of proof. One difficulty with this argument is that it is premised on a somewhat misleading picture of criminal liability. The criminal law's functional equivalent of negligently causing death is manslaughter.[83] Yet, it is well-known that manslaughter prosecutions against corporate bodies are extremely rare and even against individuals, where death results from the pursuit of business or professional activities, they are hardly common.[84] If defendants in tort cases are at risk of criminal prosecution it will be for breach of an offence under regulatory regimes such as the Health and Safety at Work Act 1974. Statutory offences here are subject to quite different enforcement regimes than those traditionally associated with criminal offences, and often do not require proof even of negligence. Unusually, a successful prosecution was brought against the water authority in the Camelford case for public nuisance. Again, no proof of a mental element was necessary. Therefore, in response to the argument that exemplary damages tread on criminal territory but without the safeguard of a higher standard of proof, it is pertinent to inquire "proof of what"? Additionally, the risk in financial terms from a criminal prosecution of this kind is very small and is indeed one of the reasons for pursuing exemplary damages in the civil case. Penalties for breach of regulatory offences are often derisorily low. The fine imposed on the water authority was £10,000 and was reimbursed by the Department of Environment. It has been argued that "The theoretical separation of the roles of criminal and civil

---

[82] Harlow and Rawlings, *op. cit.*, p. 133.

[83] It is not an exact equivalent as a higher standard of reasonableness has to be breached for manslaughter.

[84] See Bergman, D., *Deaths at Work-Accidents or Corporate Crime* W.E.A. (1991); The Independent, 25 March 1994 reported attempts to refer to the C.P.S. three workplace deaths.

law is largely illusory".[85] The discussion in the following chapter endorses the force of such a view.

Perhaps the more compelling argument against exemplary damages is that they would bring a windfall to the plaintiff. This can be addressed in two different ways. The first denies that the award amounts to an unjust enrichment on the ground that the plaintiff has taken the risk of pursuing the defendant. This has been expressed vividly in terms of the windfall metaphor: "[T]here is no windfall: the plaintiff had to shake the tree to obtain the fruits of justice; and, in so doing, he risked a large branch landing on his head rather than an apple."[86] Although this observation is useful in drawing attention to one distinct difference between civil and criminal litigation—that instigation of proceedings is at the behest of the individual plaintiff in the former but not in the latter—it is flawed insofar as it suggests that the plaintiff's loss is not a relevant part of the process, only the pursuit of punishing the defendant. The second response is to redirect the damages away from the particular plaintiff to the benefit of some wider fund. This could be as wide as the revenue or as narrow as a fund for disaster victims.[87]

The Law Commission has provisionally concluded that consideration be given to retention of the availability of exemplary damages while placing them in a principled framework.

This last section on complications of the civil liability process raises starkly some core issues about the underlying purposes and functions of legal remedies. If exemplary damages were used as a form of deterrence against corporate defendants, what relationship would they have with criminal prosecution? The punishment and deterrence purposes of exemplary damages have to be put in the context of the overall aims of tort and criminal law. The insurance context also has to be acknowledged. The reality of most tortious actions is that the insurer is the real defendant, while it is not possible to insure against criminal liability. At a very simple level it is hard to deny the deterrent function of tort law as a whole, even though the damages are assessed on compensatory principles. Consideration of these broader purposes and the interaction between them is taken further in the next chapter.

---

[85] Pipe, (1994) *op. cit.*, p. 97.
[86] *Ibid.* p. 99.
[87] Law Com. para. 6.22.

7.   Blaming as well as Claiming

> "To understand principles of liability we have to uncover the kinds of social goals adopted and the strategies used for reaching them. For this we need cultural analysis that puts every concept of normality under scrutiny".[1]

It is not just to civil law that people look to satisfy their sense of justice. A common feature of recent disasters has been a campaign to persuade the authorities to bring a manslaughter prosecution against a corporate body. This is an interesting reversal of the more usual relation between civil and criminal processes. Where the prosecuting authorities are reluctant to pursue a particular individual, civil law, with its lower standard of proof, has sometimes been used as an alternative.[2] The Law Commission, in its paper on exemplary damages, notes that "a role may exist for the civil law as a fall-back mechanism for use by private individuals to challenge a decision of the police not to initiate criminal proceedings against a private individual."[3] Disasters have presented the converse—the use of criminal law when previously civil law has been seen as the appropriate forum.

Different reasons have been suggested for this trend. Campaigning for criminal liability is sometimes thought to be used as a means of applying pressure to the civil process, but evidence from the Piper Alpha aftermath suggests otherwise. Settlements were prompt and generous and predated the pursuit of criminal proceedings against Occidental. The campaign represented something other than a means of obtaining leverage for compensation. One reason for the persistence of the *Marchioness* private prosecution was that there was little scope for argument in the claim for damages. As young adults with no dependants, the victims'

---

[1] Douglas, M. and Wildavsky, A., *Risk and Culture* (1983) p. 35.
[2] As in *Halford v. Brooks* [1992] 1 P.I.Q.R. 175, a civil case brought in relation to a child's murder.
[3] Law Commission, *Consultation Paper No. 132* (1993) para. 5.16.

deaths resulted in bereavement damages which are of limited value.[4] The bereaved relatives may well have felt that these payments were inadequate and also that the fixed limit deprived them of any opportunity of a public outlet for their outrage at the safety failures of both the Department of Transport and the *Bowbelle*'s owners. There was no public inquiry and the inquests were adjourned many times.[5] However, trying to establish what people do "want" from the legal system involves examining a deep, challenging and elusive seam of human psychology and cultural preference. Seven years after the *Herald* capsize, a family which survived was reported still to be suffering from PTSD. They were one of 20 families yet to settle with P&O. One family member commented: "You know, the worst thing is that to this day, no-one from P&O has ever written us a letter saying sorry. That would have gone a long way, wouldn't it?"[6] It would appear that bereaved relatives use law for a number of different purposes, including venting anger or frustration or both, seeking revenge, demanding compensation and wanting to prevent future tragedies.[7] As this book demonstrates, a variety of legal institutions and different types of legal process can be invoked in the search for satisfaction, a search which appears to go beyond mere compensation and becomes a quest for something like "truth" or "justice".

Amidst this diversity clear patterns emerge, which affect and reflect broader cultural attitudes. One such pattern, the increased use of *criminal* in addition to civil proceedings, is addressed in this chapter from a number of different angles. Although it focuses on criminal law, the chapter moves beyond criminal liability and brings together two broader themes emerging from the rest of the book—the changing perceptions of the collective enterprise and the function of blame through legal mechanisms. In the first section, the criminal law context in general and corporate liability principles in particular are outlined. This provides the background to consideration of corporate manslaughter. The second and third sections are concerned with the wider questions of attitudes to collective enterprises. The second returns to tort law and suggests that demands for corporate manslaughter prosecutions are part of

---

[4] See Chap. 5.4.
[5] See Chap. 2.5 for a detailed account.
[6] *The Independent*, 5 May 1994.
[7] Harris *et al* suggest that in general, personal injury claimants are noticeable for a diversity of desires, and that what most people want is a by-product of what they believe it is permissible to want: *Compensation and Support for Illness and Injury* (1984) Chap. 4.

a wider trend reflected in debates about causation in tort. And finally, the key cultural theme which has informed much of the book is pursued in more depth in an attempt to draw together the strands into an integrated argument.

1. The Rise of Corporate Manslaughter

(1) Criminal Laws

Criminal laws and criminal processes are a taken-for-granted part of the institutions of state.[8] To many people "law" means criminal law with the police ever present to enforce it.[9] At an early stage in their induction process, students of law are disabused of the misconception that most law is criminal law. A clear distinction is drawn between the purposes of criminal law, in which the state punishes those who offend on behalf of society as a whole and civil law, which is conceived as providing a mechanism for settling disputes between private citizens. While it is evident that there is a lot more to law than criminal law, what this picture fails to capture is the potential for a multiplicity of legal responses and the interaction between them in relation to the same event. Disasters provide an excellent illustration. In addition, the assumptions about the functions of different areas of law are often laid out too simplistically. Commentators point out that the parties in civil actions, particularly in personal injury cases, are corporate bodies or are backed by insurance companies. The criminal process has been less prone to such outbreaks of realism. Debate is still largely conducted through the paradigm of an offender caught by the police, tried by a jury and punished appropriately for (usually) his crime. There are important respects in which this view needs to be challenged.

Many offences, especially those concerned with aspects of industrial safety, are contained in regulatory legislation enforced on a compliance model. Prosecutions for breach are the exception rather than the norm, and the level of fines has tended to be extremely low. Although there is evidence of some change as a result of decreasing levels of public tolerance and perceptions of business safety, in relative terms breaches of safety regulations

---

[8] Lacey, "The Contingency of Criminalisation" in Loveland, I., *Frontiers of Criminality* (1995).
[9] And they are often referred to as "the law", Atiyah, *Law and Modern Society*, Clarendon Press (1983) p. 1.

would need to increase dramatically to compare with the sorts of criminal penalties imposed for conventional offences of violence.[10]

There is another sense in which the idea that criminal law punishes while civil law recompenses needs to be confronted. Increasingly, victims are perceived to have a legitimate role not just in the *processes* of criminal enforcement, but also with regard to penalty. Compensation orders are awarded in more than half of cases involving criminal damage or personal violence in magistrates' courts and in over a quarter of cases in the Crown Court.[11] The 1988 Criminal Justice Act actually requires a court to consider making a compensation order in every case involving death, injury, loss or damage and to give reasons for not making an order.[12] Although when viewed from the victim's perspective, such orders may serve a similar purpose to those awarded by the Criminal Injuries Compensation Board (CICB),[13] there are important differences. A practical distinction is that the CICB scheme does not rely on the offender being traced and successfully prosecuted. A conceptual distinction can be made between the state reimbursing a victim for its failure to fulfil its duty to maintain law and order which the CICB scheme represents, and a compensation order which asks the offender to make a direct reparation to the victim.

Reparation, as Zedner points out, appears to sit somewhat uncomfortably with the renewed emphasis on retribution in criminal justice.[14] However, she also suggests that the two ideas are not necessarily irreconcilable. Modern criminal justice systems, whose development is generally associated with the rise of the nation state, pulled away from pre-existing methods of grievance redress based on direct victim reparation, which in England took the form of the "bot."[15] She argues that "not only has the state 'stolen' the conflict, but the artifice of legal language has transformed the drama and emotion of social interaction and strife into technical

---

[10] The average fine against companies in the years 1988–90 was £1,940; Bergman, *Deaths At Work: Accidents or Corporate Crime*, WEA, (1991) and against all employers £1,134 in 1991/92: Health and Safety Commission Annual Report 1991/2, H.M.S.O. (1992). The maximum fine imposable by magistrates (before which most cases are heard) for breach of duties under ss. 2–6 of the Health and Safety at Work Act 1974 was increased from £2,000 to £20,000 in 1992: Offshore Safety Act 1992, s. 4(2)(a); fines in the Crown Court are unlimited.

[11] See Ashworth, A., *Sentencing and Criminal Justice* Weidenfeld (1992), p. 249 *et seq.*

[12] s. 104.

[13] See Chap. 4.4.2.

[14] Zedner, "Reparation and Retribution: Are They Reconcilable?" (1994) 57 *Modern Law Review* 228.

[15] *Ibid.*, p. 231.

categories which can be subjected to the ordering practices of the criminal process."[16]

These insights are particularly useful when considering the relationship of victims to corporate defendants, the types of offenders of most concern in the present context. They also provide the background for the remaining part of the chapter.

Commonly, law is conceived in instrumental terms, as a means to "protect" citizens from the behaviour of the lawless minority.[17] A moment's thought reveals that this does not accord with the actual practice of criminal law and punishment. Not only are there many other means by which social control is achieved, but any attempt to draw a causal connection between criminal enforcement and reduced crime is fraught with problems. However, another view of criminal law is that it has an ideological function: that it makes statements about the boundaries of tolerated behaviour. In the case of corporate risk-taking, it is difficult fully to separate these two conceptions. While arguments about deterrence have fallen from favour as regards the punishment of individual offenders, corporate bodies may be more susceptible. Were corporations brought within conventional enforcement patterns, the effect would be complex and fragmented. Any role which criminal law has in relation to safety will reflect and reproduce, as well as create, attitudes to risk.[18]

Much of the law which is discussed in the safety field is in fact regarded in the academy and by the judiciary as atypical and somewhat separate from "real" criminal law.[19] It is often dismissed as dealing only with "mala prohibita", "quasi" crime, as opposed to "real" crime. It is true that safety laws are distinct in a number of ways. First, they are statutory in origin, a difference which persists because of the uncodified nature of our criminal law, much of which is still derived from cases. As a result, that which is seen as the core tends to reflect the "moral" offences of earlier ages when corporate activity was non-existent or less familiar. This characteristic of our criminal law allows the distinction between "real" and "quasi" crime to persist. Secondly, unlike many other statutory offences, safety laws are enforced by separate agencies and not by the police. Each specialist agency has a specific remit bestowed by statute, contrasting with the police whose duties are

---

[16] *Ibid.*

[17] Underlined in the White Paper *Crime, Justice and Protecting the Public* H.M.S.O. Cm. 965 (1990).

[18] See Garland, D., *Punishment and Modern Society* (1990) p. 252 *et seq.*

[19] This section draws on material in Wells, *Corporations and Criminal Responsibility* (1993) Chaps. 1 and 2.

general. While both agencies and the police have large areas of discretion in respect of priorities for investigation and decisions about whether to engage the prosecution process, they differ in the overall thrust of their activities. Regulators tend to be compliance orientated, their approach likened more to the police practices in relation to juveniles, with caution preceding enforcement.

Thirdly, safety legislation is often vague and exhortatory, with terms such as "reasonably practicable" and "due diligence" softening the blow of strict liability or the absence of traditional culpability tests, (commitment to which is often more apparent than real in conventional criminal liability). Further, the offences themselves are less likely to refer to the adverse effects or results of poor practice. An offence might consist of operating an unsafe machine, for example, not causing the injury which results from that. Although there are clear reasons, based on prevention, for this type of offence definition, the reality of enforcement tends to mean that it is only when an accident happens that action is taken by health and safety officers. When a prosecution is brought the offence fails to reflect the seriousness of the harm which has been caused. In this sense these offences are inchoate rather than result-crimes.

One of the significant legal developments from recent disasters is the way that debate about corporate responsibility has burst rudely onto the hitherto off-limits territory of manslaughter law. It is not altogether surprising that when the issue did arrive on the public and legal agenda when P&O were prosecuted for the *Herald* deaths, legal doctrine was found to have difficulty in accommodating a non-paradigm case of manslaughter.

(2) Corporate Criminal Liability

Unlike the civil law principles discussed in the last two chapters, corporate criminal liability is unfamiliar territory for most lawyers and it raises questions and challenges core assumptions about the nature and purposes of criminal law as traditionally conceived. Corporate liability for crime has had a chequered history inevitably entwined with the development and perception of regulatory offences.

At first, corporate liability was confined to the regulatory sphere with some, mainly statutory, offences being regarded as capable of being committed vicariously. Later, a more general route to liability, known as direct liability, developed, with the result that as a juristic person, a corporation *itself* is capable of committing almost any criminal offence.[20] Thus, vicarious liability is narrow in its application, arising mainly in the regulatory area. However, where it does apply, its scope is broad and has the potential to render the corporation liable for the wrongdoing of any of its employees. Direct liability is the reverse, broad in application but narrow in scope and with its recognition only since 1944 has a much shorter history. In theory, a corporation can be directly liable for any criminal offence,[21] but only the wrongdoing of extremely senior company officials will render a corporation liable. Although there is a clear conceptual difference between them, with the vicarious type involving liability for the acts of another and direct liability being regarded as the criminal act of *the company*, in practical terms the sanction imposed (usually a fine) affects the corporation in exactly the same way. Vicarious liability arises from the employment relationship and is not confined to corporations. Wherever an individual can be vicariously liable, so too can a corporation.

Most regulatory offences are of the strict liability type, and do not requiring proof of a mental element or *mens rea*, while most "ordinary" offences do require proof of *mens rea*, and so it is commonly believed that courts, in deciding whether an offence was capable of being committed vicariously, were reluctant to impose such liability for *mens rea* offences. A closer reading of the history of corporate liability discloses that it was less *mens rea* which presented a problem as difficulty with the idea that a corporation might commit a traditional, felony type offence.[22] Direct corporate liability, (sometimes known as *alter ego* or primary liability), developed then as the means whereby corporations could be held responsible for non-regulatory offences.[23] In three Second World War-time cases concerned with fraud of one kind or another, corporations were themselves held liable for the fraudulent activities of their own officers. This brought to the fore the need to address the problem of how to prove *mens rea* in a corporation.

So, three major issues emerge in considering corporate liability for criminal offences. The first is: when will vicarious liability be imposed? The second is where the contours of the direct type of liability should be drawn. The third difficulty is that of translating

---

[20] Interpretation Act 1889, s. 2(1) and the Criminal Justice Act 1925, s. 33.

[21] Except murder, because of the mandatory penalty of life imprisonment.

[22] See Wells, *op. cit.*, Chap. 6. The felony-misdemanour classification was abolished in 1967.

[23] *D.P.P. v. Kent and Sussex Contractors* [1944] K.B. 146: *R. v. I.C.R. Haulage* (1944) 30 Cr. App. Rep. 31 and *Moore v. Bresler* [1944] 2 All E.R. 515.

corporate "recklessness" into a conceptual creature which law can handle.

On neither of the first two questions have courts given clear answers. Indeed, since there has been a failure clearly to separate those two questions, they inevitably shade into each other in the account below. Whereas vicarious liability for regulatory offences allows a corporation to be prosecuted in respect of the acts of any of its employees acting in the course of its business, with direct liability the difficult question has been establishing who acts *as the company*. For the purposes of discussing corporate manslaughter, it is a vital question. The cases which gave birth to the direct type of liability involved either small companies or clear criminality manifested by someone like the managing director. Modern corporations vary from the very small to the enormous multi-national. Criminal law, on the other hand, has been locked into a vision of criminal culpability premised on a responsible human individual who is punished only when he or she has acted recklessly, at least. Although this vision is far from perfect, with many exceptions in the form of strict liability offences and in other more insidious ways,[24] it has informed debate about corporate liability for "real" crime for which the direct type of corporate liability is the sole conduit. The question became framed in terms of how far up the company hierarchy to go before it can be said that an employee acts *as the company*. This is because direct liability is based on the idea of the company itself being *identified* with the acts of senior officers, rather than being accountable for the transgressions of its employees. It was not until the House of Lords decision in *Tesco v. Nattrass*,[25] however, that serious consideration was given to determining which senior officers would be regarded as being identified with the company itself for these purposes. Only those who can be regarded as controlling officers—the board of directors, the managing director and possibly others discharging duties for which they are not responsible to others within the company, are so identified. This deployed a nerve-centre of command conception of the company, in which the wrongdoing of only a small number of key personnel could be imputed to the company.

The irony about *Tesco v. Nattrass* is that it concerned a regulatory offence which, before the advent of direct liability, would have been dealt with under vicarious principles. Regulatory offences

---

[24] See generally, Lacey, Wells and Meure, *Reconstructing Criminal Law* (1990) Chap. 1.
[25] [1972] A.C. 153.

gave rise to vicarious liability partly because they tended to be strict liability offences, but also because they fitted the image of "public welfare" and therefore were not "real" crime. Yet, there is a third category lying between strict liability and *mens rea* offences, where liability is strict unless a due diligence (or equivalent) defence can be made out. *Tesco v. Nattrass* came in this "hybrid" category. The interesting point is that in classifying offences in terms of regulatory or not, hybrid offences are clearly regulatory. Yet, if the basis of classification is whether they are *mens rea* or strict liability, they are less easy to place. In determining whether an offence can be committed vicariously (in which case in relation to a corporate defendant there would be no need to go on to consider the "direct" form of liability), the orthodoxy which has developed has proceeded on the assumption that offences are one or the other, strict liability or *mens rea*, ignoring entirely the "hybrid" offence. As a result, there has been considerable inconsistency in the distribution of offences between the broad vicarious form of corporate liability and the narrow, direct type.

That is the background to *Tesco v. Nattrass*, the leading case on the contours of corporate liability for serious offences, including manslaughter. The company was acquitted of a price description offence committed by one of its store managers because the statute allowed a defence where the misdescription was attributable to the acts of "another person". The manager was not sufficiently important to represent the company for the purposes of direct liability, and therefore he must, the court reasoned, be "another person".

Recent cases highlight some of the confusion which has inevitably ensued from the haphazard way in which corporate liability has developed. Courts have been ambivalent in their attitude to corporate liability and have at times displayed unswerving and uncritical fidelity to the culpable individual model while at others have recognised its irrelevance to the question of corporate risk taking. In one case, which happened also to have Tesco Stores as its appellant, the Divisional Court sidestepped the effect of the historical and interpretive absurdities of *Tesco v. Nattrass* by emphasising the different wording in the statutes. Here, the relevant defence to an offence allegedly committed by one of Tesco's check-out assistants could be invoked if she had reasonable grounds to believe that the purchaser was over 18. (The offence was that of selling an "18" classified video to a person under that age.) The argument that only the knowledge of "controlling officers" under the direct liability theory should be relevant was rejected. It was absurd, the court said, to suggest that the directors of the company would ever have a belief or knowledge of the purchaser's age. If that argument succeeded, it would effectively mean that no national company could ever commit this offence. Thus, by implication, it was accepted that the offence was committed vicariously.[26]

In response to the Sheen Inquiry into the *Herald* disaster, a new offence was introduced of failing to take all reasonable steps to secure that a vessel is operated in a safe manner. It specifically applies to "owners" of ships.[27] The House of Lords has decided that this does not impose vicarious liability for all the ship's employees. A ship's engine had broken down, leaving her drifting within 24 hours of putting to sea. The ship's engineer had boarded the vessel for the first time less than three hours before setting sail when the minimum time necessary to familiarise himself would have been three days. It was held not to be enough merely to show, as the prosecution had sought, that the system adopted by those on the ground (or rather at sea) was unsafe.[28] The conviction was quashed therefore, but the House of Lords did say that in order to establish liability, it may be possible to show that the company had failed to establish a system for ensuring that the ship was operated safely.

This could be regarded as a major step in the direction of corporate liability which is not derived from the criminal acts of a particular individual. However, as with so many other legal dawns, the sun could set on it before anyone has fully woken up to its possibilities.

(3) Corporate Manslaughter

Institutional Resistance

If corporations have been found liable for criminal offences for more than 100 years, why has corporate manslaughter presented so many difficulties? Part of the explanation has already been given, that corporate liability was for a long period largely confined to the regulatory sphere. However, corporate *criminality* has a much wider spread and the emergence of the idea of corporate manslaughter is a response and recognition of that. "Corporate manslaughter" is a phrase which has only recently entered

---

[26] *Tesco Stores Ltd v. Brent London Borough Council* [1993] 2 All E.R. 718 (Q.B.D.), D.C.

[27] Merchant Shipping Act, 1988, s. 31.

[28] *Seaboard Offshore Ltd v. Secretary of State* [1994] 2 All E.R. 99 (H.L.).

popular vocabulary. At the time of the Aberfan disaster in 1966 there was little talk of collective criminal liability. The trend towards responding to disasters in terms of corporate manslaughter seems to have begun with the *Herald* capsize in 1987. A small activity centre company, OLL Ltd, made history in 1994 as the first to be convicted of manslaughter following the deaths of four school children in a canoeing accident in the English Channel.[29]

The varied and complex reasons for this change cannot be accounted for in legal terms. The Inquiry Report after Aberfan[30] is eloquent and categorical in its condemnation of the National Coal Board for failures which led to the disaster in the same way as the Sheen inquiry did not shirk from damning criticisms of P&O.[31] Yet, there is no contemporary discussion of a possible corporate manslaughter charge after Aberfan. The Inquiry Report does not connect its condemnation of the Board for negligence with the possibility of this having criminal consequences. Things have changed. It is clear from the P&O prosecution and from the private prosecution of the company which owned the *Bowbelle* (the dredger which collided with the *Marchioness*) that corporate manslaughter now has a cultural as well as a legal meaning. However, there is much institutional resistance to the translation of those meanings to an actual conviction, or even a prosecution. The progression from disaster to trial was neither simple nor predictable after the *Herald* capsize. The D.P.P. only reopened the case after the inquest jury returned verdicts of unlawful death. The coroner discouraged a verdict based on corporate (as opposed to individual) manslaughter[32] and, when the trial eventually took place two and a half years later, the trial judge directed acquittals on murky grounds.[33]

As to the *Marchioness* tragedy, there was neither a public inquiry nor an inquest verdict to prompt the D.P.P. into reconsidering his

---

[29] *R v. OLL Ltd* (Unreported) Crown Court (1994) 144 *New Law Journal* 1735. The company was fined £60,000 and its managing director jailed for 3 years.

[30] (Edmund-Davies L.J) *Report of the Tribunal appointed to Inquire into the Disaster at Aberfan*, (1967 H.C. 553) H.M.S.O.

[31] (Sheen Report) *M.V. Herald of Free Enterprise Report of the Court No. 8074, Dept of Transport* H.M.S.O. (1987).

[32] His ruling that corporations could not commit manslaughter was appealed by relatives: *R. v. HM Coroner for E. Kent, ex p. Spooner* (1989) 88 Cr. App. Rep. 10.

[33] The trial judge's ruling that corporations can commit manslaughter is reported in *R. v. P&O European Ferries* (1991) 93 Cr. App. Rep 73; the trial itself is reported as *R. v. Alcindor* and others, C.A. transcript, 19 October 1990. See Wells, "Corporations: Culture, Risk and Criminal Liability" [1993] *Criminal Law Review* 551.

decision not to prosecute.[34] The Marine Accident Investigation report was not published until two years after the accident,[35] on the ground that the delay was necessary to prevent any prejudice to the trial of the *Bowbelle*'s captain for failure to keep a proper lookout.[36] Two trial judges failed to agree a verdict on those charges, giving further evidence of a move from individual scapegoating to more concern with corporate bodies—in this case, the shipowners and the Department of Transport. Meanwhile, the D.P.P. had ruled out the possibility of charges against South Coast Shipping, owners of the *Bowbelle*,[37] and a private prosecution was launched as soon as the D.P.P. indicated that the case against the captain was being dropped. The case went no further than the committal stage.[38] Although the company failed in its attempt to have the trial stopped as an abuse of due process, the Divisional Court re-affirmed that the D.P.P. could always use his powers to take over and discontinue a private prosecution.

In order to explain this institutional resistance, it is necessary to remind ourselves that perceptions of crime derive from social rather than legal constructions of events. As to the latter, almost all jurisdictions include unlawful homicide as one of their most serious offences. The structure, scope and sentencing implications of such laws vary across time and place. In comparison with many schemes, the common law division between murder and manslaughter which applies in England and Wales is relatively simple, if fluid. A number of conditions has to be satisfied before a homicide will be regarded as unlawful. It needs to be caused by another person, which will include corporations as "juristic persons" but exclude "acts of God" or "natural causes".[39] Assuming cause, and absence of lawful excuse such as self-defence

---

[34] There are complex procedural reasons for the sequence of these public institutional responses: see Wells, "Disasters: The Role of Institutional Responses in Shaping Public Perceptions of Death" in Lee and Morgan, eds, *Death Rites*, (1993) p. 196.

[35] *Report into the Collision between Marchioness and MV Bowbelle on 20 August 1991*, Department of Transport, H.M.S.O. (1991); it was completed in February 1990 and published on 15 August 1991.

[36] 1988 Merchant Shipping Act, s. 32. No use was made of the offence under s. 31 of failing to ensure the safe operation of their ship against *Bowbelle*'s owners.

[37] An application for judicial review of this was rejected: *The Times*, 31 October 1990.

[38] The defence raised a preliminary question of abuse of due process, reported in *R. v. Bow Street Magistrate, ex p. South Coast Shipping Co. Ltd* [1993] Q.B. 645. The *Bowbelle* case is discussed in further detail in Wells, C., "Cry in the Dark: Corporate Manslaughter and Cultural Meaning" in Loveland, I., ed., *Frontiers of Criminality* (1995).

[39] The problem in such categorisation is rarely acknowledged in legal discourse.

or prevention of crime, a death will amount to *murder* if accompanied by intention to cause death or grievous bodily harm.[40] Manslaughter marks the border between homicides to which criminal blame attaches and those deaths regarded as accidental or to which no criminal blame attaches. Broadly covering recklessly caused deaths, manslaughter coincides to some extent with civil liability for negligence, but is narrower in its application.

The prosecution of the ferry operator, P&O, for manslaughter following the *Herald of Free Enterprise* disaster was the first involving a corporation for nearly 30 years and only the third in English legal history.[41] The paucity of such cases might seem surprising given that many of the 500 workplace deaths which occur each year are regarded as avoidable. For example, of 739 construction deaths between 1981 and 1985, the Health and Safety Executive estimated that over 50 per cent could have been avoided by positive management action.[42] However, as we have seen, the criminality of the risk-taking employer, whether an individual or a corporation, has traditionally been side-channelled, diverted into the calmer waters of health and safety offences, with their relatively low stigma and penalties.

The reluctance to consider manslaughter can be seen as part of a larger pattern whereby personal injury and violence is categorised as criminal or not. Take road deaths, for example. More than 5000 people die in road traffic incidents each year, yet few result in manslaughter prosecutions.[43] Unlike industrial deaths, these are investigated by the police, and not by a separate regulatory agency, but there is still a dual system of offences. A choice can be made between charges under road traffic legislation and common law manslaughter. The statutory offence of causing death by dangerous driving has a maximum penalty of 10 years imprisonment,[44] whereas for manslaughter the maximum is life. Until recently, the ingredients for the statutory offence were exactly the same as for reckless manslaughter,[45] yet most were pursued under

---

[40] *R. v. Nedrick* [1986] 3 All E.R. 1; intention can be inferred from the defendant's foresight that death or grievous bodily harm was virtually certain.

[41] The High Court held that a corporation could not commit a felony, as manslaughter then was, in *R. v. Cory Bros* [1927] 1 K.B. 810 and a company was acquitted in *R. v. Northern Strip Mining, The Times*, 2, 4 and 5 February 1965.

[42] *Blackspot Construction*, H.M.S.O. (1988).

[43] In 1991 the number was 5,590: *Social Trends*, H.M.S.O. (1992) Table 7.23. See also, Spencer, "Motor Vehicles as Weapons of Offence" [1985] *Criminal Law Review* 2.

[44] Increased by the Criminal Justice Act 1993, s. 67(1).

[45] Road Traffic Act 1991, s. 1, substituted "dangerous" for "reckless". Its pre-

the former, less stigmatic, road traffic legislation. In 1990, over 300 people were sentenced for causing death by reckless driving.[46] These are not included in the statistics for homicide, for which there were 607 convictions in the same year. The proportion of those given immediate custodial sentences is high in both the reckless driving and manslaughter categories (71 per cent and 80 per cent respectively).[47] However, a significant number of the reckless drivers were fined or given a community service order (29 per cent and 33 per cent respectively), sentences which were not used at all following manslaughter convictions.[48]

It is helpful to place the issue of corporate liability for disasters in the context of these other deaths in order to emphasise the significance of the social rather than the legal construction of events. When a major disaster happens it may not occur to anyone that this might come within the *legal* definition of unlawful homicide, especially if there is no particular individual as to whose recklessness it can be attributed. A disparate range of factors, amongst which the legal definition of the offence plays a necessary but certainly not a sufficient part, determines whether a prosecution is brought, whether a conviction results (especially given the reliance in the Anglo-American system on juries), and the severity of sentence imposed.

A Developing Idea

However, it is a mistake to think that turning to manslaughter as a reaction to disasters or corporate harms is exclusively a modern phenomenon. The prosecution of Cory Brothers serves to upset that assumption; it also underlines the essentially political character of the criminal justice process. Fearing pilfering during the strike of 1926, Cory Brothers, a South Wales mining company, erected an electrified fence around its property. An unemployed miner, engaged on a ratting expedition, stumbled against it and was electrocuted. Private prosecutions for manslaughter were brought by the South Wales Miners' Federation against three of the company's directors and against the company itself. The case proceeded from committal to the Assizes despite the efforts of

---

decessor, causing death by reckless driving, was held to be synonymous with manslaughter in *R. v. Seymour* [1983] 2 A.C. 493 and *Jennings v. U.S. Government* [1983] A.C. 624.

[46] Criminal Statistics, H.M.S.O. (1991).

[47] See the discussion in Ashworth, *op. cit.*, p. 105.

[48] The figures are not broken down for different types of manslaughter, so the comparison is weak.

the leading counsel of the day.[49] However, the trial judge was persuaded that a corporation could not be indicted for an offence against the person. Going further back, a dam burst at Holmfirth in 1852, killing 78 people, brought forth the following expression of regret from a coroner's jury: "that the reservoir being under the management of a corporation prevents us from bringing in a verdict of manslaughter, as we are convinced that the gross and culpable negligence of the commissioners would have subjected them to such a verdict had they been in a position of a private individual or firm."[50]

Nowadays, in order to come under the spotlight of a murder or manslaughter charge, killings have first to come to the attention of the police (or, in some cases, the Director of Public Prosecutions). Workplace deaths are rarely reported to the police by health and safety officials. The kinds of death which inevitably attract police attention are those which take place in pub, street or domestic brawls or during robberies, burglaries, or in other individualised scenarios. Most of these can be accommodated within a sub-category of manslaughter based on an unlawful and dangerous act. (This frequently overlaps with "reckless" manslaughter). An additional mechanism which helps to filter out road and industrial deaths is that as a result of an early motor manslaughter case, "unlawful act" manslaughter is unavailable where death flows from a breach of health and safety or other regulatory law.[51] For all these reasons, in respect of which it is not always easy to work out what is cause and what is effect, deaths caused recklessly while carrying out otherwise lawful activities do not often result in manslaughter charges.

Although unusual, there are instances where individual company directors have been charged in relation to deaths caused to employees or customers. Two directors of a plastic company were charged with manslaughter when they negligently caused the death of one of their workers;[52] and three directors of a coach firm were charged with manslaughter of a teacher and a 12-year-old girl when a coach owned by their company overturned.[53]

---

[49] Edward Marshall-Hall K.C. led the defence at the committal but died before the trial; his place was taken by Norman Birkett K.C. A full report of the committal proceedings is found in the *Western Mail*, 11 and 12 February 1927.

[50] See Simpson, "Legal Liability for Bursting Reservoirs: The Historical Context of *Rylands v. Fletcher*" (1984) XIII *Journal of Legal Studies* 209, p. 221.

[51] *Andrews v. D.P.P.* [1937] A.C. 576.

[52] One pleaded guilty and the prosecution accepted the not guilty plea of the other, October 1988.

[53] *The Independent*, 22 March 1990.

There may be many other recklessly caused deaths which could fit the legal paradigm of manslaughter, but which are never considered through a lack of fit with the social or cultural paradigm. The desirability or likelihood of a prosecution for corporate manslaughter following transport or other disasters caused by management disregard of safety policies or precautions are thus not matters which can be assessed from a purely legal standpoint.

After the long build-up, the trial of P&O for manslaughter eventually took place in 1990. With seven individual defendants, ranging from the Assistant Bosun on the *Herald* to the company's senior directors, as well as the company itself, defence counsel far outweighed those for the prosecution. A neat reversal of the normal balance of power between the state and the accused was thus achieved. However, the judge brought the trial to a close before the end of the prosecution's case and directed acquittals of the company and the individual defendants. He did so because he was not convinced that the prosecution could establish that one sufficiently senior member of the company's management could be said to have been reckless in the sense of creating an obvious and serious risk, one which a prudent person would have realised, that the ferry could sail with its doors open.[54] "We have heard a weight of evidence", Mr Justice Turner said, "to the effect that experienced seaborne personnel never thought for a moment that, with the system in force, there was any risk of that event happening. It was not obvious to any of those people until it happened; that is my intellectual difficulty."

Final Recognition

There has been a change in manslaughter law since the P&O trial. "Reckless" manslaughter no longer relies on the obvious and serious risk test applied to P&O. In its place the gross negligence test has been revived.[55] A recent appellate decision specifies the circumstances in which deaths caused from breach of a duty of care may amount to manslaughter.[56] The provision of a public transport service or other commercial enterprises would raise such a duty. If the breach of duty amounts to "gross negligence", a manslaughter prosecution could be instituted. Gross negligence includes the following:

---

[54] I explore this in some detail in "Corporations: Culture etc" *op. cit.*

[55] This category had been thought to be subsumed when the obvious and serious risk formulation emerged following *Caldwell* [1982] A.C. 341 and was applied to manslaughter in *Seymour* [1983] 2 A.C. 493.

[56] *R. v. Adomako* [1994] 2 All E.R. 79, H.L.

"Indifference to an obvious risk of injury to health; actual foresight of the risk coupled with the determination nevertheless to run it; appreciation of the risk coupled with an intention to avoid it but also coupled with such a high degree of negligence in the attempted avoidance as the jury consider justifies conviction; and inattention or failure to advert to a serious risk which goes 'beyond inadvertence' in respect of an obvious and important matter which the defendant's duty demanded he should address."[57]

The prosecution of OLL Ltd for manslaughter partly owed its success to this more flexible definition. Two other factors can be identified as contributing to that first corporate manslaughter conviction. Merely by virtue of being a *different* test for manslaughter than that applied against P&O, the new formulation would have been of significant assistance even if it amounted to an alternative expression of a similar concept. Secondly, the difficulties presented by P&O's distant management structure were not present with OLL Ltd, a small private company run by its managing director.

The Law Commission has recently considered corporate manslaughter and believes that the gross negligence formula enables the problems of having to find one particular officer who has the *mens rea* for the offence to be overcome. The Commission favours an emphasis on whether *the company* has failed to take account of the risk of death or serious injury. This question would only arise where the company has chosen to enter a field of activity which carries a risk to others, such as transport, manufacture or medical care. The steps the company has taken to discharge the "duty of safety" and the systems devised for running its business, will be directly relevant.[58] Although only expressed as a provisional view, it is significant that the Law Commission echoes here the recognition of corporate safety *systems* voiced in the *Seaboard* case.

If this is confusing and unsettled, that should not be a matter of surprise. A real tension exists between the paradigm of criminal culpability based on individual responsibility and the increasing recognition of the potential for harm inherent in large scale corporate activity. Regulatory offences represent one longstanding response, yet the enforcement regimes and sanctions those entail are relatively benign. Much more concern is raised when corporate criminal liability steps outside that domain and enters the field of

---

[57] *R. v. Prentice And Others* [1993] 3 W.L.R. 927 *per* Lord Taylor C.J., at 937.
[58] *Involuntary Manslaughter*, Consultation Paper No. 135, (1994 paras. 5.79–5.90).

serious offences such as manslaughter or fraud. Here the legal response has been to allow liability on very limited terms. Yet, while the *Seaboard* decision may look and feel narrow because the original conviction was quashed, with its talk of the company's systems it has the potential to presage a new era in which attention shifts from individuals (whether high or low) within the company to the *company* itself. This seems to be what the Law Commission also envisages for manslaughter. The long process leading to the prosecution of P&O and OLL Ltd is a clear demonstration that law does respond to changes in cultural attitudes.

Although the development of direct liability opened up the possibility of manslaughter prosecutions 50 years ago, it was not until the long campaign to prosecute P&O Ferries for the *Herald* capsize that the question of corporate manslaughter was properly addressed. Not only was the jury deprived of the opportunity to voice its opinion on corporate manslaughter in that case, but the way the trial was brought to an end left the issues firmly grounded in *legal* discourse. I have argued here that the complications which ensnared the trial were not those presented by the recklessness element in manslaughter, nor even by the legal doctrine of direct corporate liability, but resulted from the extraordinary threat which corporate manslaughter makes to the world we understand. Sight should not be lost, however, of the significance of the prosecution itself nor of the judicial confirmation it gave that a corporation is capable of committing manslaughter.[59]

2. Collective Responsibility

A number of different ideas have been competing for attention here. One has been to begin to account for the move towards the use of corporate manslaughter as a means of allocating responsibility for disasters. This inevitably leads into wider questions both of the need to blame and of the focus of that blame. In exploring the social institutions of blame, artificial boundaries between types of legal processes cannot be maintained. Moves towards collective rather than individual responsibility are evidenced beyond calls for corporate manslaughter prosecutions. The section below introduces arguments from American tort law as part of the background to the concluding discussion of cultural attitudes to risk.

Debates about causation in tort highlight the challenge presented by corporate wrong–doing. For example, where more than

---

[59] *D.P.P. v. P&O European Ferries (Dover) Ltd* (1991) 93 Cr. App. R. 73.

one manufacturer or company is involved in producing drugs or in polluting the environment, there are difficulties in establishing precisely who caused how much damage. In a movement which has had little impact so far in the U.K., a rule of market share liability has emerged in U.S. courts. Because of the peculiarity of generic drug manufacture, it is not always possible to identify which manufacturer supplied a particular plaintiff. Courts allowed people affected by the drug DES (which in some cases caused birth injuries) to use special "cause-in-fact" rules to overcome the normally strict causation rule in tort that only a person who is shown to have caused the plaintiff's injury can be held liable to compensate.[60] Here, plaintiffs could point to a group of possible causal actors that probably, but not certainly, included the actual responsible party.[61] Each would be liable to pay a contribution towards the damages proportional to the defendant's share of the total sales of the drug. The court claimed that this was not a breach of individual responsibility on the ground that each defendant would pay no more than the aggregate injuries caused by its own actions.[62] Yet, it is a distinct departure from traditional causation principles.

The DES litigation concerned the "indeterminate defendant"; there are also problems with "indeterminate plaintiffs". An example of the difficulties to which it could give rise is outlined by Bush.[63] A chemical leak exposes 1000 individuals to a toxic agent known to cause a particular kind of cancer. That cancer occurs "naturally" at a certain level. There is increase in the level because of the leak. In relation to any particular plaintiff, it would be impossible to establish whether it would have "naturally" occurred or was one of the increased number from the leak.

Two different arguments, risk contribution and loss of expected value, have been made to justify awards of compensation in these indeterminate cases. Risk contribution is based on the idea that liability is imposed for the creation of a risk and liability is apportioned according to the magnitude of the risk. An insurer will pay to a series or group of individual victims an amount roughly equal to the aggregate damage he caused to some of the victims in that group. The total damages paid by each defendant will approximate the aggregate harm he inflicted. Lost value relies

---

[60] *Sindell v. Abbott Labs.* 26 Cal. 3d 588, 697 P.2d 924, 163 Cal. Rptr. 132, cert. denied 449 U.S. 912 1980.
[61] See Bush, "Between Two Worlds: The Shift from Individual to Group Responsibility in the Law of Causation of Injury" (1986) 33 *U.C.L.A. Law Review* 1473.
[62] Bush describes this as disingenuous, p. 1485.
[63] *Ibid.*

on statistical evidence to assess the victim's pre-injury "value".
This is established via statistical evidence relating to the group to
which the plaintiff belongs. In some cases, the statistical probability will obviously not occur. Under this principle, however, a
claim could be made, not for actual injury, but potential injury.
Recent U.S. cases display some sympathy with both these principles.[64] In one, concerning radiation from nuclear tests in Nevada
Desert, the primary evidence was statistical correlation. It was
held that where a defendant negligently creates a radiological
hazard which puts an identifiable population group at increased
risk, a fact-finder *may* reasonably conclude that the hazard caused
the condition.[65] A settlement reached in relation to the Vietnam
veterans claiming damage from Agent Orange and approved by
a federal court was awarded to a group and distributed on a pro
rata basis.[66] *Agent Orange* "may become a precedent for future
toxic torts decisions that recognize and apply the theory of group
responsibility to both defendants and plaintiffs."[67]

The question which has exercised commentators is whether the
market share rule violates or accords with either a utilitarian or a
corrective justice philosophy of tort law. Corrective justice sees the
tort system as an expression of values of individual responsibility
for harm to others. It institutionalises an exchange between the
injured and the person causing that injury, through an expression
of regret. In corrective justice accounts of tort the *act and harm* are
significant, not attitude or wealth.

Both this, and utilitarian theories, it is argued, depend on a
concept of individual responsibility: utilitarian theory assumes
that tort law creates incentives for behaviour which minimises
social costs and corrective justice is premised on the view that tort
law exists to correct injustices committed by one individual (or
group entity such as a corporation) against another.[68]

> "Writers worry that the tort system increasingly functions as
> a cloak behind which a judge may hide while playing Robin
> Hood, taking money from a wealthy corporation and giving it
> to poor accident victims regardless of whether the corporation
> has violated the accident victim's rights and regardless of

---

[64] *Collins v. Eli Lilly*, Wisconsin SC, 116 Wis 2d 166, 342 N.W.2d 37 cert. denied 469
U.S. 826 (1984); *Allen v. U.S.* 588 f. Supp. 247 (D. Utah 1984) Fe. Dist. Crt of Utah;
In re Agent Orange 597 F. Supp 740 (E.D.N.Y. 1984).
[65] *Allen v. U.S.* 588 F. Supp. 247 (D. Utah 1984) Fed. Dist. Crt of Utah.
[66] *In re Agent Orange* 597 F. Supp 740 (E.D.N.Y. 1984).
[67] Bush, *op. cit.*, p. 1497.
[68] *Ibid*. p. 1476.

whether imposing liability will do more harm than good."[69]

In introducing these arguments here, all that is possible is to indicate directions in which further investigation can be pursued. When victims of disaster make use of legal avenues they do not engage passively in a system which has all the answers in advance. Because of their high profile and the nature of the defendants they sue, such cases may well play a part in shaping liability. However, litigants only work within the boundaries of any particular system, and the account in earlier chapters has been designed to indicate where those boundaries lie. The discussion of moves towards blaming collectivities (as seen in corporate manslaughter) and towards collective rather than individual responsibility (as seen in some U.S. tort law) demonstrates some of the dynamic possibilities of those systems. This, however, is not the appropriate place to pursue the broader issue of how best the functions of deterrence and compensation should be reflected in the legal system.[70] It is important too, in making these arguments to remember the very different welfare background against which the U.K. and U.S. legal systems operate.[71]

3. Culture and Blame: Attitudes to Risk

For now, the question of how such shifts come about needs to be explored. Whatever the individual circumstances of each disaster, there has been an undoubted shift, a change in the collective consciousness in relation to blame. It is not, however, a simple transfer of blame from the individual to the big, bad corporation. The move towards blaming corporations for major disasters bears witness to the theory that blame generally, and criminal blame in particular, is used as a way of people making sense of the world.[72] The pressure for vengeance is ubiquitous. It manifests itself in a number of ways, including greater use of civil litigation to claim compensation as well as in calls for criminal justice to answer problems ranging from terrorism through to

---

[69] Strudler, A., "Mass Torts" (1992) 11 *Law and Philosophy* 297.

[70] Harris, D., "Tort Law Reform in the United States" (1991) 11 *Ox. J.L.S.* 407.

[71] See Galanter, "The Transnational Traffic in Legal Remedies" in Jasonoff, S., *Learning from Disaster* (1994) p. 133.

[72] A number of writers point to the effect of the increasing secularisation of society on perceptions of crime and risk: Taylor, I., *Crime, Capitalism and Community* (1983), p. 107; Lee, T. R., "The Public's Perception of Risk and the Question of Irrationality" in *The Assessment and Perception of Risk* (Warner, F., 1981), p. 5.

joyriding. An increased tendency towards greater legalisation has accompanied a decline in confidence in major institutions, business and government.[73] There have been important changes in the vocabulary of public affairs.

The kinds of events which attract collective blame were not necessarily previously perceived as products of human error at all. People's responses to events are partly a product of their attitudes to risk, resulting in certain hazards being selected for attention and being socially amplified.[74] Hazards can be conceived as events which threaten things which people value, and risk as the probability of experiencing harm.[75] The move from a scientific, technical conception of risk and hazard to one based on social, cultural and perceptual dimensions is essential to an understanding of the legal consequences accompanying disasters. Harm is a socially dependent concept and the management of risk is "rooted in social institutions and relationships."[76] Once it is accepted that there is more to risk, and therefore more to disasters, and to legal responses to disasters, than a mechanistic descriptive exercise, social sciences lead to an array of different types of theorising about attitudes to risk. These range from social psychology and risk perception to cultural theorists who assert that people select certain risks for attention to defend their preferred life-styles and as a forensic resource to place blame on other groups.[77]

While cultural theory cannot answer every question, it provides a framework which is useful for considering the development of disaster litigation in general and the call for corporate manslaughter prosecutions in particular. Corporate manslaughter suggests a move from blaming the individual to blaming a collective entity. This move does not proceed from isolated individual positions. Instead, it can be approached through an institutional or group-based theory which seeks to explain how people's response to adverse events sometimes leads to a use of legal blaming mechanisms. Thus, at both ends of the scale of the blaming process it is important to acknowledge the collective rather than the individual.

Culture renders the construction of categories into a seemingly

---

[73] Galanter, "Law Abounding: Legalisation around the North Atlantic" (1992) 55 *Modern Law Review* p. 1.

[74] Kasperson, "The Social Amplification of Risk: Progress in Developing an Integrative Framework" in Krimsky, S. and Golding D., eds, *Theories of Risk* (1992) 153.

[75] *Ibid.*, p. 154.

[76] *Ibid.*, p. 154.

[77] Douglas, M., *Risk and Blame* (1992) Chap. 3.

natural, taken for granted, process. It affects the way we look at ourselves and the rest of the universe.[78] However, at the same time, in a highly interdependent society, culture is fragmented. Its reflection and refraction through the maze of social institutions will be diverse and enigmatic. Cultural theory is a social theory concerned with two things: relationships among human beings and societal relationships with nature.[79] "Whatever objective dangers may exist in the world, social organisation will emphasize those that reinforce the moral, political, or religious order that holds the group together."[80] The grid/group theory developed by Mary Douglas, and introduced in Chapter 3 above, seeks to classify people's responses to different threats.[81] Two key variables in this approach to cultural diversity are the continuums of social relationships (the group axis) and of social interactions (the grid). On the first, concern is with the degree of social incorporation of an individual within a social unit or group. On this continuum, social identity runs from strong individualism to strong collectivism. The grid axis represents the group constraints which affect individuals equally, although the individual impact of those effects will depend on how the individual is placed on the group axis. Grid constraints, which are functions of matters such as hierarchy, kinship, race, gender, age and so on, vary from extremes of restriction and independence.[82] Four institutionalised ways of responding emerge from the intersection of these two continuums: the entrepreneur, the egalitarian, the hierarchist and the fatalist. Criminal justice appears most strongly to relate to the needs of the hierarchist who represents high levels of collectivism and prescription, with a strong emphasis on central control. Fatalists, combining high degrees of individualism and prescription, experience a sense of being manipulated by a system over which they have no control. These ideal types are useful for considering how we relate to criminal justice and how it relates to us. Grid-group analysis, as Rayner notes, "follows the notion that individuals negotiating their way through the organizational constraints of actively interpreting, challenging, accepting, and recreating their social environment are limited to a style of discourse consistent

---

[78] Erikson, T., *In the Wake of the Flood* (1979) p. 46.
[79] Rayner, S., "Cultural Theory and Risk Analysis" in Krimsky and Golding, eds, *Theories of Risk* (1992) p. 83.
[80] *Ibid.*, p. 87.
[81] See Douglas, *Natural Symbols* (1970) p. 104.
[82] Explained by Milton, "Interpreting Environmental Policy: A Social Scientific Approach" (1991) *Journal of Law and Society* 4, p. 5.

with the constitutive premises of that environment."[83] Although the language is unfamiliar, lawyers may well recognise the aptness of this description.

One of the things people value most will be the set of social institutions that they personally strongly identify with or participate in. The hazards which most concern them will be those which threaten locally valued social arrangements.[84] The determination of the threat will itself be mediated by social information. Scientific knowledge is bounded by the limitations of current understanding, and also through its own blinkered vision which does not always fully interact with what might be called folk wisdom or practical indigenous expertise.[85] Furthermore, the interaction between the identification of a hazard and the processes that result (for example, the translation of worry about ferry safety into legal actions), means that those risks are further advertised.[86]

An application of this is Kasperson's theory of social amplification of risk, based on the thesis that hazards "interact with psychological, social, institutional, and cultural processes in ways that can heighten or attenuate perceptions of risk and shape behaviour."[87] What is of interest then is the interpretation of events and the communication of that interpretation in ways which lead to particular legal outcomes or the deployment of particular legal processes. Here, individual psychological and cultural group dynamics engage with each other in a continuous, fermenting, process. A further insight into the inter-relation between modern technological risk and individual responses to it is suggested by Giddens.[88] Risk assessment is translated by experts into information accessible to "lay" people, encouraging lifestyle decisions to be taken. For example, statistical probability in relation to the safety records of various car manufacturers, might be used in decisions as to which car to buy. However, this process has a sinister side, for it presages the "privatization of risks" whereby "the collectively produced dangers are 'dumped' into the privatized worlds of individual victims and translated as realities one confronts individually and struggles with through individual

---

[83] *Op. cit.*, p. 90.
[84] Pidgeon, N. *et al*, "Risk Perception" in *Risk: Analysis, Perception and Management* (Royal Society, 1992).
[85] Kasperson, *op. cit.*, p. 157.
[86] Rayner, *op. cit.*, p. 92.
[87] *Ibid.*, p. 158.
[88] *Modernity and Self Identity*, p. 111.

efforts."[89] This has implications for the blaming process. For while individuals seek to direct blame for untoward events on to outsiders, society is engaged in the opposite direction, making individuals responsible for the misfortunes which befall them when they misread the risk assessment. The presentation of statistics as certain and objective contributes to this in a metaphorical way by warding off the threat and fear of disaster by the provision of clear risk determination. The calculability of disaster, or the risk of it, is "consoling" with its "illusion of control over destiny."[90]

Theories of risk incorporating social and cultural perspectives are relatively new and the study of legal responses to disasters can both play a part in their development and draw on them for its own benefit. Attempts to understand legal processes from a static position in which the recognition of harm is taken as given are deeply flawed. It has been suggested that public acceptance of risk revolves round three concepts: trust, liability and consent.[91] In this way, a connection can be established between the already noted loss of faith in collective institutions and the tendency to use law to establish liability, both criminal and civil. A further example could be taken from medical practice. Whereas 20 years ago, doctors in the U.K. were seen largely as benevolently omnipotent, now their every move attracts critical comment and suggestions for regulation or control. Patrick Devlin, writing in 1962, captured the mood:

> "Is it not a pleasant tribute to the medical profession that by and large it has been able to manage its relations with its patients on the basis of such an understanding [that conduct be regulated by a general understanding of how decent people ought to behave] without the aid of lawyers and lawmakers?"[92]

The point is not to evaluate the merits of either approach but to note that one has supplanted the other. The interesting question which arises is how to theorise that change, how to account for it.

Cultural theories, in their various guises, offer one vehicle for tracking these shifts. "TLC" (trust, liability and consent) represents a cluster of concepts which use language that seems peculiarly appropriate to lawyers. All three affect the acceptability of any

---

[89] Baumann, Z., *Postmodern Ethics* (1993) p. 202.
[90] *Op. cit.*, p. 201.
[91] Rayner, *op. cit.* p. 95.
[92] *Samples of Lawmaking* (1962) p. 103.

given risk: can we trust the institutions which regulate technology? Are the liabilities imposed when undesirable consequences occur seen to be appropriate? Has collective consent been obtained in a way acceptable to those who will bear the consequences?[93]

This last section serves as a conclusion to the book. The argument can be summarised in this way. As the power of collective enterprise to cause harm comes to be recognised, so does the collective interest as a potential victim, of which concern about pollution is an example.[94] "New technology," it has been suggested, "produces new social responsibilities and provokes cultural re-assessment."[95] The salient message is that responsibility and blame allocation are not derivative of individual moral positions. Law and culture tolerate a push-me pull-you relationship. Risk and blame provide the fuel for its turbines. Neither disasters nor law can be taken as given categories, each is socially constructed and subject to flux. Beyond analysis and theory, though, are real people confronting real tragedies, many of which are compounded by failures to address social and economic priorities.

[93] Rayner, op. cit. p. 95.
[94] Nelken, "Criminal Law and Criminal Justice: Some Notes on their Irrelation" in Criminal Law and Justice (Dennis, ed., 1987).
[95] Douglas and Wildavsky, Risk and Culture (1983) p. 35.

182

Appendix

[An alphabetical list of disasters mentioned in the text]

Abbeystead (1984): While on a tour of the Lune/Wyre transfer scheme at Abbeystead 16 local people were killed and another 20 seriously injured when a build-up of methane gas in the underground water pumping station caused an explosion.

Aberfan (1966): 116 pupils and 28 adults died when a waterlogged slag heap became unstable and slipped down a mountainside, engulfing a Welsh primary school. In the accident report the blame was placed firmly at the feet of the National Coal Board for lack of care in undertaking their inspections.

Agent Orange (1960–73): U.S. veterans claimed damages in relation to a toxic chemical warfare weapon used during the Vietnam war.

Australia Bush Fires (1983): 72 people were killed and thousands of homes destroyed in Victoria and southern Australia, one of the country's worst fires.

Bhopal (1984): The leakage of a storage tank containing methyl iso-cynate at the Union Carbide chemical processing plant in India. The accident released tonnes of toxic gases into the area killing 3,000 people and an estimated half a million people are still affected 10 years later. An unestimated number of people have subsequently died from effects thought to be directly attributable to the disaster.

Bradford City Fire (1985): 49 people died at the football stadium when its wooden stand caught fire. Thought to be caused by a discarded cigarette igniting rubbish allowed to build up over the years under the stand.

Braer oil tanker spillage (1993): The American/Greek owned Libyan-registered oil tanker the *Braer* spilled its 84,500 tonne pay load off the Shetland Islands. Favourable winds meant that a serious environmental disaster was averted. 1,500 sea birds were killed along with some seals and otters. The main effect was financial; the salmon fishing industry and tourism lost out because of perceived rather than actual effects.

Buffalo Creek (1972): 132 million gallons of black slag, debris-filled mud and water cascaded down Buffalo Creek in West Virginia when a dam gave way. 125 people were killed and many thousands were made homeless.

Chernobyl (1986): The main unit of a nuclear reactor caught fire and because of both human and design errors, massive amounts of radiation leaked. 1/4 million were evacuated. Conservative estimate of 10,000 cancers in Soviet Union (as was) and 1000 in Europe. Two million sheep confined on 5000 Welsh holdings, down to 230,000 sheep on 340 farms by January 1994.

Chichester Floods (1994): The river Lavant overflowed, caused mainly by artificial drainage of agricultural land in conjunction with heavy rainfall causing overflow. The flood level rose to four feet leading to evacuation. The estimated insurance costs were in the region of 100 million pounds.

Clapham Train Crash (1988): 37 died and 500 were injured when two trains collided just outside Clapham station, London.

East Coast storm (1953): Freak winds drove a storm tide down North Sea. 307 died including 58 from Canvey Island. 40,000 people were rescued, evacuated or fled.

Estonia (1994): 912 people died when a passenger and car ferry lost its bow doors in high seas, rolled over and sank in the Baltic.

European Gateway (1982): Ro-Ro ferry and sister ship of *Herald of Free Enterprise* capsized following collision, six died.

Exxon Valdez Oil Spillage (1989): 11 million tonnes of crude oil polluted Alaskan coast. The cost to the operators in the clean-up and fines was $3 billion with an additional $50 billion in damages pending.

Flixborough (1974): Explosion demolished N.Y.P.R.O. chemical works at Flixborough, N. Yorks. 28 killed, 89 injured, including 53 from surrounding areas.

Great Fire of London (1666): Fire started in Pudding Lane, its spread exacerbated by easterly winds and an especially hot dry summer. Extensive damage, large part of the city destroyed, most of the civic buildings, including the old St Paul's, 87 parish churches and over 13,000 homes.

Gresford (1934): 264 miners' bodies sealed after fire prevented their retrieval.

Hagley School Tragedy (1993): 12 school children and their teacher were killed when their school mini bus crashed into the back of a motorway maintenance lorry at junction 15 of the M40.

Herald of Free Enterprise (1987): 154 passengers and 38 crew died when a car ferry capsized just outside the harbour at Zeebrugge after sailing with its bow doors open.

Hillsborough (1989): 95 spectators were crushed to death at the football stadium following the police decision to allow a large number of fans in at once.

Hiroshima (1945): 6 August 1945 the United States exploded an atomic bomb in Japan. An estimated 200,000 people were killed and deaths from radiation and poisoning have continued ever since.

Holmfirth (1852): 78 killed, four mills destroyed and an estimated 4,986 adults and 2,142 children put out of work when dam burst.

Hurlingham River Boat collision (1981): The sister boat of the *Marchioness* with the same intrinsic design faults. Mentioned in the Marine Accident Investigation Bureau's report into the *Marchioness* accident.

Hurricane Hugo N. America (1989): 18 people killed in the West Indies.

Kings Cross (1987): 31 people died and 60 were injured in the fire engulfing Kings Cross underground station, London. Cause thought to be a discarded cigarette which ignited a build-up of rubbish under the escalators. Casualties exacerbated by inadequate fire precautions.

Lockerbie (1988): Pan Am flight 103 exploded in mid-air over Lockerbie, Scotland killing 270 passengers and crew. Cause thought to be Libyan bomb placed on the flight.

Malpasset (1959): Dam burst in South of France, killing 300.

Marchioness (1989): The 1,500 tonne dredger, the *Bowbelle* collided with the 50 tonne Thames pleasure cruiser the *Marchioness*. 51 people died and 80 were injured. Both vessels were blamed for poor design and shipping practice.

Mississippi Floods (1993): The flooding spanned seven states killing over 40 people and causing an estimated $10 billion of damage with 43,000 dwellings laid waste; 70,000 people were forced to flee and 50 towns were affected. The waters rose to a record height of 46.9 feet in St Louis.

Mount Erebus (1979): NZ Airways DC10 on sight-seeing trip in Antarctica crashed into the mountain in broad daylight. 257 died. Royal Commission exonerated pilot and found primary cause to be that of the executive and ground staff.

Pen Lee Life Boat Disaster (1987): Eight lifeboat crew were killed while attempting to rescue the stricken tanker the Union Star.

Piper Alpha (1988): An explosion caused by faulty maintenance procedures on North Sea oil rig, 165 of the 226 crew were killed.

Purley Train Crash (1989): A train was struck from behind killing five and injuring 88. The cause of the accident was the colliding train driver ignoring a red light. The driver at fault was sentenced to 18 months with 12 suspended, subsequently the custodial term was reduced to four months.

Sea Gem Oil Rig (1965): North sea oil rig collapse killed 13 crew members.

Sellafield (1986): 440 kg radioactive waste discharged into the Irish sea nuclear reprocessing plant, trace levels of plutonium also present. See also Windscale.

Senghenydd (1913): 439 miners died in Wales' worst mining accident. One woman lost her husband, four sons and three brothers.

Seveso (1976): Chemical leak at Icmesa Plant, Italy caused freak reaction. Cloud of tetrachlorodiberidioxin released and led to town being permanently sealed off. Long-term damage unknown.

Storms South East England (1987): No Metereological warnings given of these October storms which caused widespread property damage and a number of deaths.

Summerland Fire (1973): 50 people died, trapped in fire at Isle of Man leisure complex.

Sydney Bush Fires (1994): Fires swept through bush on Sydney outskirts destroying approximately 120 homes, killing five people and costing an estimated $200 million to bring under control.

Thalidomide Drug disaster: Between 1957 and 1962, 8000 children born worldwide with seriously truncated limbs or limbless due to mothers taking medically-prescribed drug during pregnancy.

Three Mile Island (1979): Nuclear reactor out of control for several hours, with emission of radiation into atmosphere. Precise amount unknown for a week, 144,000 evacuated. Later emerged that the radiation was not life-threatening, and serious catastrophe averted. Primary impact was psychological stress.

Titanic Disaster (1912): Ship on maiden voyage carrying 2,224 passengers struck iceberg at 22 knots ripping 300 foot hole in its side, sank with the loss of 1,153 lives. Liner carried insufficient life boat capacity.

Windscale (now Sellafield) (1957): Three-day fire brought plant close to full-scale disaster. 250 estimated at risk of thyroid cancer as a result. Details released only in 1986.

Bibliography

Anon., "Disaster Planning in Britain" (1990) 173 H.S.I.B. 8.

Anon., "Piper Alpha Settlement" (1989) 27 *Law Soc. Gazette* 3.

Anon., "FAIs After Lockerbie" (1991) *Scots Law Times* 225.

(Cooksey) *Railway Accident: Report on the Collision that occurred on 4 March at Purley*, Dept. of Transport (1990) H.M.S.O.

(Cooksey) *A report of the Collision that occurred on 8 January 1991 at Cannon Street Station*, H.S.E. (1992) H.M.S.O.

(Cullen) *The Public Inquiry into the Piper Alpha Disaster* Cm. 1310 (1990) H.M.S.O.

(Edmund-Davies) *Report of the tribunal appointed to inquire into the Disaster at Aberfan on 21 October 1966* (1967 H.C. 553).

(Fennell) *Investigation into the King's Cross Underground Fire*, Dept of Transport, Cm. 499 (1988) H.M.S.O.

(Hidden) *Investigation into the Clapham Junction Railway Accident*, Dept. of Transport, Cm. 820 (1989) H.M.S.O.

(Marriott) *Report of the Chief Inspector of Marine Accidents into the Collision between the Passenger launch Marchioness and MV Bowbelle*, Dept. of Transport, (1991) H.M.S.O.

(Popplewell) *Final Report of the Committee of Inquiry into Crowd Safety and Control at Sports Grounds*, Cmnd. 9710. (1986) H.M.S.O.

(Sheen) *M.V. Herald of Free Enterprise, Report of the Court, No 8074*, Dept. of Transport (1987). H.M.S.O.

(Taylor) *The Hillsborough Stadium Disaster, Interim Report*, Cm. 765 (1989), *Final Report*, Cm. 962 (1990). H.M.S.O.

Department of Employment, *The Flixborough Disaster: Report of the Court of Inquiry* (1975) H.M.S.O.

H.S.E., *The Abbeystead Explosion: A Report of the Investigation by the*

Health and Safety Executive into the Explosion on 23 May 1984 at the Valve House of the Lune/Wyre Transfer Scheme at Abbeystead (1985) H.M.S.O.

Report of the Committee on Death Certification and Coroners, Cmnd. 4810 (1971). H.M.S.O.

Abraham and Abraham, "The Bhopal Case and the Development of Environmental Law in India" (1991) 40 I.C.L.Q. 334.

Alldridge, P., "Who Wants to Live Forever?" in Lee, R. and Morgan, D., eds, *Death Rites, Law and Ethics at the End of Life* (1994). Routledge.

Allen, P., "Plaintiffs and the Media" (1990) 140 *New Law Journal* 1530.

Allen, P., "The New Marchioness Inquiry" (1992) 142 *New Law Journal* 142.

Anderson, L., "An Exemplary Case for Reform" (1992) *Civil Justice Quarterly* 233.

Antoniw, M., "New System for Deductions of Social Security Benefits: A Tax on Accident Victims" (1991) 10 *Litigation* 103.

Armon-Jones, C., "The Thesis of Constructionism" in Harre, R., ed., *The Social Construction of Emotions* (1986).

Arnheim, M., "Zeebrugge: is it a good offer?" (1987) 131 *Solicitors' Journal* 606.

Arnott, H., "Justice: Hillsborough's Final Victim?" (1992) *Legal Action* 7.

Austin, T., *Aberfan: Story of a Disaster* (1967). Hutchinson.

Barrett, B., "Common Law Liability for Flood Damage Caused by Storms" (1992) 142 *New Law Journal* 1608.

Barrett, B. and Howells, R., "Legal Responsibilities for Industrial Emergency Planning in the UK" in Parker, D. and Handmer, J., eds, *Hazard Management and Emergency Planning*: Perspectives on Britain (1992).

Baughen, S., "Corporate Accountability and the Law of Tort: The Inconclusive Verdict of Bhopal", University of Manchester Working Paper no. 16 (1993).

Baum, A., Fleming, R. and Davidson, L., "Natural Disaster and

Technological Catastrophe" (1983) 3 *Environment and Behaviour* 333.

Bauman, Z., *Postmodern Ethics* (1993). Blackwell.

Beck, U., "The Anthropological Shock: Chernobyl and the Contours of the Risk Society" (1987) *Berkeley Jnl. of Sociology* 153.

Beck, U., *Risk Society* (1992). Sage.

Bedingfield, D., "The Contingency Fee System in America" (1993) 143 *New Law Journal* 1670.

Bergman, D., *Deaths at Work—Accidents or Corporate Crime?* (1991). WEA.

Bergman, D., *Disasters: Where the Law Fails* (1993) Herald Families Association.

Berren, *et al*, "A Classification Scheme for Disasters" in Gist and Lubin, eds, *Psychological Aspects of Disaster* (1989).

Bissett-Johnson, "Major Disasters: Liability and the Conflict of Laws" (1991) 7 *Oil and Gas Law and Taxation review* 220.

Braithwaite, "Train Door Accidents" (1993) 143 *New Law Journal* 1070.

Braithwaite, J., "Crime and the Average American" (1993) 27 *Law and Society Review* 215.

Braithwaite, J., "Shame and Modernity" (1993) 33 *Br. Jnl. of Criminology* 1.

Braithwaite, J., *Corporate Crime in the Pharmaceutical Industry* (1984). Routledge and Kegan Paul.

Bright, S., "Charity and Trusts for the Public Benefit—Time for a Re-think?" (1984) *The Conveyancer* 28.

Brown, J., *Valley of the Shadow: An Account of Britain's Worst Mining Disaster: the Senghenydd Explosion* (1981). Alan Books.

Bryant, E., *Natural Hazards* (1991). Cambridge University Press.

Burns, M., "How to Benefit the Many—Why We Need Class Actions in the British Courts" (1989) 139 *Scot Lag* 53.

Burton, I., Kates R. and White G., *The Environment of Hazard* (1978). OUP.

Bush, R., "Between Two Worlds: the Shift from Individual to

Group Responsibility in the law of Causation of Injury" (1986) 33 *University of Cal L.R.* 1473.

Cairns, E., "Disaster Appeals" (1991) *Sol. J.* 46.

Cairns, E., "Disaster Appeals" (1991) *Supp. Sol. J.* 47.

Calavita, *et al*, "Dam Disasters and Durkheim: An Analysis of the Theme of Repressive and Restitutive Law" (1991) 19 *Int. Jnl. of Sociology of Law* 407.

Campbell R. and Morrison W. "Class Actions" (1987) *Law Soc Gazette* 2585.

Cane, P., *Atiyah's Accidents, Compensation and the Law*, (5th ed., 1993). Butterworth.

Cassels, J., "The Uncertain Promise of Law: Lessons from Bhopal" (1991) 29 *Osgoode Hall LJ* 1.

Chesterman, M., *Charities, Trusts and Social Welfare* (1979). Weidenfeld & Nicolson.

Clark, A., "The Herald of Free Enterprise—A Defective Product?" (1987) 137 *New Law Journal* 891.

Coggi, "The Commission of the European Communities Policy on Public Information on Major Accident Hazards" in Gow and Otway, eds., *Communication with the Public about Major Accident Hazards* (1990). Elsevier.

Cohen, D., *Aftershock: The Psychological and Political Consequences of Disaster* (1991). Paladin.

Coleman and Scraton, "Unanswered Questions" (1990) *Legal Action* 8 November, p. 8.

Combs, B. and Slovic, P., "Newspaper Coverage of Courses of Death" (1979) 56 *Journalism Q.* 837.

Corre, N., "Abuse of Process and the Power to Stay a Prosecution" (1991) 155 *Justice of the Peace Notes* 469.

Cowan, M. and Murphy, S., "Identification of Post-disaster Bereavement Factors" (1985) 34 *Nursing Research* 71.

Crainer, S., *Zeebrugge: Learning from Disaster* (1993) Herald Families Trust.

Cullen, F. *et al*, *Corporate Crime Under Attack: The Ford Pinto Case and Beyond* (1987). Anderson Press.

191

Daly, "Samuel Pepys and Post-Traumatic Stress Disorder", (1983) 143 *B.J. Psych.* 90.

Davies, F., "Abuse of Process—An Expanding Doctrine" (1991) 55 *J. Crim Law* 374.

Dennis, I., ed., *Criminal Law and Justice* (1987). Sweet and Maxwell.

Department of Environment Official Working Group on Football Spectator Violence (1984).

Department on Health, *Mortality Statistics* (1992) O.P.C.S. Series DH1 no. 27, (1993) H.M.S.O.

Devlin, P., *Samples of Law-making* (1962). OUP.

Deppa, J., *Disasters and the Media: Pan Am 103* (1993). David Fulton.

Douglas, M., *How Institutions Think* (1985). Routledge and Kegan Paul.

Douglas, M., *Natural Symbols* (1970). Barrie and Rockliff.

Douglas, M., *Risk and Blame* (1992). Routledge.

Douglas, M. and Wildavsky, A., *Risk and Culture* (1983). University of California Press.

Drabek, T., *Human System Response to Disaster* (1986). Springer Verlag.

Drabek, T., "Social Responses in Disaster" (1969) *Social Problems* 336.

Duckworth, D., "Disaster Work and Psychological Trauma" (1988) 1 *Disaster Management* 25.

Dynes, R., "Cross Cultural International Research: Sociology and Disaster" (1988) *Int. Jnl. of Mass Emergencies and Disaster* 101.

Editorial, "Australia's largest oil spill: who's liable?" (1992) 6 *P and I International* 13.

Editorial, "Increase in Spill Compensation" (1993) *P and I International* 13.

Editorial, "Group Action Needed for Disasters" (1989) 139 *New Law Journal* 103.

Editorial, "Flexible System for Disaster Litigation" (1988) 138 *New Law Journal* 718.

Editorial, "Legal Aid—A Long Hard Rethink Needed" (1988) 139 *Sco LAG* 50.

Editorial, "Liability Insurance: Nervous Shock" (1991) 3 *Ins. Law Monthly* 1.

Editorial, "Liability Insurance: Nervous Shock" (1992) 4 *Insurance Law Monthly* 6.

Egan, C. and Sisk, R., "The Singular Marriage of Inside and Outside Counsel in Mass Disaster Litigation" (1987) *Int. Legal Practitioner* 45.

Epicentre, *The Future of Emergency Planning in London* (1992).

Erikson, K.T., *In the Wake of the Flood* (1979). Allen and Unwin.

Ewalt, J. and Crawford, D., "Post-traumatic Stress Syndrome" (1981) *Current Psychiatric Therapies* 148.

Fennell, "Access to Justice for Personal Injury Litigants" [1994] *Jnl. of Personal Injury Litigation* 30.

Fergus, P. and Staunton, M., "Private Prosecutions" (1991) 135 *Sol. J.* 952.

Fisse, B., "Recent Developments in Corporate Criminal Law and Corporate Liability to Monetary Penalties" (1990) 13 *Univ. of New South Wales L.J.* 1.

Fisse, B., "The Duality of Corporate and Individual Criminal Liability" in Hochstedler, E., ed., *Corporations as Criminals* (1984).

Fitton, R., "A Difficult Year For Charities" (1991) *S.J. Supp.* 28.

Fleming, J.G., "Probabilistic Causation in Tort Law" (1989) 68 *Can. Bar Review* 661.

Galanter, M., "Law Abounding: Legalisation around the North Atlantic" (1992) 55 *Mod. L.R.* 1.

Galanter, M., "When Legal Worlds Collide: Reflections on Bhopal, the Good Lawyer and the American Law School" [1986] *J Leg. Ed.* 292.

Galanter, M., "The Transnational Traffic in Legal Remedies" in Jasanoff, S., ed., *Learning from Disaster* (1994). University of Pennsylvania Press.

Garland, D., *Punishment and Modern Society* (1990). Clarendon.

Gaskell, N., Annotations to Offshore Safety Act 1992, *Current Law Statutes Annotated* (1992). Sweet and Maxwell.

Gaskell, N., "The Zeebrugge Disaster: Application of the Athens Convention 1974" (1987) 137 *New Law Journal* 285.

Gaskins, R., *Environmental Accidents: Personal Injury and Public Responsibility* (1989). Temple University Press.

Genn, H., "Dilemma of Class Action Reform" (1986) 6 O.J.L.S. 226.

Genn, H., *Hard Bargaining: Out of Court Settlement in Personal Injury Actions* (1988). Clarendon.

Giddens, A., *Modernity and Self-Identity* (1991). Polity Press.

Giddens, A., *The Consequences of Modernity* (1990). Polity Press.

Gifford, "Bilsthorpe Roof Fall Shows Mine Safety Deregulation has Gone Too Far" *The Guardian*, 25 January 1994.

Gist, R. and Lubin, B., eds, *Psychological Aspects of Disaster* (1989). John Wiley and Sons.

Gleser, G., Green, B. and Wright, C., *Prolonged Psychological Effects of Disaster: A Study of Buffalo Creek* (1981). Academic Press.

Goddard, "European Law: New Origins for Health and Safety Regulation" [1994] *Jnl. of Personal Injury Litigation* 5.

Gore, A., "Correspondence" (1994) 57 *Modern Law Review* 174.

Gorer, G., *Death, Grief and Mourning in Contemporary Society* (1977). Ayer Co. Pub. Inc.

Gow, H. and Otway, H., eds, *Communication with the Public about Major Accident Hazards* (1990). Elsevier.

Grabosky, P., "Professional Advisers and White Collar Illegality: Towards Explaining and Excusing Professional Failure" (1990) 13 U.N.S.W.L.J. 73.

Green, T., *Verdict According to Conscience* (1985). University of Chicago Press.

Grubb, A., ed., *Choices and Decisions in Health Care* (1993). John Wiley.

Hamer, M., "The Risks Of Ferry Travel" (1990) *New Scientist* 18 August.

Handmer, J. and Behrens, J., "Rescuers and the Law: The Legal

Rights and Responsibilities of Rescuers in Australia" (1992) 4 *Disaster Management* 138.

Harlow, C., *Understanding Tort Law* (1987). Fontana.

Harlow, C. and Rawlings, R., *Pressure through Law* (1992). Routledge.

Harre, "The Social Constructionist Viewpoint" in Harre, R., *The Social Construction of Emotions* (1986). Blackwell.

Harris, "Tort Law Reform in US" (1991) 11 Ox. J.L.S. 407.

Harris, *et al*, *Compensation and Support for Illness and Injury* (1984). Clarendon Press.

Hart, T. and Pijnenburg, B., *Coping with Crises: the Management of Disasters, Riots and Terrorism* (1990). Charles C. Thomas.

Hartsough, "Legal Issues and Public Policy in the Psychology of Disasters" in Gist and Lubin, eds., *Psychological Aspects of Disaster* (1989).

Harvey, *et al*, eds, *Attributions, Accounts and Close Relationships* (1992). Springer-Verlag.

Hawkins, K., " 'FATCATS' and Prosecution in a Regulatory Agency: A Footnote on the Social Construction of Risk" (1989) 11 *Law and Policy* 370–91.

H.S.E., *Arrangements for Responding to Nuclear Emergencies* (1990) H.M.S.O.

Hedley, S., "Group Personal Injury Litigation and Public Opinion" (1994) 14 *Legal Studies* 70.

Hedley, S., "Hillsborough—Morbid Musings of a Chief Constable" (1992) 51 *Camb. L.J.* 16.

Henderson, "Local Government's Role in Emergency Planning" (1986) 12 *Local Govt Stud.* 10.

Hepple, B. and Matthews, M., *Tort: Cases and Materials* (4th ed., 1991). Butterworths.

Hilliard, L., "Local Government, Civil Defence and Emergency Planning: Heading for Disaster?" (1986) 49 *Mod. L.R.* 476.

Hochstedler, E., *Corporations as Criminals* (1984). Sage.

Hodgkinson, P., "Technological Disaster—Survival and Bereavement" (1989) 29(3) *Soc. Sci. Med.* 351.

Hodgkinson, P. and Stewart, M., eds, *Coping with Catastrophe* (1991). Routledge.

Hodgson, J., "Damages for Nervous Shock" (1991) 135 *Sol. Jnl.* 620.

Holgate, G. H., "Damages for Personal Injury" (1991) 10 *Litigation* 311.

Holloway, S., *Moorgate: Anatomy of a Railway Disaster* (1991). David and Charles.

Home Office, *Dealing with Disaster* (1992) H.M.S.O.

Home Office, *Statistical Bulletin* 5/91 (25 April 1991).

Horlick-Jones, T., *Acts of God? An Investigation into Disasters* (1990) Association of London Authorities.

Horlick-Jones, T., ed., *Natural Risk and Civil Protection* (1995). Spon.

Horlick-Jones, T., "Communicating Risks to Reduce Vulnerability" in Merriman and Browitt, eds, *Natural Disasters* (1993).

Horlick-Jones, T., "Modern Disasters as Outrage and Betrayal", paper at *International Institute of Sociology Congress*, Paris, June 1993.

Horlick-Jones, T. and Amendola, A., "Towards a Common Framework for Natural and Technological Emergency Management" in Vincent and Clementson, eds, *Emergency Planning '93* (1993).

Horlick-Jones, T., Fortune, J. and Peters, G., "Vulnerable Systems, Failure and Disaster" in Stowell, F. *et al Systems Science Addressing Social Issues* (1993).

Horowitz, Wilner *et al*, "Signs and Symptoms of PTSD" (1980) 37 *Archives Gen Psych.* 85.

Houlbrooke, R., *Death, Ritual and Bereavement* (1989). Routledge.

Howarth, D., "My Brother's Keeper? Liability for Acts of Third Parties" (1994) 14 *Legal Studies* 88.

Hunnisett, R., *The Medieval Coroner* (1961). Cambridge University Press.

Hutter, B., "Regulation: Standard Setting and Enforcement" (1993) 27 *Law and Society Review* 233.

Hutter, B. and Lloyd-Bostock, S., "The power of Accidents: The Social and Psychological Impact of Accidents and the Enforcement of Safety Regulations" (1990) 30 *Br J. of Criminology* 409.

Illich, I., *Limits to Medicine: Medical Nemesis and the Expropriation of Health* (1977). Penguin.

Ison, T., *The Forensic Lottery* (1967). Staples Press.

Jansen, H., "Disaster Planning in the Netherlands, France and Belgium" (1990) 63 *Pol J.* 22.

Justice, *All Souls, Review of Administrative Law* (1988). Clarendon Press.

Justice, *Coroners Courts in England and Wales* (1986). Justice.

Kasperson, R., "The Social Amplification of Risk: progress in developing an integrative framework" in Krimsky and Golding eds. *Theories of Risk* (1993).

Katzman, M., "Chemical Catastrophes and the Courts" [1986] *The Public Interest* 91.

Kelly, A., Gibson, R. and Horlick-Jones, T., *Local Authorities, the Media and Disasters* (1992). Epicentre.

Kolman, T., "The Piper Alpha Oil Rig Disaster: Is There a Forum for Pursuers in the United States?" (1988) *Scots Law Times* 293.

Kreps, "Sociological Inquiry and Disaster Research" (1984) 10 *Annual Review of Sociology* 309.

Krimsky, S. and Golding, D., eds, Theories of risk (1992). Praeger.

Kritzer, H., "Propensity to Sue in England and the United States of America: Blaming and Claiming in tort Cases" (1991) 18 *Jnl. of Law and Society* 400.

Lagadec, P., *Preventing Chaos in a Crisis* (1993). McGraw-Hill.

Laurance, J., "Disastrous Disaster Funds" (1987) *New Society* March 20, 1987.

Law Commission, *Report on Personal Injury Litigation—Assessment of Damages* No. 56, (1973).

Law Commission, *Fifth Programme of Reform* No 200 Cm. 1556 (1991).

Law Commission, *Aggravated, Exemplary and Restitutionary Damages* Consultation Paper No. 132 (1993) H.M.S.O.

Law Commission, *Involuntary Manslaughter* Consultation Paper No. 135 (1994). H.M.S.O.

Lebedun and Wilson, "Planning and Integrating Disaster Response" in Gist R. and Lubin B. eds, *Psychological Aspects of Disorder* (1989).

Lee, "The Public's Perception of Risk and the Question of Irrationality" in Warner, ed., *The Assessment and Perception of Risk* (1981).

Lee, R. and Morgan, D., eds, *Death Rites, Law and Ethics at the End of Life* (1994). Routledge.

Levin, J., "Opren: Litigation Lessons" (1988) *Legal Action* 5.

Lewis, R., "Legal Limits on the Structured Settlement of Damages" (1993) 52 *Camb L.J.* 470.

Lewis, R., "Risk, Vulnerability and Survival—Some Post-Chernobyl Implications for People, Planning and Civil Defence" (1987) 13 *Local Govt Studies* 75.

Lewis, R., "The Merits of a Structured Settlement: the Plaintiff's Perspective" (1993) 13 *Oxford J.L.S.* 530.

Lifton, R., *Death in Life: Survivors of Hiroshima* (1967). Random House.

Lindey *et al*, "Survivors: an outreach to a reluctant population" (1981) 51 *Am J. Ortho psych.* 468.

Lipset, S.M. and Schneider, W., *The Confidence Gap: Business, Labour and the Government in the Public Mind* (1987). Collier Macmillan.

Littlewood, J., *Aspects of Grief: Bereavement in Adulthood* (1992). Routledge.

Lloyd-Bostock, S., "Attributions and Apologies in Letters of Complaint to Hospitals and Letters of Response" in Harvey *et al*, eds *Attributions, Accounts and Close Relationships* (1992).

Lloyd-Bostock, S., "Fault and Liability for Accidents: the Accident Victim's Perspective" in Harris *et al Compensation and Support for Illness and Injury* (1984).

Lloyd-Bostock, S., "Interactions between Law and Everyday Thinking in the Social Categorization of Events" in Steensma, H. and Vermut, R., eds., *Social Justice in Human Relations* (1991).

Lloyd-Bostock, S., "Propensity to Sue in England and the United States of America: The Role of Attribution Processes. A Comment on Kritzer" (1991) 18 *Jnl. of Law and Society* 428.

Lloyd-Bostock, S., "The Psychology of routine Discretion: Accident Screening by British Factory Inspectors" (1992) 14 *Law and Policy* 45.

Lockley, A., "Regulating Group Actions" (1989) 139 *New Law Journal* 798.

Loibl, G., "Transboundary Environmental Cooperation: international contingency planning/emergency assistance" (1991) *Yb Intl Environment Law* 80.

London Emergency Services Liaison Panel, *Major Incident Procedure* (1993).

Loveland, I., ed., *Frontiers of Criminality* (1995). Sweet and Maxwell.

Lundin, T., "Morbidity following Sudden and Unexpected Bereavement" (1984) 144 *Br J. Psychiatry* 84.

Lundin, T., "The Stress of Unexpected Bereavement" (1985) 3 *Stress Medicine* 109.

Luxton, P., *Charity Fund-Raising and the Public Interest: An Anglo-American Perspective* (1990). Avebury.

Lynch, B., "A Victory for Pragmatism? Nervous Shock Reconsidered" (1992) 108 *Law Quarterly Review* 366.

Matthewman *et al, Tolley's Social Security and State Benefits Handbook 1993–4* (1993). Tolley.

McBryde, W. and Barker, C., "Solicitors' Groups in Mass Disaster Claims" (1991) 141 *New Law Journal* 484.

McCool, G., "Disaster Co-ordination" (1991) 16 *Intl Leg Practitioner* 23.

McEldowney, J., "Public Inquiry into the Piper Alpha Disaster" (1991) 2 *Utilities Law Review* 2.

McFarlane, A., "Post-traumatic morbidity of a disaster: (1986) 174 *Jnl of Nervous and Mental Disease* 4.

McIntosh, D., "Defending Trial by Media" (1990) 140 *New Law Journal* 1224.

McKeogh, J., "Origins of the Coronial Jurisdiction" (1983) 6 *University of New South Wales Law Journal* 191.

Merriman and Browitt, eds, *Natural Disasters* (1993). Thomas Telford.

Miers, D., *Compensation for Criminal Injuries* (2nd ed., 1990). Butterworths.

Miller, J., *Aberfan: A Disaster and its Aftermath* (1974). Constable.

Miller, K., "Piper Alpha and the Cullen Report" (1991) 20 *Ind. Law Jnl.* 176.

Milton, K., "Interpreting Environmental Policy: A Social Scientific Approach" (1991) 18 *Journal of Law and Society* 4.

Morgan, D., "Relatively Late Payments: Damages Beyond Death and Bereavement" in Lee, R. and Morgan, D., eds, *Death Rites* (1994).

Myers, K., *Total Contingency Planning for Disasters* (1993). John Wiley.

Napier, "The Medical and Legal Response to PTSD" in Grubb, A., ed., *Choices and Decisions in Health Care* (1993).

Nasir, K., "Nervous Shock and Alcock: The Judicial Buck Stops Here" (1992) 55 *Mod. L.R.* 705.

National Consumer Council, *Group Actions: Learning from Opren* (1989).

Nelken, D., "Criminal Law and Criminal Justice: Some Notes on their Irrelation" in Dennis ed. *Criminal Law and Justice* (1987).

New, B., *Too Many Cooks. The Response of the Health-related Services to Major Incidents in London* [1992] *King's Fund Institute Research Report* 15.

Nigg, J., "Risk Communication and Warning Systems" in Horlick-Jones, ed. *Natural Risk and Court Protection* (1995).

Osborne, D., "Maritime Disasters" (1991) 56 *P&I Internat* 17.

Otway, H. and Wynne, B., "Risk Communication: Paradigm and Paradox" (1989) 9 *Risk Analysis* 141.

Pannone, R., "Speech to International Bar Association" (1989) 139 *New Law Journal* 1419.

Parker, D., and Handmer, J., eds, *Hazard Management and Emergency Planning: Perspectives on Britain* (1992). James and James.

Parks, C. and Weiss, R., *Recovery from Bereavement* (1983). Basic Books.

Pearce, F. and Tombs, S., "Bhopal: Union Carbide and the Hubris of the Capitalist Technocracy" (1989) 16 *Social Justice* 116.

Perrow, C., *Normal Accidents: Living with High Risk Technologies* (1984). Basic Books.

Petrie, J., "The Cullen Report: Lessons Learned and rec-ommendations" [1990] 9 *Oil and Gas LTR* 313.

Pine, T., "Integrated Emergency Management: Hierarchy or Network" in Horlick-Jones, ed., *Natural Risk and Civil Protection* (1995).

Pipe, G., "Exemplary Damages after Camelford" (1994) 57 *Modern Law Review* 91.

Quarantelli, E., "Disaster Crisis Management: A Summary of Research Findings" (1988) 25 *Journal of Management Studies* 373.

Quint, J., "Risk Communication on a National Scale: The Dutch Way" in Horlick-Jones, ed., *Natural Risk and Civil Protection* (1995).

Rabin, R., "A Socio-legal History of the Tobacco Tort Litigation." (1992) 44 *Stanford L.R.* 853.

Rangell, L., "Discussion of the Buffalo Creek Disaster: The Course of Psychic Trauma" (1976) 133 *Am. J. Psychiatry* 313.

Raphael, B., "Personal Disaster" (1984) 15 *Austr. and NZ Jnl. of Psychiatry* 183.

Raphael, B., *When Disaster Strikes* (1989). Unwin Hyman.

Red Cross, *Coping with a Major Personal Crisis* (Manual).

Reynolds, S., *Kingdoms and Communities in Western Europe—900–1300* (1984). OUP.

Richards, P., "Questions about Local Authorities and Emergency Planning" (1979) *Loc. Govt Stud.* 37.

Robertson, D., "Liability in Negligence for Nervous Shock" (1994) 57 *Modern Law Review* 649.

Rogers, W. V. H., *The Law of Tort* (1994). Sweet and Maxwell.

Rolt, L.T.C., *Red for Danger: A History of Railway Accidents and Railway Safety Precautions* (1955). Bodley Head.

Rosen, L., "Intentionality and the Concept of the Person" in Pennock, J. and Chapman, J., eds, *Criminal Justice* (1985).

Rosenberg, D., "The Causal Connection in Mass Exposure Cases: A Public Law Vision of the Tort System" (1984) 97 *Harv. L.R.* 849.

Rosenthal, U., "Crisis Management: second order techniques" in Horlick-Jones, ed., *Natural Risk and Civil Protection* (1995).

Rowan-Robinson, J., Watchman, P. and Barker, C., *Crime and Regulation* (1990). T & T Clark.

Royal Society Study Group, *Risk: Analysis, Perception and Management* (1992). Royal Society.

Scanlon, J., "Winners and Losers: Some Thoughts about the Political Economy of Disaster" [1988] *Int. J. Mass. Emergencies and Disasters*, March, 47.

Sefton, A., "The Enforcement of Article 8 of the Seveso Directive in Great Britain" in Gow and Otway, eds, *Communication with the Public about Major Accident Hazards* (1990).

Shaver, K., *The Attribution of Blame: Causality, Responsibility and Blameworthiness* (1985). Springer Verlag.

Shearer, A., *Survivors and the Media* (1991). Broadcasting Standards Council.

Sheridan, G., and Kenning, T., *Survivors* (1993). Pan.

Simpson, A.W.B., "Legal Liability for Bursting Reservoirs: The Historical Context of Rylands v Fletcher" (1984) XIII *Journal of Legal Studies* 209.

Singh and Raphael, "Post Disaster Morbidity of the Bereaved" (1981) 169(4) *Jnl. of Nervous and Mental Disease* 203.

Singleton, W., *The Mind at Work* (1990).

Smith, K., *Environmental Hazards: Assessing Risk And Reducing Disaster* (1991). Routledge.

Smith, R. and Lloyd-Bostock, S., Why People Go to Law: An Annotated Bibliography of Social Science Research (1990) Centre for Socio-Legal Studios, Oxford.

Sorokin, P., *Man, Society and Calamity: Psychological Ergonomics* (1990). Cambridge University Press.

Stallings, R., "Media Discourse and the Social Construction of Risk" [1990] *Social Problems* 80.

Steele, J., "Scepticism and the Law of Negligence" (1993) 52 *Cambridge Law Jnl.* 437.

Steele, J., "Two Cheers for Caparo: Ravenscroft v Rede-riaktiebolaget Transatlantic (1993) 56 *Modern Law Review* 244.

Steensma, H. and Vermut, R., eds., *Social Justice in Human Relations* Vol 2 (1991). Plenum.

Stern, G., *The Buffalo Creek Disaster* (1976). Random House.

Stowell, F., *et al*, eds, *Systems Science Addressing Global Issues* (1993). Plenum.

Strudler, A., "Mass Torts" (1992) 11 *Law and Philosophy* 297.

Sturt, "The Role of the Coroner with Special Reference to Major Disasters" (1988) 28 *Med. Si. Law* 275.

Suddards, R., *Administration of Appeal Funds* (1991). Sweet and Maxwell.

Sugarman, S., *Doing Away with Personal Injury Law: New Compensation Mechanisms for Victims, Consumers and Business* (1989).

Taylor, A.J.W., *Disasters and Disaster Stress* (1989). AMS Press.

Topping, I., "Emergency Planning Law and Practice in Northern Ireland" (1988) 39 *Northern Ireland Law Quarterly* 336.

Turner, B., *Man-Made Disasters* (1978), Heinemann.

Turner, B., "The Organisational and Interorganizational Development of Disasters" [1976] *Administrative Science Quarterly* 378.

Turner, B., "The Role of Flexibility and Improvisation in Emergency Response" in Horlick-Jones, ed., *Natural Risk and Civil Protection* (1995).

Turner, B.S., *Medical Power and Social Knowledge* (1987). Sage.

Uff, K., "Class, Representative and Shareholders" Derivative Actions in English Law" (1986) 5 *Civil Justice Qu.* 50.

Uff, K., "Legal Aid Board Consultation Paper on Multi-Party Actions" (1990) 9 *Civil Justice Qu.* 23.

Uff, K., "Recent Developments in Representative Actions" (1987) 6 *Civil Justice Qu.* 15.

Usher, A., "The Flixborough Disaster" (1979) 77 *Medical Legal Jnl.* 84.

Van Duin, M. and Rosenthal, U., "Disaster Planning in the Greater Rotterdam Area" (1989) *Disaster Management* 2.

Vincent, P. and Clementson, R., eds, *Emergency Planning '93* (1993) University of Lancaster.

Wade, H., *Administrative Law* (6th ed., 1988). Clarendon.

Wadham, J., "Abuse of Process through Delay in the Criminal courts" (1991) *Legal Action* 15.

Walker, "Criminal Injuries Compensation: A Government Betrayal?" [1994] *Jnl of Personal Injury Litigation* 47

Warner, F., (ed), *The Assessment and Perception of Risk* (1981). The Royal Society.

Warwick Inquest Group, "The Inquest as a Theatre for Police Tragedy: the Davey Case" (1985) 12 *Jnl of Law and Society* 35.

Wells, C, *Corporations and Criminal Responsibility* (1993). Clarendon.

Wells, C., "Corporations: Culture, Risk and Criminal Liability" [1993] *Criminal Law Review* 551.

Wells, C., "Cry in the Dark: Corporate Manslaughter and Cultural Meaning" in Loveland, ed., *Frontiers of Criminality* (1995). Sweet and Maxwell.

Wells, C., "Inquests, Inquiries and Indictments: The Official Reception of Death by Disaster" (1991) 11 *Legal Studies* 71.

Whitfield, A., "The Basics and Tactics of Structured Settlements" (1992) 142 *New Law Journal* 135.

Whitham, D. and Newburn, T., *Coping with Tragedy* (1992) Notts County Council/National Institute For Social Work.

Wilkins, L. and Patterson, P., "Risk Analysis and the Construction of News" (1987) 37 *Jnl of Communication* 80.

Wills, J., "Emergency" (1990) 6397 *Local Government Chronicle* 20.

Winfield and Jolowicz on Tort (14th ed., 1994). Sweet and Maxwell.

Witcomb, "An Outdated Justice" (1990) 140, *New Law Journal* 788.

Wittgenstein, L., *Tractatus Logico-Philosophicus*, trans. C.K. Ogden 1922 (reprinted 1992). Routledge.

Wolfenstein, M., *Disaster: Psychological Essay* (1957). The Free Press.

World Health Organisation, *Should Disaster Strike* (1991). Switzerland.

Wraith, R. and Lamb, G., *Public Inquiries as an Instrument of Government* (1971). Allen and Unwin.

Wynne, B., "Establishing the rules of laws: constructing expert authority" in Smith R. and Wynne B., eds, *Expert Evidence* (1989). Routledge.

Wynne, B., "Risk and Social Learning: Reification to Engagement" in Krimsky S. and Golding eds, *Theories of Risk* (1992).

Wynne, B., "Misunderstood Misunderstanding: Social Identities and Public Uptake of Science" (1992) 1 *Public Understanding of Science* 281.

Yeazell, S., *From Medieval Group Litigation to the Modern Class Action* (1987). Yale University Press.

Zedner, L., "Reparation and Retribution: Are they Reconcilable?" (1994) 57 *Modern Law Review* 228.

Index